Sketches
in his own Key

Sketches
in his own Key

By
BOB ST. JOHN

Cover by Don Collins

SHOAL CREEK PUBLISHERS, INC.
P.O. BOX 9737   AUSTIN, TEXAS 78766

Copyright © 1981 by Bob St. John

All rights in this book are reserved. No part of this book may be used or reproduced in any manner without written request to and permission from the publisher, except in the case of brief quotations embedded in a review.

First Edition

Lithographed and Bound in the United States of America

Previously published material has been reproduced by permission of the *Dallas Morning News.*

Library of Congress Cataloging in Publication Data

St. John, Bob.
    Sketches in his own key.

    I. Title.
AC8.S6637   081   81–14482
ISBN 0–88319–058–3   AACR2
ISBN 0–88319–061–3 (pbk.)

Contents

For Norma,
for Bill and my mother,
in memory of my father,
and for all those who were special
"along the way."

Sand Castles

W HEN THEY WALKED near midnight on the beach at South Padre Island it was very dark because lights had been turned out in the houses along the beach and only the moon cast light, dancing almost magically across the moving ocean. But they could see the big sand castle was gone, washed away as though it never had been there.

"Look, it's gone," said the boy, who was eleven. "Somebody worked so hard on it. Now, it's gone. Just gone."

"That always happens to sand castles," said the boy's father.

They walked for a while, listening to the violent yet soothing sounds of the waves. And then the man said, "You know why people write about sand castles in poems and songs, things like that?"

"No sir."

"Mostly, they use sand castles because they're very beautiful and difficult to build and then they get washed away by the tide. They're there and then gone, as though they never were there in the first place. But they're always there in your memory."

"I'll remember for a long time that big one we saw washed away."

"Well, remember how well it was done, how beautiful it was. That's important."

"You know, I worry sometimes about dying, being dead," the boy said. "It's hard to imagine having just one life. Just one life and I'm already eleven. I worry about you dying sometimes and how you don't seem very happy now."

"Oh, I don't think I'll be dying for a while. But, although I don't know for sure, I don't think dying is all that unpleasant. In fact, I think it might be very pleasant and that the form of life we take after death probably is very good.

"And, listen to me, son, people are up and down in their lives. But, please, don't worry about me dying or being down or unhappy now."

"I can't help it sometimes. You remember driving here in the car. You sometimes would listen to music and look sad, things like that."

"Music can make you happy, sad, make you remember good times, sad times. Music is just like that. As I've told you before, my father was killed when he wasn't very old. I don't think he ever did very much, was ever really happy. I've always worried about that, just as you are now.

"But it's different for me. I've been many places, done many things. I've had many, many good times. I've been awfully happy at times and sometimes it takes being a little sad to appreciate the times when you were very happy."

"But just one life. That's all you get."

"Well, again, I plan to be around for a long time, but say, if something did happen and I died, I wouldn't want you to be sad about my life because I've enjoyed it. I really have. I want you to know and try to understand this so you won't be so sad one day when it happens."

"Thank you for telling me that. It makes me feel better."

"It makes me feel better, too. Listen, I'll tell you what. After I die I'll tickle you on the nose so you'll know everything's all right, being dead. Just a little tickle."

The man didn't have on shoes because he didn't mind the crabs running around his feet nor the chill from the ocean water at night when it swept up across him. The boy had worn his tennis shoes because he said a crab might bite him on the toe.

"Sometimes," the boy said, "I do mean things. Sometimes this kid will make me mad and I'll say something to hurt his feelings. Just mean things. But I'm sorry for it later."

"If you're sorry then you should tell him. We all say mean things sometimes, but I think you're a fine person because you're aware of this, aware of other people's feelings."

"You make me feel better."

"When you say the things you say, the way you say them, you make me feel better, too."

The next day they saw more sand castles on the beach and some of them were well made and very beautiful.

A Small Town in Texas

As I RECALL the house that year it was surrounded, almost engulfed, by vines, some wisteria, which had been allowed to grow wild for more years than anybody could remember. Vines began growing along the fence, which was cast iron with ribs shaped like medieval spears, and were intermingled with low hung branches of trees and sticker bushes and some honeysuckle.

The house was Gothic in architecture, unkept and unlived in, with shutters that suddenly slammed in the wind. I know at that time we, the kids who lived near the house, would not have been at all surprised had lightning struck some black night, revealing words written across the entrance which would not say Kaufman Terrace, but The House of Frankenstein.

I do not know why but sounds and smells or objects or people will rekindle memories of childhood that you had forgotten or, perhaps, had forgotten to remember. But this happened recently when I stood near Kaufman Terrace, which has three stories (four counting the basement) and a pointed tower on one side. The house is now being renovated by its third owner, G. I. Hodges, who would like to restore it as it was when built in 1876. Yet, I cannot see Kaufman Terrace as it is now or as it will become but only as the old haunted house which used to scare us to death when we were second and third graders at J. G. Wooten Elementary School in Paris, Texas.

Haunted houses are a state of mind, but when you are that age they are as real as the Saturday afternoon cowboys who rode across the silver screen, wearing white hats and firing six-shooters thirty times without reloading. After school we would walk along the sidewalk by the house, and the bravest of us would sometimes climb over the fence and make a mad dash, or a dash of madness, through the yard. Even in broad daylight we got chillbumps because of all the stories we had heard and some of us believed the vines, the low hanging branches, were the long thin arms of those who had been murdered in the house.

So one time near midnight we sat on the curb under the streetlight across from Kaufman Terrace and dared, double-dog dared, and even triple-dog dared each other to run up and knock on the door. The group that night included, besides myself, Jackie Davenport and his brother, who was just a lil' kid only in the first grade, and Charlie Moore, who we called Choo-Choo because he was the fastest runnin' kid in school. Choo-Choo Charlie had flunked a number of times, and nobody really knew how old he was but it was rumored he shaved.

Choo-Choo Charlie was somewhat of a scandalous figure around the neighborhood because he had, really and truly, often been caught in the coatroom at school doing awful things, such as kissing girls. I didn't see any big deal about that. I just figured kissing girls was silly and pointless because he could have been using that time to play baseball. Shoot. Somebody said Choo-Choo Charlie even had rather kiss girls than drink an RC Cola, but I couldn't believe that. You know how rumors get started.

Choo-Choo Charlie did most of the talking and we listened, although I imagine this was more because he could whip any of us than in deference to his age. Jackie Davenport's little brother also did a lot of talking, but nobody listened because as somebody said, "He can't even whup his ownself."

Anyway, Choo-Choo Charlie had had a few narrow escapes, he often said, while dashing through the grounds at Kaufman Terrace, and told us, "Boys, one time at midnight I was a-walkin' along the sidewalk when one of them vines reached out and tried to choke me. (He paused for effect.) Only 'cause I is the fastest runnin' kid in this block did I get away by runnin' like the wind." Although sometimes I'd get to thinking that maybe Choo-Choo Charlie could be outrun, I didn't say anything about it because I didn't want to get whipped.

Jackie's lil' brother's eyes got real big then, and he said, "Onest the branches reached out and got this kid and jerked his head right off, blood flowing all over the sidewalk like a river and bones and guts and brains fallin' out and . . ."

"Shut up, kid!"

"One time I seen this woman witch with a white face looking out that tower up yonder," said Choo-Choo Charlie. "She held up her hands and had blood (he paused for effect) all over them. I swear and hope I go to the devil his ownself if this ain't true. But, being the fastest runnin' kid I was able to get away."

"You the fastest, Choo-Choo Charlie," I said. "Why don't you give me a piece of that gum you got."

"Why?"

"Well, you the fastest, that's why." Choo-Choo Charlie thought for a second and gave me a piece of gum.

"Annnnnnnnd onest this woman in the winder looked down and dropped this lil' baby out she'd been a-cuttin' up with a butcher knife, getting blood and bones and guts all over the sidewalk and . . ."

"Shut up, kid."

"And, annnnnnnd she went down and got that bloody lil' baby and fed it to her dogs and then got her butcher knife and cut them dogs all . . ."

Choo-Choo Charlie reached over and cuffed Jackie's lil' brother upside the head, knocking him over like a top. Jackie's lil' brother yelled, crawled back beside Choo-Choo Charlie, and clamped down with his teeth on his leg. "AHHHHHEEEEEEEEE!" said Choo-Choo Charlie, "that was my fastest leg you dirty little rat!'' We finally got the kid to let go of Choo-Choo Charlie's leg. He said next time Choo-Choo Charlie hit him he'd bite his leg plumb off, and his bones and guts would roll out on the sidewalk.

"You got to do something about that kid," Choo-Choo Charlie told Jackie.

"He's only a kid, Choo-Choo Charlie," said Jackie.

Finally the group decided I would be the one to climb over the fence with the spears on it and go up and knock on the door of the old haunted house. It wasn't the dares, even the triple-dog dares, that finally made me agree to do it but rather Choo-Choo Charlie saying he bet Ted Williams or Joe DiMaggio wouldn't have been scared of knocking on the door of any haunted house in the world.

My heart was leaping out of my chest, as I went over the fence, crept through the vines and sticker bushes, ever so slowly, and crouched on all fours next to the porch. God, I prayed, if you'll get me out of this I won't ever skip Sunday School again or spend the money I was supposed to put in the collection plate at the Corner Drug Store for a soda. Never again. I heard something move in the brush near me. I froze. Couldn't move. Couldn't talk. Couldn't whisper. I tried to get up but couldn't, so I protected myself as best I could by lying on my back, hands over my eyes, which were closed anyway.

Something was standing over me. Gradually, I removed my hands and opened one eye. I looked up. It must have been ten feet tall, with a sheet around it and something which looked like blood covering its face. "AIIIIEEEEEEE OOOOOOOEEEEE!" I yelled, rolling off the porch and hitting the ground running. The vines grabbed at me, tossing me to the ground, but I just flipped over and got up and started running again.

When I went over the fence, I tore my shirt, lost a shoe, and scraped my back, but I figured the thing with the blood in its face had clawed me. I ran past my buddies, who immediately were on their feet, too, running in all directions. None of us looked right nor left. We did not pass GO nor collect $200. We went home, directly to home.

The next day Choo-Choo Charlie jumped me because I hadn't knocked on the door of the haunted house. "Choo-Choo Charlie," I said, "you not fast at all. You the slowest kid I ever saw." Choo-Choo Charlie whipped me.

There were rumors in school that one of the seventh graders, overhearing our plans, had dressed up like a ghost and put ketchup on his face. But I knew what I saw and it was a ghost, pure and simple.

Recently, when I stood near Kaufman Terrace I felt chillbumps all over me.

On LAZY, HOT, slow-moving summer afternoons we rode stick horses across the old wrecking and sand and gravel yard near where I lived during those years in Paris, Texas, pretending we were the great cowboy stars of the times, such as Bob Steele, Gene Autry, the great Hopalong Cassidy, and Wild Bill Elliott, who also was Red Ryder and never shot a man in the back and sure could fight.

The old wrecked cars were hideouts and the sand and gravel piles mountains in the silver screen of our imaginations. Sometimes we lost a little terrain, a mountain or so, when the big truck came to haul off sand and gravel, but before you knew it, a dump truck brought some more. We called the beige sand piles the Black Hills of Texas.

Ritually, we went to places like the Lamar, Rex, and Plaza Theaters and watched the cowboy heroes of our heart and soul do what was right. They never lost a fight, never played dirty, always had the fastest horse, and shot a six-shooter at learst thirty times before running out of bullets.

Now most of us used three sticks, a long one and two short ones, when we played. The long stick was our horse and the short ones our guns. But there was one kid who had so much money that he always was duded out. I can't remember his name but I think it might have been Billy Gene. Anyway, everybody but Billy Gene put away their stick horses and toy guns when they went to J.G. Wooten Elementary School.

Billy Gene, however, would show up at school all decked out in his cowboy garb. He had a nice white hat, a red bandana around his neck, and a plaid shirt. He wore chaps, over his jeans, crammed into black boots with white stars on them. Strapped around his waist were two great toy silver pistols in scabbards of real leather. Those pistols shot real, live caps, I mean.

I can still see him sitting in the second row, guns hanging almost down to the floor on both sides, with his hat tilted back, like Gene Autry's was when he was about to sing. We used to argue a lot around my house whether Gene was singing to the girl or his horse. My sister, Norma, said it was the girl, but I knew it was the horse because I sure couldn't see any sense singing to a girl.

Billy Gene was just bitten by the cowboy craze worse than the rest of us. He tipped his hat to teachers and girls he passed in the hall. He never said he'd meet you on the corner after school but "at the pass." He didn't live up the street but "where the trail turns yonder."

We all had out unusual styles of running. I know I was a little knock-kneed and always seemed at odds with trying to run straight. But as a runner Billy Gene was in a class by himself. When he ran he slapped himself on the hip, as if he where whipping his horse to a full gallop, and then kinda hopped along.

Sometimes when he ran he yelled, "Hi-yo Silver, awaaaaaaayeeee!" Sometimes he yelled, "Giddy-up, old feller!" And sometimes he said, "Da-de-da-de-da-da-daaa," which he thought sounded just like action music in the cowboy movies.

But I tell you that kid really was fast, too, although not as fast as Choo-Choo Charlie Moore, who was older and bigger than anybody in our class because he'd flunked a number of times.

The best fight I ever saw was when Billy Gene challenged Choo-Choo Charlie, who naturally could whip anybody. I was somewhat of an expert on this because after watching Wild Bill Elliott whip not one but two guys with an uppercut I went after Choo-Choo Charlie. Somehow it never worked out for me like it had for Wild Bill but I kept trying, and Choo-Choo Charlie whipped me more than anybody.

One day a bunch of us at recess were walking dangerously near the girls' side of the playground. The girls were playing softball but looked silly, batting cross-handed and all that. When one hit the ball near us, Choo-Choo Charlie picked it up and wouldn't give it back and nobody could make him, that's for sure. The little girl started screaming that she wanted that softball back. Choo-Choo Charlie just smiled his watermelon smile and held the ball up high, over her head.

Then all at once out of the gray October sky came a lone rider. We heard this haunting yell, "Hi-yoooo Silver, awaaaaaawaaaaa!" We all turned to see none other than Billy Gene galloping toward us, slapping his hip. His white cowboy hat was pulled down tight on his forehead, making his ears stick straight out, and his bandana was waving in the wind. He was coming toward us a mile-a-minute, and we didn't know whether to laugh or run. Quicker than a heartbeat he leaped at Choo-Choo Charlie, knocking him to the ground. "Unhand that little lady, you dirty, rotten skunk!" said Billy Gene to Choo-Choo Charlie, whose eyes were bigger than silver dollars.

Now, I figure if Billy Gene had jumped right on top of Choo-Choo Charlie at that instant he would have whipped him because the big guy was stunned. But honor got the best of him. "I see you're unarmed," said Billy Gene, backing off so Choo-Choo Charlie could get up. He then took off his twin guns and carefully placed them on the ground. Choo-Choo Charlie, recovering, was all over him, knocking him down and then sitting on him and pounding away.

I wasn't about to take up for any ol' girl who lost her softball, but I didn't want to see Choo-Choo Charlie whip Billy Gene so I yelled, "Choo-Choo Charlie, you couldn't whup that lil' girl over there!" That sure got his attention. He got off Billy Gene and came after me. I threw my uppercut, just like Wild Bill Elliott but my derned old hand got caught in his overalls, causing no injury but some embarrassment when they came unsnapped. But Choo-

Choo Charlie, his eyes deadly cold, just snapped them back, and I went into my classic boxer's stance, backing up fast as I could. As Choo-Choo Charlie came after me, we suddenly heard from behind us the blood-curdling words "Hold it! Put up your hands or you'll be a-talkin' to your Maker."

Choo-Choo Charlie turned around and there was Billy Gene, holding two guns on him. "One more move and I'll let you have it," said Billy Gene, looking hard at Choo-Choo Charlie with steel blue eyes. Choo-Choo Charlie looked kind of puzzled, then slowly put up his hands. Billy Gene gradually backed off, holstered his guns, and went galloping off, yelling, "Hi-yoooooo Silver, awaaaawayeee!"

"That kid is crazy as a nut," said Choo-Choo Charlie, finally bringing his hands down. "He might shoot somebody, you know it."

When the school bell rang, we all walked back inside. I don't know whatever happened to Billy Gene, but I bet he never shot a man in the back.

SHE TAUGHT us music, and most of us were in love with her. She was pretty, not at all grouchy, didn't dip snuff, and tried to teach us to play "Jolly Old Roger the Tin Maker Man" on some funny plastic instrument called a recorder and to sing in tune. And we tried so hard to do those things, even if it was sissy stuff.

We were fifth graders at J.G. Wooten Elementary School in Paris, Texas, and she taught us only that one year but became the heroine of our dreams and fantasies. For instance, I would be sitting in her music class, my blank eyes staring at the floor, and imagine, that some thugs who smelled bad were trying to beat her up and steal her piano. She would cry when they took it away, and suddenly, I'd appear.

"Let me take care of this," I'd say, then knock them all out, give her back her piano, and carry her off in my arms. I never was sure in those days where I was going to take her or what we were going to do when we got there, but I guess we'd have played the recorder and sung. In tune, of course.

She always was getting ideas to use for plays that we would do before our parents. Although it might come as a surprise to my friends, I, too, once was a star of stage, playing a prominent role in one of her productions. I was Mr. Sunshine. I wore a crepe paper robe and a round pasteboard hat, both of which were bright yellow. Because the robe was a little short, my white sweat socks and tennis shoes showed, but I didn't think much about that as I was worrying about my one line, "Hi, I'm Mr. Sunshine."

I felt I had the line down perfectly but blew it the night of the play. I stood in line on the stage with Mr. Moon and Mr. Stardust and Mr. Tree, stepped forth on cue, and said, "Hello, uh, uh, I . . . I'm Mr. Sunshine." Everybody in the audience laughed. I didn't know why and asked my friend Palmer Poteet, who made A's. "Don't worry about it," he said. "You did just fine. It was a most unusual theater audience tonight."

"Fine, haw-haw," said Choo-Choo Charlie Moore. "You shore was funny, kid. Your face got so red is why they all laughed. Haw-haw-haw. You shoulda said, 'Hey, I'm, Mr. Redfaced Sunshine.' Haw-haw-haw." Then he folded to the floor, laughing hysterically at the image.

But actors have bad days, too. There's no business like show business or some such. The beautiful music teacher gave me another chance, casting me as the tragic Don Jose in her version of the opera *Carmen*. No, we did it in English. Really, I mean, don't you think she was ambitious and imaginative enough using a bunch of snot-nosed kids in overalls, bowl haircuts, etc., in *Carmen*.

Don Jose was a soldier and so my costume consisted of bluejeans and a blouse which belonged to my teacher. (She had painted soldier's stripes on it and made me tie it at the waist, but it was still much too big in the chest.) She also painted a mustache on me. I carried a sword, which we called a "sward," and a dagger made of rubber. The only way I agreed to wear the blouse was if she'd let me wear my Detroit Tigers baseball hat that I'd ordered with a coupon in *The Sporting News*. And she did saying it might just look a little like a soldier's hat.

We had dress rehearsal the afternoon of the play, scheduled to begin at 7 P.M. sharp in the massive, historical Wooten auditorium, which would hold an SRO crowd of forty-five. Choo-Choo Charlie almost destroyed my confidence that afternoon when he grabbed my blouse and said, "Hey, kid, you playin' Carmen or Don Jose? Haw-haw-haw." I wanted to blast him but he was older, bigger, and faster than all of the rest of us.

We had several musical production numbers, and I actually learned the songs and wrote my speaking lines down in ink on my hands, just in case I forgot them. Our big musical number was the "Toreador Song," which we sang when the bullfighter, Escamillo, who stole Carmen from me, came around. The beautiful music teacher was proud of the way we sang that song, but Choo-Choo Charlie, who played a soldier with a non-speaking part, kept messing it up.

"Toreador-ra, Toreador-ra," he would sing, "don't spit-a on the floor-ra." Then he'd laugh his head off, and the beautiful music teacher would make him stand in the corner. Choo-Choo Charlie stood in the corner a lot.

And, sure enough, during the play that night when we were all singing "Toreador," the fiend, he did it. I looked at him and caught the last few words, ". . . spit-a on the floor-ra." Then he giggled and went and stood in the corner without even being told to do so by the beautiful music teacher. Choo-Choo Charlie knew his place.

But the show, the play as it were, must go on, and did. In the final scene, a big one for me, I was supposed to stab Carmen as she tried to enter the arena and see her rat-bullfighter-lover do his thing. The beautiful music teacher had told me to stab her in the breast, but I couldn't figure out where that was so she said just stab her in the back. When Choo-Choo Charlie, laughing his head off, told me the breast was the same thing we knew by another name, I sure was glad I would be allowed to stab her in the back. Anyway, I ran after her as she was about to enter the arena, which was supposed to be off stage, and stabbed her in the back with a little too much vigor. But I had been thinking what a rotten deal it was for her to run off with the rat-bullfighter so I let her have it.

"Ouch-ouch-ouch!" she yelled, tears coming into her eyes. Then, suddenly remembering herself, she grabbed her breast and fell to the floor, dead as a doornail. I guess I stabbed her so hard in the back that she felt it all the way to her breast.

I was supposed to cry, "Carmen . . . Carmen . . . I loved you." But the girl's name was Nancy and I cried, "Nancy . . . Nancy . . . I liked you."

The curtain fell. Nancy got up and said I had stabbed her too hard and slapped me on the left ear. When the curtain went back up to a standing ovation, I was holding my ear which was still burning. We all bowed, acknowledging the applause, and Choo-Choo Charlie fell to his knees, put his head on the floor, and did a somersault. I knew the beautiful music teacher couldn't wait to get him back into the corner.

She left us after that year and went to work in a big city, but to this day I can still play "Jolly Old Roger the Tin Maker Man" on a recorder.

T HE OTHER DAY when I was giving my library its annual ten-year cleaning, I climbed a ladder and looked back at the farthest corner of books, near the ceiling, and came across some of the old Dell paperbacks, which I know now were not hiding but only resting there in the dust of nostalgia. There were *Bill Stern's Favorite Baseball Stories, Bill Stern's Favorite Football Stories,* and baseball and football books with cover pictures of Ted Williams, Joe Page, Charley Justice, Leon Heath, and a 1949 *Complete Baseball,* showing Lou Boudreau on one knee, leaning on a bat he used to help the Cleveland Indians win the 1948 American League pennant.

I had been in the fifth or sixth grade when I bought the book showing the great Lou Boudreau for twenty-five cents. Seeing it again reminded me how cluttered and complex my life has become because all I ever really wanted to do was play third base for the Cleveland Indians (or Detroit Tigers). In those days if you did not want to be a baseball player there was something terribly wrong with you, the most serious thing being you were a girl.

I organized my own baseball team at J.G. Wooten Elementary School. Now the school had a softball team, but I wouldn't play anything but baseball, or hardball as the softball players called it. I tried to run my team as the great Lou Boudreau might have run his. Although we often would have only eight guys, I'd post the batting order each Saturday morning on the backstop at the baseball field on the school ground and spent many of my weekday nights calling around town trying to get games scheduled.

My best hitter came from the poorest part of town, although we never judged degrees of social status. His name was Choo-Choo Charlie Moore. He was older than the rest of us and came to play in overalls and without shoes. But it bothered me that he batted cross-handed.

"Hey, Choo-Choo Charlie, you a-battin' cross-handed again," I'd yell.

"Shut you mouth or I whup up on you," Choo-Choo Charlie would yell back. So he was a discipline problem, not only for my baseball team but also in school. Many was the time we'd just get seated in class in the morning when some little girl would scream from the coatroom and then rush out and whisper something to the teacher. A moment later out would come Choo-Choo Charlie, a silly grin on his face, and we knew that the "Kissin' Bandit" had struck again. The teacher would then grab his arm and march him down to the principle's office. Soon you'd hear a great, fearful noise echoing down the halls as Choo-Choo Charlie got a swat with the big, black belt. We'd expect to see him come back, all bleeding, but he never did. He'd walk back into the classroom, grinning. "Never felt a thing," he'd say. "Never felt a thing."

Another of the great burdens I had to carry was that I couldn't whistle. Everybody on the team would whistle encouragement to the pitcher. I couldn't. I tried and tried but I'd just blow out air. No sound. I think I was thirty before I learned to whistle, putting my tongue and teeth just right and letting the shrill sound come out of my mouth. It sure didn't help my managerial authority with the team when I couldn't whistle.

Wooten also had a football team, which played in a league with the other elementary schools. I was the only one on the football team who couldn't whistle, too. I honestly can't remember us winning more than one or two games, but we seldom lost a fight. We had not only Choo-Choo Charlie, although he'd miss a lot of games because he was out picking cotton, but two other real tough kids, the Glenn brothers, James and Clarence. James was our tailback, our best runner, and Clarence, called Bubba, played on defense, despite having a crippled hand and foot. Bubba was at least a head and a half taller than anybody else.

I also was in the backfield but had to block a lot more than run. I didn't like to block Bubba in practice, not only because he was crippled but also because he was bigger than I was—not necessarily in that order. But one afternoon at practice the coach kept yelling at me to knock Bubba down when we ran a sweep. So I kinda stumbled and threw myself under him, sending both of us tumbling and James loose for a touchdown.

But Bubba jumped up, yelling and going berserk. He started kicking at me with his good foot while I was still on the ground. I curled up in a ball and let him kick away, not only because was crippled but also because he was a lot bigger than I was. Again, not necessarily in that order. So Bubba was just kickin away when James came back from making a touchdown. James saw what was happening and screamed, "Leave Bubba alone! You a-pickin' on a po' lil' crippled boy!" With that pronouncement James jumped on top of me and started pounding away. When Bubba heard James say *cripple,* he began to cry.

So there I was on the ground, like a turtle, with James pounding away on my helmet with his fists and Bubba crying, screaming and kicking me. After about ten minutes the coach broke it up and said, "A lil' fightin' is good for the spirit. But we don't pick on no cripples here." Everybody nodded approval, except Bubba who started crying even louder. I didn't much like football after that and just looked forward to baseball season.

Paris had a baseball team in the East Texas League, later going into the Big State League. We'd go out faithfully to watch it play because it was the closest we could get to the great Lou Boudreau, the great Ted Williams, or the great Joe DiMaggio. There was a custom then of passing the hat around in the stands and taking up a collection for players who hit big home runs.

One night the almost-great George Sprys hit a home run. After the game we were walking the ten-odd miles back home when who but the almost-great George Sprys walked up behind us. We were ecstatic. We talked and he bought us ice cream with one of the one hundred coins they'd collected for him that night. He said he'd had trouble finding a ride back to the hotel and had just decided to walk. I told him about our team, and he promised to come out the next day and help us at practice.

The next day was Saturday, and we were out bright and early. We posted a lookout, and everytime he'd see somebody walking toward the school ground he'd yell and we'd start hustling. By mid-afternoon some of the guys, including Choo-Choo Charlie, Bubba and James Glenn, James and Joe Davenport, James Carstophen, and Eddie White, wanted to go on home.

"The great George Sprys said he'd be here and he'll be here," I told them. "So he's a little late. You think all he's got to do is come play baseball with a bunch of snot noses like us."

We waited until dark, but the almost-great George Sprys never showed up. In fact, after everybody else left I waited until almost 9 P.M. When I found those old paperbacks the other day and dusted them off I got to thinking that the great Lou Boudreau would certainly have showed up that day.

W E SAW THE brand spankin' new car sitting outside the school building, which wouldn't mean that much unless you'd seen the old one. Fess valued that new car a close third behind his wife and daughter.

Fess was the name we gave to the principal of J.G. Wooten Elementary School, also called Second Ward. I do not remember whether this was short for professor or fessin' up. Now Second Ward was in a somewhat poor part of town and not far from the vinegar factory. When you were downwind from the factory you could smell vinegar in the air, and as a small boy, I often thought that was the way air smelled. My family was far from the poorest in the neighborhood. Adjacent to the school was a section in which dirty, naked kids were bathed on Saturday nights in washtubs over fires built in front of lean-to houses.

So the new car looked much more out of place than the old one. You could hear the old one coming blocks away. It coughed black smoke, clouding its wake. Only one of the four doors closed and stayed shut on its own; the others were tied with old sheets. Its upholstery was burned by ashes from Fess' ever present cigar. He used the car to take the seven members of our basketball team to places such as Honey Grove or Roxton for games.

We identified Fess with the old car so much that it was shocking to see the shiny new car sitting outside the school that morning. Often thereafter we would see him take a handkerchief out of his breast pocket and remove any dust he saw, or thought he saw, on the car.

He made rules about our riding in the new car. Members of our basketball team had to take off their shoes before getting in, and Choo-Choo Charlie Moore had to wash his feet because he didn't wear shoes in the first place. Fess allowed no horsing around in the new car and promised anyone who did a lick with his big, black belt.

Considering the neighborhood, Fess had an awfully tough bunch of kids with which to deal. He did most of his dealing with the big, black belt. As I think back, that was probably the best way because, had we not feared him, we not only wouldn't have learned English but would have taken over the school.

Fess liked his job very much. He loved his wife, daughter, and the new car. His daughter was in my class, and we were kinda sweet on each other for a while. So I escaped the belt, although I deserved it at times. That should have taught me a valuable lesson in life but it did not.

Anyway, by the third grade she figured out she could do a lot better and jilted me for an older man, a fourth grader. That was hard to take, although not as hard as the time somebody stole my Lou Boudreau baseball glove.

Fess prided himself on English and taught the course himself for the sixth, seventh, and eighth graders. His students were known as having the best preparation in English when they went to Paris High School, which speaks well not only for Fess as a teacher but, maybe, his belt, too.

Usually, Fess would open class by telling us how lucky he was to have such a beautiful daughter "sitting right there on the front row." I don't think it embarrassed his daughter at all because she was used to getting his praise, in public and at home. He'd also tell us how smart she was which, as I look back, might have been another reason our romance ended. I was not near the head of my class. She used a lot of big words, and I had trouble relating to anything over four letters. I always wondered how she turned out because Fess sure did love her. He told us how much he loved his wife, too, and you could tell he loved that shiny new car.

What seemed like a hundred years later I went back to Paris to see what Fess had been up to. Second Ward was gone, replaced by a welfare office. Fess had lost his job for reasons that never were clear. His daughter had died of cancer before even reaching her prime.

I felt awful about these things and drove out to see Fess. He no longer lived in the best house in what had been Second Ward's district but in a broken-down, unkept place. I got out of my car and started walking toward the door but stopped. Parked nearby was a car that looked like the one I had seen so long ago when it was so new and shiny. It was old, falling apart.

When I saw the car that day I could not go in to see him.

Suburbia,
Cabbages and Kings

She was a pretty girl, not fat at all but quite large and more womanly than girl-like, although she was only sixteen that year we often used her as our baby-sitter. She had green-gray eyes, as I remember, and auburn hair, and we often talked about what a lovely woman she was turning out to be. Had she dressed in heels, as a woman, she would have looked to be in her early twenties, but she wore very plain, schoolgirl clothes, which always seemed out of place on her.

She had come highly recommended as a baby-sitter and always was prompt and well-disciplined and did the little extra unrequired things, such as washing the drinking glasses used by the children and left in abundance like toy soldiers on the cabinet.

Although we talked to her parents on the telephone, I don't think we actually ever met them. Her mother was a voice through a half-closed front door, her father, if he answered, would always say, "Wait, I'll let you speak to my wife."

At first the girl was very shy but the more she came to sit with the children, the more she began to talk. We talked in the car when I picked her up and when I took her home, and she also visited with us the brief minutes before we went out and after we came home. She was always very detailed about the children, what they had done or said, and carefully put down phone messages.

Once a neighborhood gossip had said the girl was an "A" student but had a difficult time at home. She said the girl's parents expected her to do too much. She said the girl did a lot of cooking, although her mother didn't work. She said the girl also took care of her two small brothers and was required to do more than her share of housework. But the girl lived in a large, fine house and such talk didn't seem logical. I also knew the gossip watched a lot of soap operas and was re-reading *Oliver Twist.*

One night it was raining very hard when I took the girl home. At first the rain splattered the windshield in a blinding way but then began to fall slowly, softly on the street and dark green lawns of the neighborhood.

"I so love the rain," she said. "It's so refreshing. Sometimes I dream I'm in a cottage in the English countryside and the rain is coming down. I can see it sweeping across the hills but I'm very snug and cozy by the fire in the cottage."

"I'm sure that will happen," I said. "It's a nice thing to want."

"Mr. St. John, I think I'd like to be a writer, perhaps a poet. I . . . (her voice became excited) . . . I . . . we're reading *Hamlet* in school. I love Shakespeare, the language."

She became quiet for a minute and then recited: "Oh, that this too, too solid flesh would melt, thaw and resolve itself into a dew, or that the Everlasting had not turned His cannon against self-slaughter. How weary, stale, flat and unprofitable seems to me all the uses of this world."

She was very still, seemed embarrassed, and said, nervously, "We have to learn so many lines from *Hamlet,* but it's easy, really."

Before she went to the door she said she had written some poetry that she wanted me to read and would bring the next time she sat for us. But the next time she sat for us she said she was too embarrassed to bring the poetry, so I made her promise to bring it when she came back again.

That night we were late getting home. She had said she had an 11 o'clock curfew on school nights, but it was half past that hour before we ever got home.

It was my fault. I'd lingered, had one more drink at a friend's house. The girl was at the door and ready to go when we got home. I told her I'd been selfish, that I was very sorry I'd made her late. She said that was all right and tried to refuse the extra $5 I handed her. She said I owed her only for an extra half hour, but I insisted she keep the $5.

When I had driven her to the front of her house I said, "I'd like to come in and talk to your parents, to explain to them why you're late. That it was my fault, in no way yours."

"Oh, Mr. St. John, that's not necessary. My parents are sound asleep by now. The 11 o'clock curfew is something I've established for myself. I do things like that. I also make lists of things to do each day and each week. I make lists of stories or books to read, music I want to listen to, and things to do around the house. I also want to stay in condition, you know. I jog every morning before school and keep a chart. A healthy body . . . a sound mind. Don't you think people should have lists?"

"Sure. I do, sometimes. I'll jot things down on scraps of paper, here and there, and usually lose them. What I need to do is make a list of the places where I leave my lists."

"Mr. St. John, what you could do would be to get yourself a tablet and put your lists down on it. Then you could put it in the same place each time when you were finished with it and you'd know where it was."

"I think that's a fine idea."

Before she left she asked me if I'd ever been on a long ocean voyage and said she'd been thinking how much she'd enjoy doing such a thing. She said she'd like to sit on deck, in a soft chair, and look out onto the ocean and write poetry.

"Do it," I said. "You'll be able to do that. You'll take a fine voyage, and a young man will fall madly in love with you while watching you on the deck writing poetry.

He'll like poetry, too, and you'll wear a beautiful dress and dance in the ballroom. And everybody will whisper how lucky the young man is, how beautiful you are."

"Oh (she laughed), that would be so nice. I like so much to dream of such things."

"I know."

For a long time that year we couldn't get her to baby-sit. Her mother said that she was sick or busy and no longer was baby-sitting. It was difficult to get information out of her mother, and finally we started using other baby-sitters. After a while I called to see about the girl, but the phone had been disconnected. The gossip was that she had gotten pregnant, married a man in his late twenties, and, of course, dropped out of high school. She had been a junior, and the next year when her class graduated she wasn't on the list.

One day many years later in the supermarket I saw a woman, very much along in her pregnancy, pushing a cart down an aisle of endless cans. Two children, one about two and the other perhaps five or six, followed her. I thought I recognized her. She looked very tired, and her auburn hair was unkept. I thought it was the girl who had been our baby-sitter and, smiling, walked toward her.

She looked at me, then quickly turned the cart around and hurried around the corner into another aisle. I suppose I had been mistaken, that it wasn't the dream-filled girl who had sat for us so often that year.

YOU KNEW THEM without knowing them by looking at the car. It was one of those paneled station wagons, simulated wood, mid-70s model, with what looked like new tires, and they had stopped by the roadside park on Highway 35, South.

The back of the car was fallout from what had been organization. The license plates said they were from Illinois, which is not the sunshine state.

It was mid-afternoon, and the woman, who had gotten out of the car and sat on a picnic table, looked haggard. She put her feet on the bench below her, put her elbows on her knees and her chin in her hands. Her husband stood near her, stretching, then opening a beer which he began to sip. Two small children, maybe five and four, ran around the area, looking everywhere and nowhere in their happiness of escaping the confinement of the car.

Obviously, they were on the Great American Vacation and it was Thursday, so this must be the roadside park on Highway 35, South.

They said their name was McNeil and they had driven from Illinois, taking an easy week to get where they were south of Dallas. They wanted to see Texas and would stop at the coast and spend a week. They had heard it was cheaper to stay on the coast in Texas than in California or Florida, and even on vacation you had to watch your money a little. McNeil seemed friendly in a nervous-laughing way. Mrs. McNeil did not seem particularly friendly, but I could see that she was tired.

"You've got five, six hours left if you go to the coast near Corpus," I said.

"That far?" Mrs. McNeil asked. "I'm worn out now. These kids are driving me crazy, you know."

"Honey," McNeil said, " we'll be there in no time. No time flat."

"Well, you could stop over in Austin," I volunteered. "Rest a while. I know this park with a creek, a lot of trees, rock paths. You could rest and the kids could run around. And, if you stayed over, you could go down on the Colorado River for a while. Austin's a great place. Maybe you could go up on Mt. Bonnell, where there's a fine view of the city and the river."

Mrs. McNeil, who did not want any volunteers and wasn't taking any prisoners, looked at me coldly and asked, "You a plain clothes tour guide or something?"

"Come on, honey. He's only trying to be nice."

"I'm sorry," I said. "I'm sorry. I didn't mean to interfere."

"How far's San Antonio? Say, from Austin," said McNeil.

"Oh, maybe eighty or eighty-five miles," I said. "The San Antonio River runs through downtown and you could stop there and eat at one of the restaurants on the river. It's pleasant there on cool nights and . . ."

"Rivers! Rivers! Rivers!" Mrs. McNeil said. "I don't want to see another blankety-blank river! The Mississippi River, the Colorado River, the San Antonio River! The River-River-River! No more rivers!"

"Hey, honey, come on," McNeil said. "This is vacation. Have a beer. Come on, have a beer. Okay."

"I don't want to see another blankety-blank river. You kids stay out of the driveway there. Hey! HEEEEYYYYYY! Will you get those kids back? You're their father, blankety-blank. In case you forgot, you, too, are a parent. Get your nose out of that beer and get those kids back. BAAAAAAAAAAAAAACCCK!"

"Honey, this is a vacation."

"Your vacation. Look at me. That motel last night . . . the bed was so soft it was like sleeping in a hammock. Get those kids out of the road!"

"Honey, that motel was all right. It was reasonable."

"Am I having fun yet? Tell me if I'm having fun yet," I said.

"What do you mean? What are you talking about?" the woman asked.

"I don't know," I said. "I really don't. This friend of mine, Laurie Stowers, always used to like to say, 'Tell me if I'm having fun yet.' So I just thought of it."

"Why?"

"I don't know."

"Honey, this man's trying to be nice."

"Listen, mister, I'm sorry if I've been rude, but the kids are acting up and it's been hell."

"I can understand that."

"Kids," Mrs. McNeil yelled, "make sure you go to the bathroom if you need to before we leave. Now's the time. We're not stopping for a long time. We're going off . . . TO SEE ANOTHER BLANKETY-BLANK RIVER!"

I left and sat in the car to watch them leave. They got into the car, drove to the end of the roadside park.

Suddenly, the man slammed on the brakes and burned rubber as he backed up, stopping almost at the same place they had been.

One of the kids got out of the car and ran toward the bathroom.

His MOTHER lived alone in an apartment with old pictures, both on the wall and in albums, her television set serving as a kind of daily timekeeper and her telephone linking her to the outside world, as did the soap operas she often watched.

She phoned him almost daily, just to keep in touch, and asked him when he might be stopping by to see her. "Today or perhaps tomorrow?" she questioned, hoping. He told her he would try to stop for a while, perhaps tomorrow, but that he was very busy, that he had this or that going.

"Well," she said, "it seems like I never see you anymore. It seems you could stop by sometime."

"I will. I'll try to get by the first thing next week."

But he got very busy with something unexpected the first thing next week and didn't go by to see her. "I'm sorry," he said. "It just came up. I can't help it. Maybe next week, the first thing next week."

Sometimes when he went by to see her she got out the old albums and showed him the pictures, some fading and torn at the edges. In some pictures he had a crewcut; in others he wore a baseball hat, tipped back on his head, and held an old glove, a bat, and a bottle of water. She said his hair looked a little too long nowadays.

"He never got into any trouble," she told any visitors who came with him. "I read nowadays that kids are always getting into trouble, but he never did."

"I waited until adulthood to get into all the trouble," he said, smiling. "I was saving myself while I was growing up."

She smiled, understandingly, even if she didn't understand. When she cooked supper for him, the smells reminded him of long ago times. She cooked with the same seasoning, so the smells were the same as those he remembered from boyhood. But when he went to see her he usually was on his way to somewhere else and didn't stay very long.

Often he felt guilty for not going to see her more, for not staying longer. Guilt had been such a part of the religion, the place and the time in which he grew up. He was almost forty before he stopped feeling guilty for not feeling guilty.

"Well, listen," he said. "I guess I'd better be going."

"So soon," she said. "Maybe next time you can stay longer. It was nice to see you again. It wouldn't hurt you to stop and see me every once in a while. The others do."

"I will. I'll phone you tomorrow and stop by the first thing next week. Things will slow down soon, and I'll drop by more often."

He had a son, twenty-one, who lived not far from his house. Maybe fifteen miles. He phoned his son. "Are you dead? Alive? Are you in limbo or what?" he asked.

"Oh, hi, Dad. I meant to phone you."

"Well, I just haven't heard from you in a month, so I wondered if you were dead or alive."

"I've been meaning to come by. There's just a lot of things going on now. I've been on the run. I'll try to get by and see you first thing next week. Okay?"

THE MOTHER of my children, who over the years has accumulated more college hours on more subjects than anybody else in America, has gone this month to study in Mexico, so my kids, Scott (15) and Todd (13) and I (unknown) are bacheloring it, preparing gourmet meals for ourselves.

I'm having trouble pushing my frozen TV dinners. Frankly, I love frozen dinners. I yearn for their hard, icy taste, and elegant blandness. Sometimes I like them so much I think I could just eat them cold, unheated. I don't mean to get carried away, but nowadays you can get full frozen dinners—featuring turkey, fish, Swiss steak—or, if you're not very hungry, you can just pop a pot pie into the oven.

The boys often kid me, a lot, saying I just eat frozen dinners because I can't cook. Of course, they're too young to understand that there's an art to cooking TV dinners. I mean, you have to have the oven at just the right temperature and leave them in just the right amount of time or they'll be cooked in the middle and still cold in the far corners.

But the kids have gone on strike against my frozen dinners and have taken over the kitchen. Scott has begun calling himself Monsieur Scott and declared that he is a chef. The other night he prepared our entree while talking to his girl friend on the kitchen telephone, which has an extremely long cord. When he'd finished cooking, the phone cord looked like a spider web.

He also asked his friend Brian Mock over and prepared this concoction which he called, "Lost Steak a la Scott." As nearly as I could determine without an extensive investigation, he put the steak in a pan and then poured on various kinds of soup, plus a special sauce he devised. When he took the steak out of the oven it made funny noises.

"I can't eat that, I'll die," said Todd. "And you can't give it to the dogs or they'll die."

"I don't know whether to try to talk to it or eat it," I said. I slowly approached the dish, bent over it very carefully, and said, "Friends. We are your friends. Where did you come from?"

Brian Mock backed away. "Uh, I forgot, " he said. "I've already eaten."

"Just remembered, huh?" I asked.

"Coward," said Scott, as Brian hurried out the door.

We all ate a little. I mean when you're hungry you'll eat anything. Right? What was left we put outside for the dogs. The next morning it was still there.

Todd proclaimed the other night that he was the dessert man. We were out of butternut ice cream and the great energy-giving M&M's with peanuts. However, he said he would prepare an "overnight pudding." He worked in the kitchen for about forty-five minutes, while talking to himself and listening to the Texas Ranger baseball game. When he'd finished, the pudding was, I believe, a kind of yellow color as he put it into the refrigerator. The next morning it was greenish, and honestly, it appeared to have something growing in the middle of it.

"You don't put flower seeds in pudding," snapped Scott.

"I don't know what went wrong," said Todd. "I can't understand it."

"Think of it this way," I said. "If you were still in kindergarten you could take it to show and tell."

"Very funnnneeeeee."

"Tonight," announced Scott, "I have a new idea for steak."

"I'm working," I said.

"I'm going to the Ranger game with Nick Druga," said Todd.

"Maybe Brian Mock can come over to eat," said Scott.

But we all stayed, grim but loyal. Actually, I think the steak he broiled would have turned out all right except that Scott decided to talk to his girl friend on the telephone in the bedroom instead of the kitchen. You might say the steak was a little overcooked, frizzled and hard as a rock.

"Ahhhh-so, what have we here?" I asked, looking at what apparently had been meat.

Scott got this sickly look on his face, then grinned, and said, "Beef jerky of course. I was making beef jerky."

We put it outside, but again the dogs wouldn't eat it. I guess what I'm trying to say is that we're having frozen TV dinners tonight.

He is out there somewhere, doctor. I know it. I know he is. Oh. Sorry. Sorry. I'll relax, lie down again. No, doctor, I like him. I really do. There's no, noooo animosity. It's just . . . just he, well, fixes everything. It makes me look bad. I can't fix anything. And he's always so clear-eyed and healthy. Clear of mind, body, soul, spirit, and eye. Yeah, right. Like Roger Staubach.

I bet Roger Staubach fixes everything.

He lives near me and watches my house. I know he does. No. Not Roger Staubach. The guy. Well, not long ago I was in the bathroom, shaving. I was late for work. I had on a new pair of shoes. Suddenly, I got this odd sensation on my feet. I looked down. Water was all over my shoes. It was all over the floor. My first thought was to take one thing at a time and go ahead and finish shaving. But water was really getting all over the floor. Right, the dike had broken. Right.

I looked under the sink. The pipe was leaking. Really leaking, doctor. I got a pan and then another, putting one under the leak and shoveling water into the bathtub with the other. I did this for some time and thought of the Law of Diminishing Returns. I ran for the phone and called the plumber. He couldn't come for two hours but told me to go outside by the hydrant and turn something that would shut off the water to the house, thus stopping the water from leaking out of the pipe.

I got my screwdriver, which my mother gave me when I was a kid, and ran outside to cut off the water. I found the hydrant behind some bushes. There was no cutoff. He saw me. I was afraid he would. He came jogging out of his house, quickly diagnosed the problem, and ran back into his garage. He reappeared with the proper equipment, raced to the manhole nearest my yard and used the proper key to open it, and then took the proper tool and shut off the water.

"Are you all right?" he said, walking over to me. I was by the bushes. "Hey, thanks a lot!" I said, enthusiastically. "You saved my life."

"It's nothing, really," he said. All the kids in the neighborhood were there. Listening. Watching. "Well, I'm off to work," I said. He looked at me and pointed out, "Your shoes. They're . . . they're full of water."

"Nothing," I said. "It's really nothing." I jumped into my car and drove on to work, where I hid my feet under my desk all day. My new shoes were too little the next morning, doctor.

Another time, my lawn mower stalled. I couldn't start it again. Okay, I admit it. I yelled. Screamed. Yelled. It still wouldn't start. I fell to my knees, tears in my eyes. I lay prostrate and looked up. He was there. I tried to hand him my screwdriver, but he wouldn't take it. He took a small wrench, did some adjusting, and then started the lawn mower. All the women in the neighborhood were watching.

Doctor, you don't know. It's embarrassing. Really embarrassing. Most kids say, "My daddy can do anything." The other day I heard one of mine saying, proudly, "My daddy can't do anything." Then he added, "But he can hit free throws."

I can doctor. I can really hit free throws. Sorry. Sorry. I'll lie back down. I know. I know, doctor. As my brother said, not long ago, "So what? So you can hit free throws. As near as I can tell there's not a great demand in the world today for guys over forty who can hit free throws." I gave that a lot of thought, doctor. He's probably right. But it's just . . . just . . .

Oh, yeah. Once right after I'd bought a brand new shiny Volkswagen . . . What? Right. With radio, heater, bumper guards, white sidewalls, "Love It or Leave It" bumper sticker. Anyway, it wouldn't start one afternoon. I tried and tried. The battery, brand new, wouldn't even turn over. I got out of the car, slid down the side to my knees, and buried my head in my hands. Just as I was getting up to go get my screwdriver, he appeared. Jogging footsteps.

"Something wrong?" he asked. "No," I said. "Why?" He looked at me, then the car, and said, "Car won't start? I had a Volkswagon once. What you got to do is rock it. Rock the car, the VW."

I got up and rocked the car. It wouldn't start. "Here," he said. "Let me try." He rocked it. It started. I looked around to see if anybody was watching. The blinds slammed shut next door. "Well, my daddy can hit free throws," I heard my kid say.

No, no, doctor, I'm all right. I'M ALL RIGHT, YOU HEAR ME! He's fixed everything. Plumbing. Toys. Bikes. My typewriter. My camera. Everything. I . . . I . . . I'm late for work, doctor. Same time, next week. What? That. My screwdriver. Yeah, I might need it.

SHE WAS A large woman who looked to be in her thirties and wore a gray suit. Her hat, small and fragile, seemed to be bobby-pinned to her dishwater blond hair, done up in back. She wore pinkish lipstick and had a sour face. I wondered if her shoes were too tight.

A boy of about five followed a half step behind her. She held his hand, like a leash, and seemed to be pulling him into the cafe where I was having morning coffee. He, too, was dressed up, wearing a miniature suit and clip-on tie.

It was Sunday, so I thought they probably had stopped for breakfast before going to church. Watching them sitting side by side at the table next to me, I remembered that when I was a kid in East Texas we'd say "You've got on your Sunday-go-to-meetin' clothes" about people who got all dressed up. The large woman and small boy definitely had on their Sunday-go-to-meetin' clothes.

"Now you behave yourself," the woman told the boy. "Do you hear me?"

"Yes, Mother."

The waitress came, left them each a glass of water, and took their orders for pancakes. The woman told the boy he didn't drink enough water and that this was a good time to start. The boy took a drink from his glass and then blew bubbles into it.

"Stop that!" snapped the woman, and everybody in the cafe heard her. "Put that glass down this instant!"

"Yes, Mother," he said, looking angelic.

"I told you to behave. We've just gotten here and you're already embarrassing me."

"Mother, I'm hungry. My tummy is hungry."

"Be quiet! I told you if I brought you here for breakfast you'd have to wait. You said that was all right.

That's what you said. I hope you don't start lying to your mother, telling her things you don't mean."

"Yes, Mother."

"Would you like one of those crackers with syrup on it, to hold you until the pancakes come?"

"Yes, Mother."

The woman tore open a small package of crackers in the middle of the table, took one out, carefully poured syrup on top, and handed it to the boy. He turned it sideways as he started to put it into his mouth. Some of the syrup fell on his shirt, just to the right of his clip-on tie.

"Oh no! Now you've done it! I told you to be careful. Oh, my goodness, now you've ruined your new shirt. I paid good money for that shirt and . . . oh my goodness, look at it. It's enough to make me cry. Now aren't you ashamed? Well, aren't you?"

"Yes, Mother."

The woman got up and stood over the boy. Her calves and ankles were very heavy, and her shoes looked too small for her feet. She held his shoulder with her left hand and took a napkin with her right hand and dipped it into his water glass. Then she scrubbed his shirt and mouth.

I could tell she was squeezing his shoulder very hard with her left hand because his eyes bulged and his mouth opened. He looked like a goldfish, coming to the top of a bowl. When she sat down again, the boy rubbed his shoulder.

After the waitress brought their pancakes, the woman carefully put butter and syrup on them. She told the boy he knew how to eat properly and to put his napkin in his lap. He said the napkin was wet, but she told him again to do it, and he said, "Yes, Mother."

After holding his fork correctly for a couple of bites, the kid got bored. He cut a piece out of the pancake and pretended his fork was an airplane zeroing in on a target, which was his mouth. He made an airplane noise, the whistling noise of bombs being released and then the sound when they exploded.

"I don't believe this!" the woman said. "I knew I shouldn't trust you . . . you . . . you . . . you little snit. I wish your father could see you. He taught you how to do that, play silly games while you eat. I just wish he was here to see the damage he's done. I take you out for a nice breakfast of pancakes before church and you do this to me. You little snit! I'll never take you anywhere again!''

"Yes, Mother.''

"Don't you yes-mother me.''

"Yes, Mother.''

The kid then held his fork correctly, ate about half his pancakes, and said he was full, that his tummy said it was full.

"You didn't finish half your breakfast. Now eat! Eat all your food! I'm paying good money for your food and you waste it. Aren't you ashamed, wasting food?''

"Yes, Mother.''

"I've learned my lesson. I'll never take you out to eat again. Your manners are awful. Just awful. Next Sunday, you can just stay home and have cereal. And you won't get any of those fancy brands anymore either . . . the chocolate coated junk. You'll get . . . you'll get Wheaties, young man. Do you understand?''

"Yes, Mother.''

She seemed to feel better after pronouncing the awful sentence on him. Everybody felt better when the large woman and small boy left the cafe. I still thought her shoes looked too tight.

THEY WERE showing pictures of their overseas vacation, which both said was great, the best time they'd ever had, and they hoped I wouldn't find all the pictures boring. But I would be the first to see them. The very first.

I thought that was fine. I wanted to see the pictures and hear about their trip, the one for which they'd saved and planned so long. The pictures were spread out on the kitchen table. Some were very bright and cheerful, some were a little out of focus, but they were all interesting. During their ten-day whirlwind tour of Europe they had taken so many pictures that I wondered how they had had time for anything else.

"Listen," he told me, "you've just got to go. It's tremendous, the best vacation, the most fun we've ever had. Right, honey?"

"Right. It surely was. So different and so beautiful. Here, look at this group of pictures from Ireland . . . the rolling greenery. See the rock fences. No, we didn't spend much time out in the countryside. We just got the bus driver to stop so we could take these pictures. They're good about that. Next time I'd like to spend more time out in the countryside. Next time."

"You got awful sick," he said. "We stopped at this pub. Had a little time and drank some Irish beer and, boy, she got sick. Ha-ha-ha. She was sick for two days. Just kind of hanging on."

"Oh, come on. You make it sound awful. I wasn't THAT sick. It was just the excitement, I guess. You wait so long for something and then, well, it's happening. Happening right then. I so love Europe."

"Me, too. Here, look at these shots around London," he continued. "Oscar Wilde lived here, right in that place. And here's Churchill's home. That's something, isn't it. We didn't have that much time, so I'm glad we got these pictures."

"We were going to the theater," she said, "but he lost the tickets. We got there, the tickets didn't. We went back to the hotel and by the time we got back to the theater, the play had been on for forty-five minutes. That was a stupid thing to do, leave the tickets."

"Well," he said, "that happens. You didn't have to get so mad. You bitched at me for two days, and then pouted for two more. You pout just like your mother."

"Why do you bring up my mother?"

"Because, after I lost the tickets, you said that next time you'd go to Europe with her instead of me."

"Well, you just about ruined the best vacation we ever had. We'd so looked forward to going and you just about ruined it."

"Shoot me! Kill me! Cut my fingers off, one by one! I said I was sorry."

"Here's the inn where we stayed in Scotland," she continued, ignoring him. "Such a quaint, beautiful little place. It was almost like going on another honeymoon for us. We just loved it.''

"The only thing I'd change is that I'd have bathrooms in every room," he said. "They had a bathroom down the hall, but you had to share it with the other guests and that can be, well, awkward.''

"You'd find something wrong with anything," she said. "It was a fine little place, and we just loved it.''

"We had a wonderful time," he said. "And here, look here. This is the cafe where we ate. Everything was just like, you know, in the old movies you see about Europe. The food was great, except what . . . I guess it was the mutton. I really didn't like it very much.''

"I told you not to order mutton. But you have to try everything. And, really, did you have to get into it with the waiter?''

"Well, he was rude.''

"You didn't have to make such a big deal out of it. I mean, after all, everybody was looking at us. There we were, the ugly Americans. It was so embarrassing I couldn't enjoy the food.''

"If you'd had mutton you wouldn't have enjoyed it anyway.''

"Here. Here's Parliament. Look. The shots are a little pale, but, you know, there was no sunshine in London. But Parliament. Such tradition. Isn't it stately? No. We didn't spend much time there. We had to be going on. But we want to go back so the next vacation there we can take our time, you know.''

"Oh, look at you, standing there in the pictures. You didn't have to look so sour. I told you to smile. You look like you're mad at the world. Really.''

"Well, I was just very tired, dear," she said.

"It was wonderful, the best vacation we've ever had.''

"Honey, where are the pictures from Paris? Gay Pareeee. We were rushed, but I thought we got some pretty good shots.''

"Let me look. They're around here somewhere. Paris was wonderful, except you got mad and started pouting.

Really, will you ever outgrow pouting? Yes, we had such a
fantastic time."

"It was the best vacation we've ever had."

"We've got to go back, soon. It's worth whatever it
costs. Right dear."

I<small>T WAS TIME</small> to go. He was packed and had said goodby
to his grandson, who had run outside and down the block
to play. It was his grandson's way of escaping, of not
watching. Everybody has escapes, he thought.

Two suitcases. After a lifetime he had two suitcases
full of clothes, belongings, and a few of his favorite books.
He would read them again. And again. Odd, he thought,
how perspective changes for everybody.

He had collected books since he was in his mid-teens
and taken such good care of them. Besides the graying, the
fading of everything, that comes with age, the books had
remained in such good shape, spotless and unsoiled except by time. But that had ended when he had been
brought to live with his son's family.

His daughter-in-law had decided to keep a few chickens in a shed she had built in the backyard. The dog had
broken into the shed one night and killed all but one of the
chickens. She had no place to put the remaining chicken
until the shed was reconstructed so she had put it into the
storage room in the house, where his books were kept.
They were in open boxes, scattered about because he
often went there to browse through them. The chicken
had done its do on the books.

At first he had been angry for what he considered a
thoughtless, blatant disregard for the property he most
treasured. But then he had begun to laugh, seeing the
chicken manure on his books as symbolic of what had
become of his life.

He had reached seventy and his back hurt a lot. He
had injured it playing ball in his teens and it had been a
lifelong problem, which surgery had not particularly
helped. But in recent years his back had gotten worse,

reaching the point where he couldn't get out of bed without help nor move around without a walker. It was so degrading to be like that, but it had happened. Old age, he thought, should be a time of philosophizing, of great dignity. But if you had a bad back it wasn't.

After his wife had died five years ago, he had lived alone in the house that he had begun to buy shortly after their marriage. At first he'd gotten along all right by himself, although moving around had been difficult. His two sons came to see him, bringing their families, every couple of weeks, and they often phoned to check on him. He read, watched football on television, and took walks while he was able.

Then the time came when his back wouldn't loosen up at all, when he couldn't get out of bed. He could handle arthritis in his hands and his joints, but not in the back. So his son had come and gotten him and after selling the old house, he'd moved into their guest room.

He had been there six months. At first it was fine, although he knew he was a burden. His daughter-in-law, who was working and trying to take care of her husband and fourteen-year-old son, had little time to take care of him. She constantly was busy, doing something for somebody, seldom herself. And he had to have help.

His corncob pipe, old and stained, bothered her. He was becoming more forgetful each year and continually left the pipe lying around. She would find it on the arm of a chair, the mantel, the kitchen table, anywhere and everywhere. Once he heard her through a closed door yelling to his son about "that damn pipe!" He tried to remember to keep it with him but forgot. It was symbolic, really.

Nobody talked to him that much, except his grandson. Sometimes when he walked into the room his son and daughter-in-law would become quiet. They were polite, cordial, but he knew they didn't know what to do about him. He had no place to be. But his grandson would listen to him, and he told the boy all he knew about sports, books, and how life once had been. He hoped what he told the boy would help.

His grandson looked so much like his son. He remembered that when his son was in his teens, they'd had a lot of trouble with him. He'd stolen, gotten into trouble repeatedly. Several times he'd had to get out of bed and go to the police station to keep the boy out of the juvenile home. Even the boy's mother had about given up on him.

Still, he kept faith in his son, who finally had gone to college at twenty-two, had gotten three degrees in English, and now was teaching at the university. It had been difficult to send the boy to college, and he'd had to spend the money he was saving for a retirement home on the lake. But it didn't matter. After his wife had died, he couldn't have lived at the lake anyway because he couldn't get around.

His son and daughter-in-law argued a lot. They argued about their son, about him, about who was treating whom badly. Etc. Etc. He knew his presence didn't help. And now he couldn't help feeling rejected, moody, because they had decided it was best to put him in a home for the aged. God, he hated that, the final indignity. Strangers would see him as he was now—a cripple, a person who couldn't even get out of bed without help.

He thought about how he had stood by his son during some awful times, and now his son wasn't standing by him. He felt sorry for himself, awfully sorry for himself and knew, because of this, his perspective was clouded. His son and daughter-in-law felt guilty. They had tried but just couldn't take care of him. They didn't have the time, the resources. So they all had talked and decided it was best for him to go to the home, where people knew how to take care of him. His son told him he could watch television, read.

So it was time to go. As they drove down the street he waved to his grandson, who had stopped playing football long enough to watch them drive past. His grandson just stared, then quickly got back into his game. His daughter-in-law had begun to cry. His son's voice was shaking and he guessed he might cry, too.

Finally, he thought, none of us is wrong.

THAT FIRST year they'd go to movies downtown and then, after the show, take long, dreamy walks on fall nights that were neither too hot nor too cold and look into the store windows, wishing and thinking about the things they didn't have.

But there are no movies downtown now, and people no longer take walks there on fall nights that are neither too hot nor too cold.

For them in the old days the store windows were a looking glass. There had been one particular store for people with a great deal of money where they stopped often, looking into the window at the fine things, worn by staring, uninterested mannequins with too-white and too-pinkish skins. They'd look at the things in the window and at their own reflections.

One night the window displayed a scene in which a mannequin with too-black hair stood over a fine glass table, upon which were two fragile cups, so small and dainty they hardly could have held more than a sip or so. The mannequin had on a long, white evening dress, flowing shiny and softly to the floor. The dress cost $850.

"Oh that dress is so lovely," she said. "So very lovely. Buy me that dress sometime when we're rich and famous. We are going to be rich, aren't we? Of course we are. And look at those cups and . . . and the glass table. Would you buy those for me, too? Would you buy me everything in the window?"

"Sure," he said, "I'll give you everything in the window."

"Oh, thank you," she said, seeing clearly his reflection.

They were married and as the years passed they were happy and unhappy, had money, did not have money, bought things and did not buy things. They were suburbia.

Another day in fall after the movies no longer were downtown and suburbia had engulfed the things and people around it, had expanded, moved outward and onward like locust, they went back downtown one evening.

They ate at a restaurant which closed early because not many people came downtown at night anymore. After they had eaten and left the restaurant they, unconsciously, began to walk. She said she felt a chill and wished she had brought a sweater, so he gave her his coat because he felt warm, actually too warm.

They seemed almost drawn, hypnotically, to the store window in which they had seen the mannequin in the long, flowing white dress so long ago. They stood there for a while and saw their reflections. Then they saw a display of fur coats, some lying against a velvet background and one worn by a mannequin . . . and then their reflections again.

"You never did give me what we saw in the window that night," she said. "You promised but you never did."

"Well, I did. I gave you everything in the window."

"No, you didn't."

They stood there in silence for a few more minutes. Then she saw their reflections again, his reflection.

"I'd forgotten," she said.

The Shell Games

THEY WERE TALKING at a nearby table, voices overheard in a small and clean cafe . . .

"I so love these teacups," she said, holding hers as though it were a fragile, wounded bird. "They're, well, very pretty, almost . . . well, dainty. Aren't they? Aren't they dainty? Not like the ones you ordinarily find in cafes."

"I don't know why I'm drinking tea," he said. "I don't usually drink tea, hot tea I mean. But you know that. And, ah, the cups. They remind you of another cup, another place."

"You're going to make fun of me."

"No, I'm not. They remind me, too. But you just can't go back, you know. Everybody knows that. Thomas Wolfe wrote it very lyrically a long time age. People know it to be true but try it anyway. You can't go back. We can't go back. It wouldn't be the same."

"But . . . but we could try. We could go back, even for a little while, and try. I've missed you a lot. You don't know. You just don't know."

"Yes I do. I've missed you, too. You'll always have a place there, inside me."

"We could go back and try. Remember how beautiful it used to be, how fine the weather was in autumn in

Austin. And . . . and we walked along the Colorado River. The river is still there. We could go back (she smiled weakly). It'll be autumn soon. Soon.''

"It's been so very hot this summer, still is. I think there might not be an autumn this year. Oh, sure, we could go back and it might be fine, but I don't think it would be the same. That was a different time of our lives. We were different then. More innocent. Much more innocent. I think if we went back and walked along the river the mood no longer would be so dreamy, our feelings so pastel. Besides, it would rain.''

"We do so need rain now. Remember you used to like to stand in the rain. And you don't have to be so mean when you talk to me. I . . . I don't even know what happened to us. It just happened. I'm sorry it did.''

"I'm sorry. I'm sorry, too. It was nice. I don't know what happened, but it just happens to a lot of people. We both changed a little. There were a lot of outside things, a lot of negative indentations.''

"God, I feel indented. You were nicer then. Now, you're being mean to me.''

"I'm not trying to be mean. You just can't go back. Can't be the same because it's not the same time and place.

"Oh, the least you could do would be to try. Remember when we used to take long walks? I don't remember us ever driving much. We walked, like in that park, the one with the oaks, the rock paths, and little creek.''

"And the picnic tables under the trees. You could lie on them and look up through the branches all the way to the sky. It was just off Lamar, not far from Caswell Tennis Center. Yeah, I remember.''

"Oh, maybe we couldn't do that again. Maybe you're right.''

"I have this friend who also lived in Austin. He was married there, lived there, and then they came to Dallas and split. He said after they'd split that they had tried again. They had gone back to Austin for a long weekend and went to the old places, did the same things they had done before and had had a good time.''

"See. See. We could do that. We could go back.''

"Let me finish. He said they left and drove back to Dallas, and just as they got back to the city limits, something happened. He said they looked at each other and both knew it was no good. They'd fooled themselves. The magic really hadn't been there again. They'd tried, been actors in a play . . . played their old parts, themselves when they were young and lived in Austin. And then they got back and became the people they are, not were. The old feelings were gone."

"Everybody's not the same. Maybe we could do that and it would be all right. Maybe."

"I wish. I really wish. If I thought for a minute it would be all right again, I'd grab you right now and we'd go. I feel like somebody in a John Cheever short story I read. It was about this couple close to breaking up who had gone back to the places they'd been when things were all right. But what they had wasn't there anymore, waiting for them. The pages they'd once read were blank."

"Maybe. But just maybe."

"Maybe we could have a relationship charging windmills."

"Well, you used to charge windmills."

"I know."

"Well, look. It's dark out there. So dark. And I don't want to go. We could try."

The waitress brought more tea and the woman prepared hers ever so carefully. She fingered the cup, holding it gently, softly in her hand. "I so love these cups," she said. He looked at her, the way she was holding the cup and wondered if they could go back again.

THEY SAT IN EARLY evening at the bar on the edge of the French Quarter in New Orleans, overlooking the Mississippi River, and she asked for another drink. She had had two and when she was about halfway through the third said she wanted to get up and dance.

"Sure," he said. "Sure. They don't dance here, in case you hadn't noticed, but go ahead. Get up and dance."

"I just might," she said, looking at him questioningly. "I just might."

They sat in silence for a while, looking out over the bar and through the window at the riverboat, brightly lit and passing slowly as if flowing in time with the river. The lights of the boat were bright, glowing on the night waters like diamonds on black velvet. "That's so pretty," she said. "Let's ride on it sometime. Look . . . it looks like a giant Christmas tree floating down the river."

"We will," he said. "Sometime we will."

"It would be so much fun. Soooo much fun. We've been here for seven, eight years and never ridden the riverboat. You said when we moved from Dallas that we'd do the fun things here. That it would be fun."

"We will," he said. "Sometime."

"Why don't you loosen up, like me. Why don't you have a good time."

Never looking up from the beer he was sipping, he said, "I am. I'm just fine."

"You don't want me to have a good time, do you? Well, maybe I'll just get up and dance. Maybe I'll get up, right here and now, like one of the strippers over on Bourbon Street. Maybe I'll get up off this bar stool and start taking off my clothes right now."

"That's what you ought to do. Why don't you do it?" There was silence again; then he said, "Let's go on and eat. It's time. Reservations are for nine."

She got up off the stool, staggered slightly. "Uh," he said, "if you don't feel good, why don't we just go on home, stop, and get something on the way? Why don't we do that?"

"Noooo way. This is a night out for me. Are you afraid I'll get drunk and embarrass you? You don't want me to have a good time."

"No. Have a good time. I want you to have a good time." He smiled at her. A Dentyne smile.

"Loosen up your tie," she said. "Why don't you loosen up your tie?"

They walked down the street in the Quarter, which was full of people going in the same and opposite directions. Music was coming onto the street from behind almost every door.

"I used to be a good dancer," she said. "I was in ballet, took it for five, six years. I took tap, too. Watch. Watch this . . ."

She began to dance along the street, around a pole, swinging on one arm, hanging on as though it were a brass ring. She was in time with the music coming from behind a door, a trumpet sound, low and brassy. "Da-da-da-da-da-deeeeeee Sweeeeeeet Georgia Brownnnn . . . da-da-da-da-DEEEEE . . ."

She got up on her toes, took a few steps, and then came down again and started tapping. Three guys passing started clapping time. She laughed and kept on dancing. He walked along the street, mostly looking down at the ground. Then she took off a scarf from around her shoulders, put it on her hips, and started wiggling, sisssssss-boooooom-baaaaaaaa.

She looked over at him, then stopped. She took his arm and said, "You're mad at me. You're sooooo mad at me."

"No, I'm not. I want you to have a good time. I'm not mad."

"You're mad. I know you're mad. But I can't be like you. I'm just having a good time. You get out. Go to the office, see people. I'm at home all week. I want to have a good time. Loosen up. Why don't you loosen up?"

"I'm loose," he said, looking over at her. "I'm having a good time. Here's Broussard's. Maybe, if you're not hungry, we ought to go on, stop on the way, and get something to eat. I'm not hungry. I'm full. The beer filled me up."

"Wellllll, I'm starved. And heereeeee weeeeee areeeee." She walked into the restaurant and noticed that the man checking reservations had left his station. She jumped behind the man's station, looked at her husband, and said, "Sir, do you have reservations? Oh sir, I didn't recognize you. And is your lovely wife with you, the famous ballerina. Sir, we indeed are honored, and might I say, you have our best table."

People standing nearby grinned, one woman in a long dress laughed aloud, and he smiled a little, although his eyes did not seem to smile. The man came back and, checking reservations, led them to their table. When the waiter came and asked it they'd like a cocktail, he said no but she said, "Weelllll, my good man, let me have a martini, shaken, not stirrrrreeeeed."

She had her martini and then became very quiet, as though thinking she might be somebody else, someplace else. They ate, he very quickly, then they left Broussard's and started walking back down the street to their car.

The air seemed to revive her. She did a fast tap number and then began singing, "Chiiiicaaagooo, Chiicaaagooooo, that toddlin' town . . . Chiiiicaaagooo, Chicaaagooo . . ."

"It's not Chicago," he said. "It's New Orleans."

"Newwwww Orleeeeannnnns, New Orrrlleeeeannnsss, that toddlin' town," she sang.

They crossed Royal, went down a side street toward the parking lot where they'd left their car. She was dancing along the sidewalk, sometimes swinging out from a post onto the street. He walked on the sidewalk close to the store fronts, hands in his pockets and looking neither right nor left.

MIKE JONES LEANED over the table, cupping his fourth beer as though it were a crystal ball. He stared at the reflection in the glass, which distorted his face as though it were a balloon, busted and all stretched out. Randy Galloway leaned back in his chair, looking out into the dimly lit room. He saw nothing that anybody else could see.

I didn't look into my beer nor lean back in my chair but just sat there, sipping beer and watching blankly as people came into Joe Miller's establishment, where time sometimes stops. Galloway and Jones, of course, are members of the *Dallas Morning News* sports department, and I used to be.

"I was ready," said Galloway. "Ready! I'd trained and would have won. It was the White Rock Marathon, 26.2 miles, December 2, 1978. I remember every detail. Now the weather was . . ."

"North Dallas High versus Woodrow Wilson," I said. "Bottom of the last inning. Cloudy, muggy day. I was up. Count was 2–2. Howie Reed was pitching. And you know . . ."

"Know. KNOW! Yeah, I know," Mike said. "I was a sophomore at ol' KHS, Kilgore High School, US of A, year 1960. Even before it happened I'd made this great play from my defensive end position. I'd tackled that Palestine kid in the end zone for a safety. When I ran off the field, everybody congratulated Timmy Jack Whatsisname. They thought he did it, and would he tell them? Would he tell them? Noooooooo. But listen, hey, a receiver got hurt and they put me in. We were on their three. The quarterback threw me a short pass in the end zone. I was wide open. It would have won the game but was tooooooo long. I dove, missed it by this far, this far (he held out his hands at full wingspan). But I . . ."

"Uh," I said, "I got to go to the bathroom. Order me another beer, *por favor.*"

"This far," said Jones, now holding his hands three feet apart. When I got back from the bathroom, his hands were two and a half feet apart, and Galloway, his eyes glazed, was saying, "How could it happen? How could the weather do that to me? It was humid and muggy. Everybody knows you can't run a marathon when it's humid and muggy! That kid won it. Tommy Marino. Just a kid. If the weather hadn't been bad there's no way he'd have beaten me. No way I tell you! No wayyyyyyy! Let me tell you . . ."

"Yeah, let me tell youuuu," I said, my voice sounding like an echo. "It was my big chance. The thing (my voice began to shake) is that the ball hit the outside corner and I didn't even swing. Didn't even swing!" I dropped my head in my hands, my voice became little more than a whisper. "We were behind 2–1, runners on third and second, and I didn't even swing. My God why!Whyyyy! It was a strike, a called third strike. Just a punch hit to right and I'd have been a hero. And . . ."

"This far," said Jones, holding his hands a foot apart. "I dove and missed it by this far. It would have won the game and that blankety-blank Timmy Jack wouldn't have been the hero. He'd . . . he'd have been nothing. A . . . a gnat and . . ."

"That little gnat, Tommy Marino," Galloway said, just after emptying his glass. "But the weather got me and I . . . I didn't finish in the top 2,000. But, listen . . ."

"I got to go to the bathroom," Jones said. "Bob, order us three more beers. Bob? Bob, are you there?"

"There I was," I said. "Howie Reed. Three-two count. I hit the outside pitch, and that so-and-so made a leaping catch against the fence. This close. It was this close to being a home run."

"This close," said Jones, standing up and holding his fingers an inch apart. "This close." His head dropped onto his chest. "I dove, stretched out the length of my little body and . . ."

"My body was aching all over because of the weather," Galloway said. "But I was determined. No, nooooo I didn't win. Tommy Marino won. But I was close. I was in the first 100 finishers. And if it hadn't been for the weather . . ."

Joe Miller came by and muttered something about a hockey match in which he'd played in Canada.

Galloway never looked up, shaking his head slowly. Sadly. "Joe," he said, "that kid Tommy Marino beat me by a foot. A foot. If the weather had been right I'd have more than made up that foot and wonnnnnnnnnnn. But it's a game of inches. It's . . . It's . . ."

"By inches," I said. "Inches and it'd have been over the fence. I hit it solidly. It was high and far into the darkening sky . . ."

"It was a high and far pass coming out of the darkening sky," said Jones, slowly returning to the table and muttering. "I had it on my fingertips. On my fingertips . . ."

"The weather was . . ."

"Soooooo close . . ."

"Hey, guys," Miller said, "let me buy you a drink and tell you about the time I was playing hockey and . . ."

"Goodnight, Joe."

"Goodnight, Joe."

"Goodnight, Joe."

HE CAME EACH night and sat for hours by the table near the jukebox in the back and played the same sad songs over and over, as if in replaying them they suddenly would change, end happily, and everything would be all right. Of course they didn't change, and everything wasn't all right.

He usually wore an old cowboy hat, pulling it down over his forehead to the point where he could see out but nobody could see in. Nobody knew where he had gotten the hat which, tilted forward, gave him an almost whimsical look as he stretched out in the chair. He was a metaphor.

After more years than he could remember his marriage had broken up, which had come as a great surprise to him, although I suppose such things never should surprise anybody. But the impact went right through him, leaving a hopeless, gnawing feeling inside that would not go away. He felt useless and his life became an endless blank and he had no place to go except back into the past, where he had been.

But the man and two women liked him, felt for him, and although they could not stop him from going back into the past, they did all they could to keep him from staying there. They spent long hours sitting with him at the table by the jukebox, trying to make him feel important again, trying to convince him that after a while it all would be better and that what had happened to him had happened to many people. They took him in and made it better. They became his bond. He became theirs.

Now the man had been his friend for a long time. Like the man in the cowboy hat, he had three children at home, but his marriage had not broken up. Yet, the man had reached the point in his life when he was forever questioning what he had started to do and was very disappointed in what he had done, and he stopped by the bar a lot on his way home, looking for something he did not find. But now he always found his friend in the cowboy hat sitting there at the table by the jukebox in the back and wanted so much to help him.

One of the women was a barmaid at the place. Once she had been very trim but had gone through a divorce a few years before, lingered for a while, and then let herself go. She drank a lot before she went home to her nearby apartment, ate a lot after she got there, and was very lonely. The man in the cowboy hat always had been nice to her, and now she thought about him a lot, talked to him a lot, and wanted to help him.

The other woman was young, in her early twenties. She was coming off an affair with a man who led her to believe she lacked compassion and was a very cold person. She was a beautiful young woman who always put on a party face, ready to jump at a good time on a moment's notice. But she hid behind the party face. Just underneath, she worried about lacking compassion and being cold. When she saw the man in the cowboy hat at the table by the jukebox she felt a great deal of compassion for him and didn't know what to do with it, so she, too, started talking to him a lot, spending time with him, and missing many of her parties.

After a long time the man in the cowboy hat seemed to be feeling better, almost like himself again, and even smiled when his three friends tried to be funny. He came and went and sometimes felt better but still dragged his foot in the past. One night when the bar was about to close, the young woman said what the hell, grabbed the man's hand, and took him home with her.

She began to like him very much. As they did things together, the man in the cowboy hat began to relate again to the present. The young woman felt compassionate and warm, and he helped convince her this was so, that she truly was this way. She felt much better about herself.

The barmaid looked forward nightly to seeing the girl and the two men. They talked to her and made her feel more important. She started taking more time with her hair and went on a diet.

The man whose marriage had not broken up listened to the man in the cowboy hat talk about his children at home, about how much he missed them. He started going home earlier. And earlier.

I lost track of all of them. But I saw the young woman in the bar the other night and found out the barmaid had gotten married and seemed very happy. She also said the man whose marriage had not broken up was spending more and more time with his family. And the young woman said she had gone back to school, gotten a degree, had a fine job, and felt very good about herself.

"I'll always feel good that we helped him because he was truly a good person," she said about the man in the cowboy hat. "But, no, I haven't seen him in a long time. We kind of all went our separate ways. Yeah, I'm glad we helped him."

"Both ways," I said. "It worked both ways. Consider what he did for you."

She thought for a minute, then said, "You're right. Of course you're right."

Recently, I saw the man in the cowboy hat sitting at the table by the jukebox in the back. Alone.

HE HAD STOPPED by the beach house I had rented during a recent vacation on South Padre Island and said he guessed he'd go back to Dallas in a few days. At the time the beach was still unravished since the winds had not yet turned westerly and shoved the Mexican oil spill ashore, fouling the sand.

We sat in late afternoon on the porch, mesmerized by the sights and sounds of the waves washing ashore, and he started telling me what I already knew, although it was all right to be told again, because I don't know anybody who isn't self-indulgent at times.

He said he had brought her there a year or so before and taught her about the ocean and beach and helped her see things she hadn't seen before. He told and then showed her that the birds along the beach weren't just sea gulls, that the small ones walking on straw-like legs and running away from the waves were sanderlings and that, mostly, the gulls were scavengers along the beach and that the terns usually were the divers for fish in the water. When she had said she had never really noticed sand dunes before, he had told her to look again more closely. And when she did, she had seen that they were beautiful, as were the vines and flowers growing on and around them.

"Sometimes," he said, "we'd walk along the beach, right out there. We'd go at maybe two, three in the morning or very early in the day as the sun was coming up. You know, right out there."

And he said he had pointed out to her how mystical the faraway lights of boats could be and how the ocean could be so many things. He said he had told her to watch the ocean and feel its being so she would know it could be strong and fierce and peaceful and calm and God-like. We had talked before about how the ocean can have a calming effect, sometimes helping a person regain strength and perspective, and he said he had told her that, too.

"Oh, well," he said, then became quiet for a few minutes, staring toward the ocean.

And then he said, "We were out there, see, right out there, in the water one day and a porpoise crossed near us, going south toward the jetties. She started screaming because she thought it was a shark. I tell you (he laughed) she got out of the water like she had a motor on her back.

"When she calmed down I explained that the porpoise was very intelligent and did not harm man in any way. She laughed and said, 'But what about woman?' (He laughed again.)

"Then we went fishing and she saw a porpoise circling the boat showing off, and she started talking about how intelligent they were.

"Oh, what the hell."

He said that when they had left a year or so ago they'd said they always would come back together and do the things they had done again. But it had ended between them, and they had not come back together.

"These people I know told me she was here a couple of months ago," he said. "She'd brought a guy with her. I don't know why they told me but they did. I guess because they knew I didn't care anymore.

"They said they saw her walking with him along the beach and watching the birds. I guess they all weren't just gulls anymore. I guess they weren't. Well, you know what was happening, don't you?"

"Sure," I said.

"She was telling and showing him all the things that I had taught her."

"I'm sure it makes you feel odd."

"I'm not sure. Sometimes it makes me mad, as if nothing we had was important at all, and if it wasn't, I'm not sure what was. And sometimes it's just like, well, things are nice if you pass them along to somebody else."

I thought that probably one day the guy she had brought to the beach a month or so ago would bring another girl there and tell her the things she had told him.

"Oh, well," he said. "sometimes I think I understand."

"Sometimes I think I understand too," I said.

"I guess I'll go back to Dallas in a few days," he said.

W HILE WE HAD coffee the day after Christmas that year, he told me what had happened. I had been curious, but as we talked, as I listened, I began to feel a little like Nick Carraway in *The Great Gatsby*.

I had known both of them a number of years, him much longer than her, and they were fine people, very much alike in that they both were dreamers, idealists, and all those things, I suppose, of which realists are not made. He sometimes affected an almost macho image and once had boxed, but there was a night I had seen tears come to his eyes when he accidentally killed a bird, which had sluggishly flown into the grille of his car. She told me she sometimes cried watching old movies on television. She said she had seen *A Portrait of Jenny* about five times on television and cried over it about ten times. She almost cried again when she told me about it. She almost did.

I knew they had a great deal in common, so I had introduced them late one afternoon over a drink. The had hit it off immediately, picking up on each other's subtleties and humor, neither having to stop to explain anything to the other, although their conversation confused me at times because my wave length was not the same.

They were so easy with one another and saw through each other's acts and phoniness, which had impressed others greatly. They joked about this and laughed at themselves. I always have liked people best who could laugh at themselves. And it was as if they alone knew the great secrets inside each other. When I got up to leave, they asked me not to go, but as far as they were concerned, I had not been there for a long time and I knew it was past time for me to go.

I very much liked the story he told me over coffee, the day after Christmas that year.

"I have," he said she had told him, "invented you for Christmas."

"I think I invented you, too," he had said. "But what then, when it's over?"

"You'll go away," she had said. "I know you will. Like . . . a puff."

"Well, Christmas isn't over and nows are important."

But for both of them the past was there, lurking, just a thought away.

She had been divorced after a short marriage, and his marriage, which had lasted much longer, was smoldering, the flames soon to go out. His wife had moved away, taking their son to live in another city. He talked a lot about the boy and missed him very much. He once had told me so many things reminded him of the boy. He said he'd be driving along the street, see a small boy riding a bike or playing a game that small boys play, and that an awful, hollow feeling would stab him inside.

82.1-495

56

The bartender said that the night I introduced them they had gotten very drunk. He said they had giggled a lot, finally holding hands across the table like a couple of kids. He kept telling her he had to go before he turned into a pumpkin. He kept telling her that if they drank any more they'd start talking to ducks. But he did not turn into a pumpkin, and they did not talk to ducks.

And he told me over coffee that for the two days of Christmas that year they had reached out to one another. He said they seldom slept but had spent hours on hours sitting by the fire and talking about childhood, their parents, friends, and the silly things a person did that, perhaps, he never told anybody about . . . or found anybody else who would listen.

"I know," he said she had said, "I know. You're going away, disappearing. But you're nice for Christmas . . . a pumpkin for Christmas."

"Ducks are people, too," he had said. "Let's go talk to ducks."

For Christmas she gave him a great pumpkin. "You can talk to it, put a hat on it, take it for a ride in your car, or just let it sit there," she had said. "You'll never be lonely again."

He gave her a duck to talk to when she got very drunk. They both laughed a lot, cried some, and loved for the two days of Christmas that year.

"It went so well," he had told me over coffee the day after Christmas, "that I still don't believe it. Do you?"

"Sure," I said. "I believe anything."

"It was," he said, "the best of Christmases."

"So what now? Will you see her tonight, this week? Let's all meet for a drink."

"Nothing. Nothing will happen. We said goodby this morning."

"You kid me. What'd you do that for? You said things went so well, that you got along so well."

"You don't understand," he said, looking at me over his cup of coffee. "It wasn't real. We invented each other just for Christmas."

PEOPLE WALKED along the river, which dissects downtown San Antonio in its slow, timeless fashion. Some would move up and down the banks, covered on the surface only by concrete. Others would stop and look at people in foot-paddle boats or go into one of the many shops or sit at tables at outside cafes.

This is a pleasant, almost festive area much of the time but it also draws lovers and dreamers. Rivers, if they're big enough can hypnotize you, transfix you, because, I suppose, they were there long before we were and will be there long after we're gone.

During one of the lower ebbs of my life I walked along the river, generally feeling quite sorry for myself. Friends have told me that when I'm like this, my shoulders sag, my head droops, and I walk with a kind of pathetic shuffle of feet. But this isn't the point.

I could see a clown coming far away. See him long before I actually heard him talking and joking with the people he passed. He would grab some of them, and after others had passed, he would sneak up behind and scare them.

Frankly, I am ashamed of the way I felt and how it was causing me to think. But I saw no humor whatsoever in grabbing and scaring people, and although again I am sorry my perspective had reached such depths, I had decided that if the man with white, red, and black paint on his face did this to me I would swing up in a low arc, catch him on the lower side of the face, and perhaps send him tumbling into the river. Then he could not grab or sneak up behind and scare people.

He drew closer and we finally met in a darkened place under a bridge. As he saw me coming he moved slightly backwards, as though aghast, then walked in a long path around me. Even looking down I could see out of the corner of my eye that he was mimicking me. I finally stopped and watched him. His shoulders sagged, his painted face was down, and he slowly shuffled his feet along.

I saw my image on a painted clown with baggy pants and torn shirt and started laughing. I couldn't stop laughing, and soon the clown was laughing, too. I thought laughing at clowns had passed me years ago but I guess not. I suppose you laugh at clowns when you laugh at yourself.

Clowns touched us all, when we were very young, at the circus that came each year. They would fall clumsily and stand on their heads and whatever. It is not all that clear in my mind whether the circus just stopped coming or was paled by changing attitudes and progress. Perhaps we grew up and stopped going because we no longer thought the clowns were that funny. Sometimes the circus still appears, as if poof out of the past. But nobody goes. Nobody sees the clowns. Now they are sometimes seen at shopping centers or sports shows where they give away balloons.

When we become adults clowns are seen and then again they are not. They are somewhat, I think, like a balloon or kite in a park on Sunday afternoon. You see them, watch them float upward on a gust of wind, but perhaps do not remember the style or color.

I did not know the man behind the clown's face who was walking along the San Antonio River that day. I'm sure I will not see him again, although I will see myself in him.

Yesterday,
When We Were Young

So THERE WE were again, after twenty-five years, and just for a while, for ever so brief a time, we indulged in a nostalgia with people we had known, of dreams realized and others lost or so faded that if you thought that much about them they'd crumble like an old, yellowing newspaper clipping.

Oh, sometimes it was a little sad because we were of the sentimental generation, but most of the time it was happy, very cheerful. We had again found a warm place that we had known so long ago. We were at the 25th annual North Dallas High School reunion, Class of '55. Of course, right away I must tell you that, unlike the others, I was only eleven when I graduated. I knew you wouldn't believe me.

It was interesting to see how some people had changed so much, yet not at all. I had not changed in a way and was late for the inaugural cocktail party at the DAC Country Club. When I finally got there and walked into one of the banquet rooms, I thought I must be in the wrong place. Why, these are old people, I thought. But I was in the right place. We were older.

Fortunately, all the guests were wearing name tags with their high-school pictures on them. But some were not wearing their glasses. It was funny, really, watching some people walk up to each and bend over to look at a name tag, squinting. I don't think we are vain, but I suppose we are at a somewhat vain age.

We talked about the times of charcoal sport coats and pink shirts, of Jo Stafford and Nat King Cole and the days when North Dallas High School had won a football championship, had actually contended in the city races, of cars we had had, of teachers and coaches we had liked, of successes and failures, and of love affairs we had thought would last forever. Funny. I got the impression some of them had.

The reunion ended with a big dinner-dance at Dunfey's. They played the music I still like best, such as "Stardust," "Autumn Leaves," "Canadian Sunset," "Let It Be Me," "Too Young," and so on. I just about got up my nerve to dance, but they were playing "Stardust" at the time and that was too fast.

Actually, since my wife was out of town, I attended the dinner-dance alone. I'd planned to walk in, say, "I'll have a table for one," then just talk, watch, and observe. But when I first got there, I went over and sat down and announced, "Well, here I am. Nothing's changed. It's been twenty-five years and I still can't get a date." We all laughed, but then I got to thinking that it wasn't so funny.

Billy Travis, a year or two ahead of us in school, dropped by to say hello. We'd played baseball and basketball together, and I'd also double-dated with him some in high school. I was sure Billy's family must have had a lot of money because he drove an almost new car and owned a *Playboy* magazine.

"Bobby," he said. "Still no date, huh. Maybe I can fix you up with somebody."

"Tell her I have a good personality."

Personality or not, I now jog and work out in order to keep my weight the same, I explained to Cindy Hutchinson Hamilton. I pride myself on this, to a degree, playing for a tie, you might say.

"I don't know what happened," she said. "It's usually just the opposite. But notice that all the women have remained very trim and all you guys have gotten fat.''

"Thanks a lot," I said.

"Well, Bobby, hold in your stomach."

I held in my stomach and danced with Lou Ann Campbell Porter. The music was slow. "Well," she said, "I want to congratulate you. After twenty-five years you've almost gotten down the two-step. But . . . why don't you let me lead?"

I always liked Liz James Strain. We recognized each other's face but weren't all that sure about the name. We danced and, honestly, I was doing my best but stepped on her foot. "Ouch," she said. "Now I remember you, Bobby St. John."

After twenty-seven years I got to kiss Susan Mara Oaks. Susan went through high school without ever kissing a boy. She had a few dates with a friend of mine, Mike McKeogh, who liked her a lot. He lives in New Orleans now and couldn't attend the reunion.

But in fact, he used to say he didn't mind that much if she never kissed because he didn't figure it was hygienic. Anyway, at the reunion I came up behind her and planted a big one on her cheek. Then I phoned McKeogh and told him what I had done.

"You rat, pervert," he snapped. "I leave town for twenty-five years and you can't wait to kiss Susan."

"I'm sorry. How can I make it up to you?"

"Tell me what she looks like now."

We all were sorry when the lights were turned up and the reunion was over. I felt a lot like I had when I broke up with this girl I liked at a big Valentine Dance at North Dallas. That must have been, oh, yesterday.

But the 25th North Dallas High School reunion, Class of '55, was a lot of fun and so was its after-glow. I'm glad I went because it was so pleasant to pass that way again.

I TELL YOU, that Lucille was something, all right. I always will remember that summer we dated. Painfully. In the first place, her ancestry was full-blooded Italian, and nobody ever had warned me that Italians can have bad tempers.

My family had moved to Dallas from Paris, Texas, and I always thought pizza was the name of an Italian actor. Honestly, I'd never in all my days in Paris seen a pizza or spaghetti. I'd met Lucille at North Dallas High School, and one summer night she asked me over to dinner to meet her parents. I wanted to impress them with my worldliness so I got a brand new burr haircut and, using a knife and fork, practiced my table manners in front of the mirror.

They had pizza, with dishes of spaghetti on the side. And garlic bread. I had no idea how you were supposed to eat pizza or spaghetti. I waited for somebody else to start eating so I could find out, but they all were waiting for me. So I picked up my knife and fork and started cutting and eating the pizza as though it were steak. Somebody snickered and everybody started laughing. Because I didn't know what else to do, I also started laughing, like the silly fool I was.

I can't remember but I imagine when I left the table that night I had spaghetti hanging from my ears. Anyway, Lucille walked me to the door, laughing, and said, "You're different."

"I know," I said. "I know." Then she puckered up to kiss me goodbye but just ended up smacking me lightly on the cheek. She whispered that my breath smelled like garlic.

That summer I was playing a kind of amateur semi-pro baseball and hitting very well. So, I took Lucille to a Sunday afternoon doubleheader we were playing at Buckner Park to try to impress her. I would show her what my world was like, the world of baseaballa. I impressed Lucille by going one for eight, striking out twice, and popping up to the third baseman with two out in the bottom of the ninth, the tying run on third and the winning run on second.

Now in my teenage days I had a terrible temper. I thought it was macho in those days. Since I played sports, had boxed a little, and had the temper, I felt my reputation of macho was fairly well established. So, as I finished my infamous performance before the small crowd and Lucille that Sunday, I watched the third baseman come in to catch my pop up. Then I pounded my bat on home plate and broke it. It was the best bat I ever had.

Teammates and spectators cleared the way as I, the Crazy who had broken his bat on home plate, stormed to my car. I'd had a bad day, but at least my image was still intact for posterity. Lucille, all five foot one and 100 pounds of her, walked over to me as I leaned up against my car, pouting.

"Hey," she said, tapping me on top of my lowered head which was on my slumping body, "weren't you supposed to hit a home run?" I gritted my teeth and ignored her.

"Hey, I'm talking to you. Look at me. Weren't you supposed to hit a home run?"

I gradually looked up, into her eyes. Then I yelled, "Will you shut up!"

I never knew from where it came nor that it was coming, but eyewitnesses later told me. And told me. And told me. Lucille doubled up her fist, drew back as far as she could with her right, and connected with a picture-book hook on my left cheek. I saw stars; my knees buckled.

Gradually, I slid down the side of the car and just sat there on the seat of my pants, blinking. As the cobwebs cleared I thought, I don't believe this happened. I shut my eyes tight, and when I opened them again my worst fears were realized. Lucille stood over me, her fist doubled up and her face set, a miniature conqueror. Some of my teammates stared in disbelief, snickering, then laughing. My image was shot.

"St. John," said one guy, "you need any help?"

"Lucille," said another, "why don't you pick on somebody your own size?"

Neat. Great. Just great. I sat there on the ground by the car for a long time, and as the sun set slowly in the west, I got up and crawled into the car. I could feel my eye swelling and knew full well that it would turn black as the ace of spades.

"Hey," said Lucille, sliding into the seat beside me. "I'm sorry if I hurt you. Just don't ever tell me to shut up, okay."

"Sure. It's all right. I can play on Tuesday night with a black patch over my left eye."

"Hey, you will phone me again, won't you?"

"Listen, I'll do whatever you tell me to do," I said and we both started laughing.

We laughed a lot and fought a lot that summer, but I never did tell her to shut up again.

SHORTLY AFTER my family moved from Paris to Dallas, I couldn't sleep because street cars passed throughout the night, moving down the track to their own cadence of whining wires and rattling steel on worn tracks. After we had lived in Dallas for a while, I couldn't sleep unless the street cars passed throughout the night.

The street cars are gone now, but they opened the door to a great education in human nature for me and others of my generation who rode and watched and listened. When you are twelve or thirteen you observe things and they affect you a great deal, even if you don't understand them until later.

I spent a lot of time riding street cars to the transfer spot, from which the buses went to Spence Junior High, downtown to the big movie houses such as the Majestic and Palace, and on the death-defying ride across the Trinity River bed to Burnett Field, where you could watch the New York Yankees and Cleveland Indians play an exhibition game if you skipped school.

A large club was situated on the corner just before the street car turned onto Columbia, where we lived for a while in an apartment in a big, old house when we first moved to Dallas. The club had huge neon lights that never changed, even if the name did, and there always was loud music coming through thin doors from inside, and people gathered outside, talking, smooching, fighting. I was more into baseball then but noticed that some of the women outside were attractive, while others had aged like Pepsi Cola.

One night after I had seen a John Wayne movie at the Majestic, the street car stopped by the club to let passengers off and wait for the light to change. A man staggered out, waving his arms wildly, throwing punches at invisible adversaries . . . at devils, if you will. He had on a fancy Elvis shirt and faded work pants. His hair was slicked down with the tonic of the day and, I imagine, he had on shaving lotion that smelled faintly of roses.

He whirled around, almost falling, looked back toward the club, and yelled, "I can whip anybody here! Any of you . . . I can whip you six days a week and twice on Sunday!" He drew himself up as tall as he could and walked toward the street car, which was stranded at a red light.

Those of us on the street car watched him from our theater with a dirty face. And he saw us looking at him and, although he was only a few feet away, yelled, "I can whip any of you on that street car, too!"

I thought he was going to come onto the sreet car and whip all of us, but the light changed and we left. He was still yelling. I wished I were John Wayne because I'd have jumped off the car and knocked him flat and saved the girl, except I didn't see any girl to save. It was years later when it occurred to me that perhaps the man wasn't yelling but crying out and that he might have wanted to be John Wayne, too.

One Sunday a large black woman got onto the street car, carrying a big, cracked, imitation leather purse and a Bible. There were strips of paper sticking out of the Bible, marking many places for her. She had a nice peaceful smile but no seat. I sat four rows from the back of the street car next to a man in clean, starched work clothes. I had, of course, been taught manners but was confused about the times.

When the street car turned, the woman almost fell. I jumped up and told her to take my seat. "Sit down, kid," the man next to me said. "Just sit back down. It's all right. Let her stand."

I later wished I had told him I'd do exactly what I wanted to do, just like John Wayne would have done, but I didn't have the guts. I was tired but I said, "Oh, I'm just tired of sitting. I'll stand up for a while. Ha-ha-ha."

After the woman sat down next to him, the man cursed and got up, moving to another part of the street car. I knew he was angry, but it worked out all right because I sat back down next to the woman. I really was tired.

The side door was stuck so I had to get off the street car at the front. As I started off, the conductor handed me two tokens for free rides. I thanked him and then spent a long time trying to figure out why he'd done that. But, heck, it was two free rides.

It was wild, watching and listening to couples that got onto the street cars. Some, I noticed, would just sit there, never saying a word to each other. I didn't know whether they had nothing to say or didn't need to say anything. But I thought that when I got older and had a wife I sure would talk to her, especially if she were a baseball fan. I always figured I wouldn't marry anybody who wasn't a baseball fan.

One couple, two rows up across the aisle, got into a big argument. "I'm leaving," the woman said. The man looked at her, very hatefully I thought, and said, "Good. Just don't let the doorknob hit you in the tail on the way out."

"I'm packing when I get home."

"You do and I'll drag you back by the hair of your head!" he said.

"Do you have to talk so loud. People are listening to you. I'm leaving the minute we get home."

"So leave," he said. "Leave." The guy sure couldn't figure out whether he wanted her to leave or not. I supposed, at that time in my life, neither of them were baseball fans and didn't have much to talk about.

One night I rode the street car with a Latin couple. I couldn't understand what they were saying, but the man had his arm around the woman and they talked softly. When the street car stopped at their block, the man got up and very carefully helped the woman out of her seat. She was a lot, rather than a little, pregnant, and I thought it was nice that he helped her. He also held her arm as she got off the street car and they held hands as they walked off into the darkness. Baseball fans, for sure, I thought.

There were so many things I saw, some of which I didn't know I was seeing at the time, while riding street cars. But the street cars don't pass anymore.

SOMETIMES WE would hear them talk about her in whispers and hushed voices from another room, but what they said wasn't any big deal to us because we were kids then and knew only that she was so very nice to us, that she loved us and showed it.

She always showed it. We all called her Aunt Ree, although her real name was Marie, but I suppose when you're very young you sometimes have trouble with big people's names, and so you just shorten them to suit your pronunciation. Still, even after we, the nieces and nephews, became adults we still called her Aunt Ree. I think she liked that. It made her special, being given a special name, because everybody but the kids called her Marie. Just Marie.

Aunt Ree was a very shy person around other adults, even her brothers and sisters. And if you were a stranger about the most you would get out of her was a pleasant smile, a "Hello," and a blush. When the adults were around she seldom talked but would sit for hours in a rocking chair under a lamp and read her Bible or sew. She'd crochet or sew scraps of cloth together so they would one day become a quilt.

I still remember the chocolate fudge she made for us when we were kids. She made a lot of fudge and also popcorn and pies. She was tireless when it came to children. She would tell us stories and laugh and cry right along with us when they were happy or sad. She was just like a little girl, laughing in a high, little girl's voice. She so loved to play Chinese checkers. She'd get right down on the floor with us and play for hours.

As we grew older, the talk, the words, they whispered about her began to take shape. Her past had not been happy, which was such a shame because anybody who loved kids as much as she did had so much to give.

There were five children in the family of my grandfather and grandmother. There was only one boy. My mother was the youngest, and my Aunt Ree the eldest, of the girls. It was said that Aunt Ree had been very fragile since childhood, that she had been sick a lot. It was said that my grandparents greatly sheltered her, shielded her from the outside world. This wasn't difficult to do because the family lived in the very small farming community of Maxey, about nine miles outside of Paris.

I suppose at that time nobody knew that when you shielded somebody from the bad you also might have shielded them from the good. But when she reached womanhood she met a man, a first man, and they were married, moving to Oklahoma.

And it was said that the man treated her badly, despite warnings from my grandfather. They had no children and had not been married all that long when the man ran off with another woman, leaving her. Just leaving her. My grandfather packed an overnight bag, put on his big black hat, and drove to Oklahoma to get her and bring her back home. She never left again.

My grandfather died when I was less than three, but Aunt Ree continued to live with my grandmother from the time she was a young woman until she reached the twilight of her life. She always called my grandmother "Mama." For all the time I can remember, my grandmother and Aunt Ree wore clean, starched, cotton dresses. You could smell the cleanliness.

Aunt Ree baby-sat all of us. She was dependable; she always was there. All those years, as far as I know, she had no life outside of sewing, attending church, cooking, and entertaining the kids. She never dated again, never went to a movie. Nothing.

When my eldest son was very small I took him to see her and she played Chinese checkers with him, the same games, the same way she had when I had been his age. God, she was a dear woman, but I don't think any of us ever told her that, told her that we loved her. When I was fourteen or fifteen, this finally occurred to me, and I sat down and wrote her a letter. I told her she was one of my very favorite people in the world and that I loved her dearly.

Aunt Ree died about five years ago. Except for her clothes, she left precious few possessions. But the letter I had written her was in her jewelry box, which was almost empty.

NOT LONG AGO I drove down the narrow, winding road to the small graveyard near the community of Maxey, about eleven miles from Paris, Texas, and saw on the tombstone that her full name was Lula Amanda White Wheeler. It's odd, really, but everybody always called her Lula, and it never really registered with me that my grandmother's name was Amanda, which is a beautiful and fitting name.

So many images of her passed through my mind, where they always will be. I could see her in the wooden swing on the porch of the high-roofed frame house in which she lived in Maxey or inside her home, slowly moving in timeless fashion in her rocking chair. She was a small woman and her gray-white hair would be done in a bun in the back and she'd be wearing one of her spotless, starched cotton dresses which were long and loose. She would wear those dresses because she always had and did not care what anybody else thought or wore as the times changed.

She was such a fine storyteller, and if I'm able to tell a good story sometimes, I think it's due more to her than to any education I've gotten. I would sit for hours while she rocked and told stories of how, as a girl, she had come in a covered wagon with her family from Arkansas. After she'd married my grandfather, they moved for a while to Indian Territory in Oklahoma. She always pointed out, though, that even the renegade Indians there never bothered them because my grandfather always treated every man fairly, and that their kitchen and water well were open to all.

She loved to tell about how my grandfather ran the general store and post office in Maxey, after they'd moved there. And how, when it snowed, he'd hitch a horse to a sled he'd built and take her and the children riding through the countryside.

"You have seen the pictures on the Christmas cards of snow-filled countrysides and horse-drawn sleds," she'd say. "Well, it was just like that."

My grandfather died when I was less than three years old, and my grandmother spent the last thirty-odd years of her life without him, but I bet there never was a day when she didn't think about him, talk about him when she could.

When I visited her, which was often, she might be churning butter in the kitchen or cooking over the pot-bellied stove. She loved to cook and bake pies, she washed in a tub and hung the wet clothes on a line to dry "because it makes them smell so much fresher."

She was always reading the Bible, quoting Scripture, and sitting down during idle summer evenings and playing the organ my grandfather had given her after they'd gotten married. As I remember, her favorite song was "The Old Rugged Cross," which she played very well, and she sang in a fine soprano voice that at times would sound almost like a bird.

When they told her she was going blind she made a concentrated effort to memorize the parts of the Bible she didn't already know by heart so they would be there to comfort her even in the semi-darkness that would replace her eyesight. She would read hours on hours with the Bible almost against her face.

Relatives kept saying she was going to die ten years before she ever did. They said she was dying when she started to lose her eyesight, and again when she fell and broke her hip. She never walked for the nine years she lived after suffering the hip injury, but it wasn't about to kill her or make her give up.

There always seemed to be a relapse or another sickness that should have killed her, but they never did. Time just ran out on her in 1975 when she was 103.

During her final year or so, when she couldn't talk at all, a lot of people thought she wasn't coherent, but I knew she was because she'd always squeeze my hand during my visits with her, as though we shared a great secret. When she finally died she looked so very peaceful that I figured she had been thinking about my grandfather.

W E SAT FOR peaceful hours in the shade on the front porch of the general store-post office and watched people as they passed down the dirt road on foot, in wagons, or in an occasional car. The wheels made a certain grinding sound on the dirt road, spewing gravel and dust. We were in no special hurry for anything. We might have gone fishing.

Sometimes my grandfather sat down by me on the steps of his general store and post office in the small farming community of Maxey, near Paris in Northeast Texas; at other times he went inside, brought out two straight chairs, and leaned them against the front of the store.

We sat in those chairs on the front porch for hours. My grandfather puffed on his corncob pipe and thrilled me so much when he gave me a corncob pipe, just like his. I leaned back in the chair, tried to emulate his slight rocking style, and puffed on my corncob pipe, just as he did.

Women then wore bonnets and long, full cotton dresses, and men wore work shirts, jeans or overalls, and big straw or felt hats. The person I most liked to watch pass was Uncle Buck Williams. He was not actually my uncle nor anybody's that I knew of, but everybody just called him "Uncle" and that was all right by me. Uncle

Buck was an elderly man with a long white beard and rode by on a horse that appeared to me to be as big as an elephant. I thought I sure would like to have a horse that big, although I wasn't sure I wanted a long white beard.

My grandfather's general store, like similar stores everywhere in those days, served as a window on the world for the community. It contained all kinds of things. Oh, there was milk and cream and bread and all the food essentials. And there were shoes, new and shiny and black, and shirts and dresses. But the best things were the striped peppermint sticks and chewy candy in the sticky wrappers, which always seemed to end up on the bottom of my foot no matter where I threw them.

My grandfather often let me reach behind the glassed counter and take out all the candy I could hold in my hand. I used to wish I could be grown up so my hand would be bigger. He also allowed me to go to the barrels, hidden in the shadows in back of the store, reach into the darkness, and pull out a cracker to eat. I had a lot of trouble back there, in the shadows. I'd reach in to get a cracker, only to be stung by a nail.

It's odd, really, on the surface anyway. I can't remember things that happened yesterday but, for some reason, can recall the time and place when as a very young boy I used to sit on the porch with my grandfather at his general store. I don't know that much about memory and the mind, nor what we store there. But I have read that we begin recording impressions as newborn babies and that a sight, a smell, or almost anything can rekindle them. They were rekindled for me not long ago when I drove through Maxey, although nothing that was there of my grandfather's is still around.

However, the memory of him is, and his name. People in his day had great names. My grandfather's name was Washington Wheeler and my grandmother's was Lula Amanda White Wheeler. Their names are carved on large, well-kept tombstones in the old cemetery on a road outside of town.

Men who were boys when my grandfather was alive remember hearing their parents talk about him. He was a

Mason and also a deacon in the Baptist church, a small, white frame structure that was continually repainted. Most people in the area did not have much money, but it was said my grandfather gave away groceries and clothes to the needy and never expected nor asked to be paid back.

I believe I can remember once when a man and his wife came into the store and left, holding packages and groceries, with tears in their eyes. I believe I can remember the man stopping, patting me on the head, and saying he hoped I grew up to be a fine, God-fearing man like my grandfather.

Death, taxes, and the march of time took everything my grandparents had . . . the store, the house, the stock, the land, everything. But I still have that corncob pipe.

THERE WERE SOME bad times, especially in later years, which I suppose none of us really ever understood except perhaps on the surface. Or, maybe we just got tired of trying. I know I didn't understand until I was well into my twenties and by then it was far too late.

Of course, he had the Scotch-Irish in him and so he always liked his cup of drink or ten. In fact, he got to liking drink too much and it reached the point where, if he didn't have any, he always felt as if he were stepping barefooted on cold, hard linoleum. Drink made it feel like soft, warm carpet — at least for an imagined little while.

Because he drank, everybody called it "madness", although now my friends and I might do the same thing and people would say that we're just newspaper people or writers or artists and that we have the "fine madness' in us. There is, of course, the great difference in perspective: he being "mad" and we being "deep, sensitive, funny, silly" and in roles that we are supposed to play.

But back then, before I was in my early teens, we lived in a small town in East Texas, and in those days, some relatives and people at the church would whisper about you if you took a drink. I imagine that, at times, they would whisper so you could hear. I also remember one Sunday the preacher wore a red tie, and they whispered about that, too. So I'm sure he heard the whispers and, at first, said, "So what?" And then, perhaps, "What the hell!" And then, perhaps, he said less and less.

Although he was taller, slimmer, and better looking than I, my father did leave me with his Irish face and eyes. But I don't know the whys about him, really. Perhaps it is just something that can happen when you think things are a certain way and they cannot be . . . or you see something, reach for it and find an empty place.

He always was going to do something. He always was going to buy something for us, do something for us, but he seldom did, although I know his intentions were good. I remember as a boy waiting daily for the mail to bring a baseball game he said he had ordered for me. It never came, and then one day it showed up, and I never told anybody that I knew my brother had bought it for me. But I do remember getting the best bicycle I'd ever seen one Christmas after he told me I would. It was shiny, new, perfect. Now I realize that it must have been a terrible financial drain on him, but when you are very young, things only are shiny and new, not financial drains.

He had very little education and was raised in a very small rural community by a grandmother, after his parents had died or disappeared or whatever. Everybody always said he was a very good mechanic. Even the people who whispered about him would give him that, at least. "Ohh, meee, but he surely is good at his trade. He surely is," they would say.

He never read Tolstoy, Hemingway, Faulkner, as his children were to do, but when he was at home he would spend hours sitting in a chair, which always looked uncomfortable, reading pulp paperback novels that he bought at the drugstore. Sometimes he would read two or three a night. He especially liked Westerns, and always wore cowboy boots.

I remember overhearing conversations in which he'd tell those who asked that cowboy boots were the most comfortable things, that they especially were good to wear when you had to drive long distances. Odd. I never thought about that until I started wearing cowboy boots. I realized he was right, though, when I was working on a book about rodeo cowboys a few years ago . . . and would drive long distances.

Anyway, one day many years ago he stopped just before he left on a trip and told me he was going to buy me new tires for an old junker I was driving to school. He said that he could get this good deal and that I certainly needed tires because it was dangerous driving with the ones I had. I knew he wouldn't buy the tires but went along with it as though he would. On that trip, while driving through Royse City, he was hit by a bare train on a bare track and killed in the middle age of his years.

I don't know. I suppose because of Father's Day I got to thinking about him and how he always meant to do what he said he would do for us. I didn't understand for many years but now I know that this was enough and that he had bought the baseball game and the tires.

THAT YEAR WE lived in Austin in Bill Brammer's house on a hill up from Caswell Tennis Center. Everybody has their best time and best place and that was it for me, although there have been good and bad times since and there will be more of them.

It is that way for so many I know who have lived in Austin. Perhaps it is because we lived there when we were younger and thus were more romantic and seemed to be living in some kind of novel or a movie that always had music in the background and a happy ending.

Oh, the house wasn't that much. My landlady, Nadine, Brammer's ex-wife, had it painted a kind of pinkish color, which I thought was neat, although admittedly some felt this color scheme did not add much to the neighborhood. That worried me then about as much as the price of milk, which was not at all.

At night it was nice to sit on the back porch, listening to music and drinking beer and watching cars slowly climb up the hill, their lights like a giant, slow-moving necklace. It was a dreamy time, that year we lived in Austin.

And then, some sixteen years ago, Brammer was the inspiration for us all. His book, *The Gay Place,* which I always have considered the best novel written by a Texan, was the talk of literary circles, and those of us who would be writers thought about how one day we also would do such a book. In fact, after a night under the trees at Scholz Garten, we would talk about how we would be getting to the novel the first thing in the morning. It's just that there seldom was a first thing in the morning.

Brammer, of course, died in early 1978, the sad thing being what he must have gone through trying to write another book like *The Gay Place.* He never could. But he left us all something, especially those of us who have lived in Austin.

We had many things to do then. There always was a cause, such as marching in front of the capitol for civil rights or settling some political issue. Looking back, I think that some of our causes might have been taken in order to march to a different drummer, although we didn't know it at the time.

Oh, we did try and I believe John Updike is only partially correct when he calls us and our times "The Silent Generation." We just didn't take over the president's office at universities or throw ourselves under the wheels of movements but, had we thought about it, we might have done so.

If you were in love, the thing to do was go listen to Ernie Mae Miller sing your favorite song, such as "Moon River" or "Days of Wine and Roses," at the New Orleans Club on Red River Street or drive out to the bottom of Mt. Bonnell, park and walk to the top. You could sit there and look down at the city on one side and the Colorado River, soft as velvet, on the other. After reading Brammer's book, I found myself climbing Mt. Bonnell very early in the morning to watch the sun come up and turn the capitol building pinkish, just as he wrote it would.

On a recent visit I drove out, parked, and climbed up Mt. Bonnell, breathless, only to notice that a road had been built up there. Now, couples just drive to the top in their cars, park and look. I guess I looked awfully silly climbing up the old trail when all I had to do was drive. But I guess I'll always climb.

They used to say we had our own United Nations in the sports department of the *Austin American-Statesman*. The staff included Ed Knocke, Lou Maysel, Charley Eskew, Joe Heiling, George Breazeale, and a St. John. After I won an award for a sidebar I had written, somebody told me I should have seen the one Brammer once did when he worked for the *American*. I looked it up and it was better than mine.

There were so many good things that year. But the worst thing was having to be at the newspaper at 5 A.M. to help the sports-desk man write headlines for the afternoon paper, the *Statesman*. Since I never could wake up, on time, the poor guy would have to phone me, somewhat frantic. The phone would wake me up, and I'd throw on what clothes I could grab in the dark and run for it. I would tell my wife, Katherine, to please go answer the phone and tell the guy I'd left a long time ago and must have had car trouble. I had a lot of car trouble in those days but it was a very used Valiant I drove. I wish I still had that car.

Anyway, at times I would run into the newsroom at the crack of dawn with one loafer, one tennis shoe, a blue sock on one foot and a gray one on the other. Often, I would grab a jacket and wear it without a shirt. But I always was late, and sometimes when I'd get there, the sports-desk man would have already written the headlines for the afternoon paper. I'd tell him I'd had car trouble and apologize and say it would never happen again, that I'd be on time the next day.

He finally got to where he wouldn't talk to me. One day he just shook his head and said, "I hate you sometimes."

"I know," I said. "Sometimes I hate myself, too." But I didn't.

The house I lived in that year still is there, although it has been painted a more sensible gray. They have changed the songs on the juke box at Scholz's and the New Orleans Club has disappeared from the face of the earth. Most of the people I knew when I lived in Austin that year have moved to Dallas or Houston. Brammer is gone and Mt. Bonnell is full of cars. The guy who helps the sports-desk man write headlines for the *Statesman* is there by 5 A.M.

But sometimes I still wear one gray sock and one blue one.

Hands
Across the Border

ACROSS THE TIRED old lady, the Rio Grande, in Nuevo Laredo, there's a small cantina near a park with a big clock in the center. *Novios,* or sweethearts, were walking there on a recent Sunday afternoon as though nobody else were in the world. Three, four people were asleep on the ground with newspapers, like drawn shades, over their faces.

Card tables, surrounded by folding chairs, were placed under the trees at the cantina, and a small boy, perhaps ten or eleven, was helping his papa run the establishment. But business was very slow. I was there and a lone Mexican man sat at a nearby table, looking deeply into his glass as if for a solution.

I ordered a Superior, a light Mexican beer, and the boy brought it with a glass. I had watched the boy get the glass from his papa, then wipe and shine it with a clean rag. I usually just drink beer from a bottle or can, but the boy had been so meticulous in shining the glass that I felt it would be an insult not to use it. When I did, he smiled and seemed to be happy.

An American couple walked past the cantina, looked in, and walked on down the street. Minutes later they were back, still casing the place, and decided to stop. I think they did so because they saw me, a gringo, there. The couple ordered two beers, saying sure, Carta Blanca would be fine. Most tourists drink Carta Blanca because they have heard of it but it's a heavy beer, and I don't care for it. The small boy wiped two glasses very clean and brought them with the beers. The couple whispered, their faces almost touching, and decided not to use the glasses. The boy shrugged and looked at his papa behind the bar. His father nodded, shrugged, too. The man looked as if he were about to fall asleep and probably would have had he not been working. I started to go over to the American couple, whose accent indicated they might be from the Midwest, and tell them the glasses probably were cleaner than the ones they used in the United States, but it was too much trouble.

Business was not good. The afternoon was lazy, slow-moving. I knew the boy's papa was not asleep because he bent over, putting a record on an old player. The record sounded very scratched. The music was from the *corrida de toros,* the bullfight. I had been disappointed when they stopped having regular bullfights in Nuevo Laredo because I like them, sometimes even the bad ones. Oh, they still have them on special occasions but only with *novilleros,* those whom we might call amateurs, the ones who are still learning and have not yet become matadors.

But the brassy bullfighting music was good and caused me to order another Superior. The boy stood by his papa, becoming dreamy. Seeing that his customers were satisfied, he walked away from his papa, directly to the back of the cantina. He took off his soiled apron. Suddenly, he held the apron as a matador might his cape and began swinging it, as if he were passing a bull. After making two successful passes he turned his back on the bull and walked the cocky walk of a matador. He paused, bowed to a beautiful and rich woman in the third row, and then tossed her his hat, dedicating to her the bull.

He returned to action, twirling and spinning the cape around him in a classic veronica. I suddenly remembered that as a boy I had hit rocks with a stick, pretending I was knocking home runs in Yankee Stadium. Kids are much the same anywhere.

I started to get up from my chair and saw the man behind the bar look around for the boy. I walked to the bar, handed him my money, and asked him, please, to leave the boy alone for a while. I told him he had a fine place and that I would come back often. He seemed satisfied for a while.

I walked to the back, closer to the boy, and suddenly yelled, "*Ole! Ole!*" I had hoped to encourage the boy but instead embarrassed him by yelling what they yell at bullfights when a matador does well. I had not meant to do so but I had broken his dream.

M OST PEOPLE WITH whom I talked did not know what had happened to Flora Calderon. Years ago when she had run the midwife hospital on Hidalgo Street in Laredo she was felt to be some kind of saint and, certainly, was a word-of-mouth legend. But she seemed to have disappeared.

"Flora Calderon?" said Odie Arambula, managing editor of the *Laredo Times*. "She had the midwife hospital here with a shingle hanging out and everything. I know of no other such place. A very nice old lady. There is no telling how many babies she delivered, how many needy mothers she helped."

It is said that Flora Calderon delivered thousands of babies. She also would place unwanted babies in proper homes and even adopted some of the homeless ones herself. When the money wasn't there and someone needed help, they could turn to Flora Calderon. But she was no longer on Hildago Street.

"I don't know," said Arambula. "Maybe she died, although I don't remember hearing about it. But she would be quite old by now."

A midwife, one who delivers babies and helps women in childbirth, is called a *partera* in Spanish, that is, a person who is in the profession of midwifery, *parteria*.

Certainly, it is one of the world's oldest professions. It is much more common in Mexico than in the United States. But a midwife is licensed, and by checking with city officials, I finally found a deputy who said, "I think she might live on Davis Street. No, I am sorry. I know nothing else about her."

"Many do," I said.

"Yes," he said. "Many do."

Davis Street, in the shadows of downtown Laredo and short blocks from the Rio Grande, is not among the affluent sections of town. Dust hangs in the air, stirred by passing cars, and small apartments are very close, as though nudging one another for more breathing room. There is a small cantina, a cafe, almost empty.

I parked and then walked along Davis, asking about Flora Calderon, but did not have much luck. Between two box-like, brown brick apartments young teenagers were playing volleyball without a net. Their English was better than my Spanish and they had, indeed, heard of Flora Calderon. In fact, she lived right there, in the small brown brick building. Talking in broken English, broken Spanish and by the use of sign language, one said she would get the señora who would meet me at the front door.

A small, bent, elderly woman with sheet-white hair answered the door. She also could not speak much English, and I cursed myself for letting my Spanish get worse and worse over the years from lack of use. The two teenagers, Elba Gonzales and Martha Alicia Collazo, came in to help, and with everybody contributing, we communicated.

In the small front room were two filing cabinets, straight chairs, a license in a frame on the wall, and a large desk, behind which Flora Calderon was trying to sit down. Her body was arthritic, and she moved in a kind of slow motion until I went over and helped her sit down. She said, indeed, she was still working and would continue to do so until age stopped her. She had taught one of her daughters, Juanita, the trade and she was a big help.

"I have done this for forty-five years now," she said. "Before, I would deliver maybe eight babies a week. And now, maybe three. I had to move here from Hidalgo because I lacked money, and as you can see, this is a very poor *casa*. I deliver babies in the back room and we do what we can, as you must know."

"From what I've heard of you, señora, I am sure you do as much as is possible."

The old woman now has five children, the youngest of whom is six. I wondered how she could take care of a six year old but I'm sure she does as well as she can. She said she was sixty-five, but looked older, although hard work can add age. She told me she came to Laredo from Victoria, Mexico, when she was a girl of eight and learned to be a *partera* from a local doctor. I asked her why she had chosen that profession, and she smiled and said, "Because it is a very beautiful thing for me to do."

Her voice cracked slightly and she continued, "I love babies, all babies, and it is a wonderful thing to see life come into them. They are beautiful. All of them are so beautiful."

She said she charged $2 for a visit and different prices, according to the financial status of her patients, for delivery. She looked at me, grinned, and said she would charge me, maybe, $250. I told her I did not believe there would be a need but (patting my stomach), if so, it would be worth a lot more money than that. The teenage girls giggled.

"I am sorry," Flora Calderon said again, "but this is a very poor *casa* and I have nothing to offer you but some tea. But I am glad you would visit me and talk."

"No. It is not poor. It is a very rich house, señora, because you are here."

HIS NAME WAS Manuel, although it could have been Juan or Jorge, and he lived in an old mobile home near a stream on a ranch of some four hundred acres, eight or nine miles from a small community in the Hill Country. Wild fern grew cliff high and, in patches, bluebonnets and Indian paint brushes carpeted the ground.

He spoke very little English and had come across the border illegally, but he liked the ranch, the country, and his work, which was to build fences, clear brush, and do whatever else needed to be done. You would see him carrying an old ax swung over his shoulder and hear him whistling strange songs as he went out to find and cut down trees to trim and use to mend fences. He did his work very well.

It was not clear from which province in Mexico he had come, but obviously, he had gone through the usual channels, the ones in which somebody would ask a certain man in a certain place if he could supply Mexican farm laborers. The smuggler, called a *coyote,* would say, yes indeed he could, for a fee, and after a dark night workers, called wetbacks, would appear with very little other than the clothes on their backs. But they would be more than ready to work at anything.

When Manuel had come to the ranch, his boss, the *jefe,* had taken him into a small community and bought him two pairs of work clothes. He also had bought him some groceries, a few things with which to cook, and a radio. He told him he could live in the old mobile home all by himself, which at first Manuel found strange because when he was growing up in Mexico the nine members of his family had lived in two small rooms. But often he had heard from workers who came back from the United States that life there was much better, if the *coyote* kept his word and got you there and if the *jefe* was a fair and honorable man.

From Monday through Friday he would work from very early until mid-afternoon and then come to his mobile home and, alone, make tortillas and cook beans and corn. Sometimes he would have fish he had taken from the stream or one of the tanks in which they had been stocked by the owner of the ranch.

At night the sky was clear, very wide and uncluttered. The air was fresh, also uncluttered, and at times made him feel very good. But at times only a thought away were his wife and baby, whom he had left in Mexico. His longing for them often made his chest feel heavy around the heart, and sometimes, because he was alone, tears would come into his eyes.

And so he would try not to think about them, which had nothing to do with his lack of feeling but only survival. He liked where he was but did not like being alone in the night. Daytime was more open but night closed in on you.

Sometimes late at night he could bring in a San Antonio radio station, which carried the music of his country and made him feel as though he were closer to home. At times he would sing along with the songs on his radio, to everybody and to nobody. He would think of dancing with his wife, the first time he had met her, but when it hurt too much he'd try to think about something else.

He had a good job, which paid much better than any he had had in Mexico. He was only twenty-two but had worked regularly from the time he was twelve and, in his country, had sold flowers from a cart and worked in a mine. He still coughed a little from the time he spent in the mine, but the fresh air on the ranch was helpful.

The small boy who lived with his father in the Big House on the ranch would pass by the mobile home on his way to fish. The owner of the ranch lived in San Antonio and leased the house to the small boy's father, who made his living by staying up late at night and putting words on pieces of paper with an old typewriter and selling them somewhere. Manuel never was sure where the small boy's father sold the pieces of paper with words on them but it didn't seem healthy making a living that way. If Manuel could speak the English words better he would suggest to the small boy's father that he bring his equipment outside to work so he could get more sunshine and fresh air. Sometimes gringos did funny things.

Always Manuel would smile and wave at the small boy when he saw him pass. Once after he had come home from work he offered the small boy a sweet he had made by putting coloring into water in an ice tray and freezing it. Soon, they became good friends, although neither could understand the other's language. They would communicate with a few common words, by nodding and pointing, making sign language, and by laughing a lot.

Manuel taught the small boy to make tortillas and some tricks about fishing.

After a few weeks on the ranch Manuel began to look forward to Friday afternoons when his work was finished. He would clean up, slick down his hair with oil, put on cleanly starched work clothes, and hitch a ride into town with the small boy's father.

At the same place in town each week he would meet others from his country who had crossed the border to work. They would drink beer, tell stories about their old and new lives, and sometimes play cards.

On Sunday afternoon the small boy's father would pick up Manuel and take him back to the ranch. At times his head would hurt a little from too much beer, but he would fall asleep and dream. He would try to dream of the time he could bring his wife and baby to live with him and sometimes he would. At other times he would dream that something terrible had happened to them and wake up, sweating and afraid. And alone.

Every few months the authorities would run a big bus through the area, rounding up the illegal aliens and sending them back to Mexico. A few would run, but many would just sit and watch the bus as it came through the countryside toward them. Fate was inevitable, they would say. From a lifetime of being poor, rundown, you become a fatalist.

I do not know whether Manuel was taken on the big bus. I do not know if he eventually brought his wife and baby to live with him but I am glad he taught the small boy how to make tortillas and hope he enjoyed the beer he drank on the weekends in the small town near the ranch.

T HE *Ferrocarril al Pacífico,* the Chihuahua to the Pacific railroad, winds its way snakelike from the border to the West Coast, crossing the desert, passing through Chihuahua City, climbing through the towering Sierra Madres and, finally, settling down to Los Mochis, only a short drive from the coastal village of Topolombampo on the Gulf of California.

It is a very practical trip, for shipping lumber and supplies, but also can be a romantic trip if indeed you are in no special hurry and do not mind delays . . . if indeed you are, at heart, a dreamer of fine dreams. So Bo Linn caught the *Chihuahua al Pacífico* that day in late afternoon at the depot in Ojinaga, a small Mexican town just across the Rio Grande from Presidio. His life never would be the same again.

Bo was twenty-two at that time, preoccupied as many are his age with having a good time and raising hell, and he had just begun to work for the railroad in the United States. One day, waiting for rail cars to be added in Presidio for the trip north, he looked across the Rio Grande and wondered just what was out there beyond the border. He had been struck by wanderlust, that unseen malady which lies somewhere within us all, active or dormant.

So it was decided, on a lark, that when he got some time off he would make the train trip so many had talked about as far as Chihuahua City. Jimmy Collins, also with the railroad, would come along, and they would have a great time. It was agreed that they would meet on the same date, about the same time, the following year at the International Bridge. And oddly enough, although they did not communicate on the matter, both kept the date.

Linn is a wide, husky man of about five eight or five nine, with a belly that always hangs over his belt. He can be rough. Yet, he also can be a reflective, sometimes mellow man. I think in another time, another life, he might have had the soul of a poet. He can pick up a guitar and sing sad or happy songs and talk about books you would not have expected him to have read.

The afternoon that Bo met Collins for the trip on the *Chihuahua al Pacífico* the old train jerked away from the station but soon smoothed into a constant, almost hypnotic rhythm. Bo and Jimmy had facing seats and were alone because, although the train was crowded, the Mexicans did not particularly want to sit next to the robust looking, red-faced gringo and his smiling friend.

When Bo turned away from the window and looked down the aisle, he saw her. He became almost transfixed.

He felt she was the most beautiful girl he'd ever seen. She had soft tan skin, fine Castilian features, and soft brown eyes that seemed to be brightly lit from within. He was frozen, fixed, dumbstruck, and could not take his eyes off her. When their eyes met she turned quickly away.

Abisué Ramos had not reached her twentieth birthday that day. She was returning home from college to visit her family, aristocrats who owned a large rancho outside Chihuahua City. She sneaked a glance, subtle and virtually unnoticed, at Bo when he turned back toward the window. This is strange, she thought, but he looks like the man I once saw in my dreams.

When Abisué noticed an old woman trying to keep her balance in the aisle she quickly got up and gave the woman her seat. Bo, watching, took his feet off the seat across from him and told Jimmy to also put his feet on the floor. He took out his handkerchief and wiped the seats clean. He then motioned to Abisué to take the seat next to him. She acknowledged his offer and sat down. Bo, who was reared in San Angelo but moved to Slaton (near Lubbock) had spent a lot of time on the border and taught himself to speak Spanish.

"Señorita, is possible you are going to Chihuahua City?"

"Yes, I travel for there, señor."

"Ah, as fate would have it I too travel for there."

They felt awkward, fell silent. Bo glanced at her and then turned quickly when she glanced back at him. She did the same. It was as if they were viewing separate tennis matches. The old lady who had taken the seat from Abisué chuckled and whispered something to the person next to her.

"Uh, could it be, señorita, that you live there?"

"Yes, this is true, señor."

"Señorita, please do not think me too bold but it would please me greatly if I could learn where you live so that I might come to see you."

"No, is not possible, señor."

Assuming she was Catholic, Bo drew the sign of the rosary and was surprised to learn she was Protestant in a Catholic-dominated country.

"Señorita, pardon me for asking, but I, too, am Protestant and is it that you intend to go to church on Sunday?"

"Yes, of course, I will do this thing."

"Then, perhaps, it is that I could come also."

"No, is not possible."

"Ah, then perhaps it might be that I could come to your home and meet your family. This would please me because I do not mean to offend you in any way."

"No, señor, what you ask I cannot do."

"I do not mean in any way to offend you, señorita. But if it happens that you change your mind, I am lodged at the Victoria Hotel in Chihuahua City."

When the train stopped in Chihuahua City, Bo got off, watching Abisué walk away with the people who met her. He felt strongly for her and thought about her for a long time after she had gone but believed he never would see her again. He did not know, of course, that she, too, thought a great deal about him. He has this roughness about him, she thought, but, too, there seems to be a sweetness about his manners toward me, a tenderness inside. It is so strange but he looks like a man about whom I once dreamed. But she reasoned that she must be proper and not get in touch with him and that she never would see him again.

Now Chihuahua City, capital of the state of Chihuahua, is just over two hundred miles from the border. From the northeast, the city opens into a desert-like terrain, but from the other directions it is hemmed in by the towering Sierra Madre Occidental. It is a beautiful, historical city and typical of Mexico once you get away from the border, which is not really Mexico, nor the United States for that matter, but in a kind of perpetual limbo, part of each and belonging to neither. There are many rich mines in the area and so the city is affluent, although as in other parts of Mexico, you find the wealthy and poor and no middle class.

The family of Señorita Abisué Ramos had money. Their rancho was one of the more prominent in the area. After she had gotten home from the station, she visited her mother (her father had died), her sister, brother, and brother-in-law, but her thoughts were with the gringo she had met on the train.

Linn and Collins had gone out on the town the night they had arrived in Chihuahua City. When they returned to the Victoria after the night had wound down, there was a message waiting for Bo. A Señorita Ramos had phoned, inviting him to the rancho of her family.

Bo went to the rancho the following night but, being a very proper family, the Ramos did not allow him to be alone with Abisué. Even when it was decided that they could go out to dinner, Señora Ramos made sure they were accompanied by her daughter and son-in-law. They sat at adjoining tables in the restaurant. Later when they went to a movie, the relatives sat three rows back of them. But Bo and Abisué were allowed to talk privately as they stood outside the door of the ranch house. They talked for almost three hours, watched but not bothered by those inside. There was strong feeling between them. They were in love and knew that they would see each other again, no matter what.

Bo, completely taken, borrowed a guitar and stood outside Abisué's window the next night, serenading her. They call this giving the *gallo*. He asked her to marry him and she said, yes, this was what she, too, wanted.

When Bo got back to Texas and told his parents of his plans, they were beside themselves, unable to understand that their son was not marrying one of the border prostitutes, one of the girls of the neon lights. He could not make them understand because they knew nothing of Mexico, only of what they had heard about the border.

He did not have the money to go back to Chihuahua City. He corresponded with Abisué, but after a time the letters were not enough. There was pressure from his parents. Bo became depressed, despondent over the situation. He gave up. And, as the young sometimes do in the frustration of blank walls, he threw himself under the wheels of any relationship he could find. He met and without adieu married another woman.

He phoned Abisué to tell her what he had done. She cried. And cried. Her brother grabbed the telephone and told Bo in no uncertain terms that he had disgraced his sister, his family, and that if he ever saw him again he would kill him.

Bo's marriage lasted about a month and a week. After his divorce, Bo was out hunting one day, trying to forget, when a strong feeling came over him. You fool, you absolute fool, he thought, what did you do? He left his friends, his gun, and found a telephone. He spent two and a half hours making calls to Chihuahua City until he discovered that, indeed, Abisué had not married and was working as a bookkeeper for a tire company. Although he had not talked to her nor written for over a year, Bo phoned Abisué at the tire company.

"Abi, this is Bo Linn. Can it be that you remember me?"

"Yes, señor."

"Will you marry me?"

"Yes, señor."

But after they had talked for a while, the madness of the moment subsided, and she told him he must come to see her, that they must talk first. Bo, broke, went to the bank in Slaton to borrow money. The bank was closed, so he went to the house of a bank official. He apologized for disturbing the man but told him he had to have $300 right away. He had decided to go to Mexico to get married. The banker, stunned, gave him the money.

Bo chartered a plane and was in Chihuahua City the next day. When he got to the ranch, Abisué's mother slammed the door in his face. But her sister let him inside the house. She told her mother that Bo was there at the request of Abisué, who then came into the room. Señora Ramos was told of Bo's intentions to marry Abisué.

"What is this crazy thing I hear? I forbid you to see this . . . this person. Marrying him, ah chihuahua. You will be the death of me. Marriage is out of the question. I forbid it."

"Mama, I always have obeyed your wishes. But I am now twenty-two years old and must do what my heart says for me to do. Once in my dreams I saw such a man as this Bo Linn. It is God's will."

Her mother said it would not work but saw that it was fruitless to argue with her daughter. So in the end the Ramos family relented, staging a large, expensive wedding for the railroad man from Texas and their daughter. They were married almost two years to the day from the time Bo had first left Chihuahua City.

Bo took Abisué to meet his parents, who still lived in San Angelo. When he had phoned, saying they were coming, his mother had said she wanted no part of them, no part of the marriage. Bo took the middle path, driving his new bride to see his parents in the middle of the night. They got them out of bed, and when his mother saw Abisué, she embraced her and everybody cried.

Recently, I went to see Bo and Abisué in Slaton for the first time in years. Bo, a conductor for the railroad, had gained a little weight and grown a beard which gave him a Hemingwayish look. Abisué was still trim and beautiful. They had two sons who stood around very politely as we visited. After dinner Bo got out his guitar and sang me a song he'd written about Christmas.

I looked at my watch and imagined it was about time the *Chihuahua al Pacífico* was making its stop in Chihuahua City.

T HERE IS A *mercado,* a market place, down the street from the Carta Blanca brewery near the outskirts of Matamoros, just across the river from Brownsville. Narrow, European-like streets run from four directions into the market, which is colorful and full of people, buying and selling. Many small, box-like shops are back to back, side by side, and those who sell goods stand outside the stores and are remindful of the hustlers who used to wait on downtown streets and try to talk guys into going to Boys Town or barkers outside the clubs in the French Quarter who plead with passersby to duck under hot, neon signs to see Miz Fanny do something or other.

"What you like to buy, sir? We have it here, plenty good. You see, you look, okay, see the best prices money can buy, hokay. You come in and look."

In recent years I must have become a tourist who watches tourists. Many know, but many do not know, that in most places in Mexico, especially the markets, you bargain with the sellers, attempting to find their lowest price. This is accepted protocol. The sellers, of course, know a gringo sucker is born every minute and will try to get everything they can, which in their case is a form of the law of survival.

For instance, the boss or *jefe* will purchase goods for a certain price. He will then add what he feels he must make as a profit. Then he will put on a price tag which is much higher. The closer the salesperson gets to that price tag, the more money he makes on his commission. There is a great desperation in many of the salespeople, who not only hustle but sometimes plead. Some will physically block your path as you pass their shop. I deal as best I can with the hustlers, but sometimes feel sorry for the pleaders, which I've found results in a direct hit on my pocketbook.

The afternoon I was in the *mercado* in Matamoros the shops, as usual, contained various artifacts, pictures on velvet, clothes, ponchos, pottery, onyx, and the heavy agate with various colored layers adaptable to bookends, ashtrays, jewelry boxes, and many other things. A chess set made of onyx, like one I had seen on sale for as much as $30 in the United States, had a price tag at one store in the *mercado* of $27.

"You like it, I wrap it up," said the man, wearing a brightly colored shirt outside his slacks, which were very wrinkled. "It is the best deal in town, a special price for today."

"It is very pretty but I don't want it that much," I said. "In fact, I think I'll just move on down the street and check out prices in other stores."

"Hokay, you like it señor. For you today is a special. I let it go for $22.50, my lowest price."

"But, ah, I am very poor and can give you only $7 for the set."

"How can this be, señor? Why, look at those very fine boots you wear. The cowboy hat. You must have much *dinero*, no."

"Well, the boots aren't that expensive. Besides, they were given me by my father on his deathbed. 'I leave you nothing but these boots,' he told me."

"Ahhh, señor, you father must have been a very rich man to have boots such as those."

"He was a man who died very poor, owning only his boots and a broken-down horse."

"Señor, for you this day only, this minute only, the price is $15. I wrap it up quickly before my *jefe* sees what I am doing and fires me."

"I cannot find it in my heart to give you more than $8. But I tell you what. For $20 I will take the chess set, a poncho, and a leather belt."

"Nooo, señor, for these things a special deal is $27."

"I will give you $50 for the chess set, a poncho, a leather belt, and your store."

"Ahh, señor, you joka with me. Hokay, take the chess set for $11, my absolute lowest price."

"Ten."

"Eleven."

"Sold."

With a great deal of shopping around I found out the price for the onyx chess sets in the *mercado* that day was $10 to $11. Eventually, the same price was reached in other stores, too. I walked around the market for a while, talked to the salespersons, and found most of them, at the bottom price, would make $1 to $2 commission on the set.

Before leaving the *mercado* I walked past the open door of the store in which I had bought the chess set and heard an American woman telling her husband, "My oh my, how beautiful these chess sets are."

"You like these?" asked the same salesman who had waited on me. "They are nice, as you must know. Beautiful work, no? Today, we have the special price of $24.50. As you can see the price tag is $27. Today only, for tomorrow the price will be full again."

"Oh dear. Can we get this, honey?"

The man smiled and pulled out his money. As they walked out of the store, the man asked his wife if he should have tipped the salesman. His wife said she wasn't sure but did not believe this was necessary.

The salesman saw me watching him, grinning. He smiled, shrugged. I smiled, shrugged.

Along the Way

Until recent times Henry Zollner, aided by his wife, Zula, and family, ran what was called a hobo ranch in Rockwall County. Zollner hired hobos to work his place, paid them wages, and gave them room and board. Men would come off the highway, the freight trains, the roads and always find work, for a day, month, a year or years. Through word of mouth the place became known as the "Hobo Ranch," and during its heyday perhaps thirty years ago, as many as 200 to 250 workers were there at one time; the turnover was something like 2,000 a year. In October 1978, the Zollners had to close down the ranch that had been operating in the family for more than a hundred years. They said the minimum wage and welfare got them.

But all the hobos who came had a story, a past. "The world is full of skeletons of people nobody knows . . . nobody knew who they were, what they were," Zollner once said.

IT NEVER WAS clear from whence the man had come. But from the first it was evident he was different, that his background was different. His speech was very correct, disguising the status he had come to know. As others, he had come to the hobo farm to work, pick cotton, make a little money and then move on, either escaping from a past that was too painful, too difficult to cope with or, perhaps, riding the crest of wanderlust that was gripping the country prior to World War II.

He was a tall, thin man with neatly trimmed white hair, a face made tan by the sun, and soft blue eyes. Zula Zollner said she couldn't remember exactly how the man had gotten to the ranch, whether by thumb, by hopping a slow-moving train, or by some other means.

"He talked so well," she recalled. "So proper. He almost had a British accent. But Henry didn't ask the men who came about their past. Certainly, there was some curiosity about the man because he was so different from the others, but we felt it was his business."

The man kept mostly to himself. He was not rude to the other workers but didn't seek them out to socialize either. He read a lot, sometimes took walks alone, and on Saturdays turned the radio to the Metropolitan Opera.

Soon the Zollners discovered that his value wasn't in hard labor, so they used him as a kind of overseer some of the time and also as a bookkeeper. "He was a superior bookkeeper," Mrs. Zollner said. "He kept such neat, accurate books. So precise. Sometimes he shocked you with his knowledge about certain things. It was obvious he was well educated."

At times on weekends the man left the Zollner Ranch, which isn't far from the community of Fate in Rockwall County, and went to Dallas. He stayed in the finest hotels, ate at the most expensive restaurants.

"He dressed very well," Zula said. "He had a number of suits, fine clothes. He left for his weekends, returned, put on work clothes, and went back to work.

"One day I drove to pick up Henry at the store. The man came with me. While we were waiting for Henry, I mentioned something about a movie in which Bette Davis was the star. Suddenly, he went into this long discussion about Bette Davis and why she didn't really do anything for him, why she left him cold. You just never knew what he would talk about next. I think, in a way, he liked to shock us.''

The media heard about the hobo ranch and came to do stories. Writers interviewed many of the transients; photographers took their pictures. Once a photographer took a picture of some of the workers and the man was in it. When he heard his picture had been published, he went to the Zollners and asked them to keep the media away from him, not to let them take his picture. He remained upset about the picture for a long time but there were no repercussions.

The man became ill and the Zollners put him in a nursing home in Royce City. In 1941 he died, leaving some fine clothes, a gold watch, and a Bible.

When people came to work for the Zollners, they were asked to leave a sealed envelope with the address inside of a person who could be notified in case anything happened to them. Most did. The man did not. But they found out the name of his brother, a famous surgeon who lived in Massachusetts. When the Zollners contacted the brother, he said he wanted only the gold watch and the Bible, to give the clothes to those who needed them. The man was buried in an unmarked grave near Rockwall.

''Of all the men we had here, he's one of the ones we can't forget,'' Mrs. Zollner said. ''I don't suppose it matters now that he's dead . . . been gone so long . . . if you print his name.''

''No, I don't think I should,'' I said. ''He wouldn't have wanted me to.''

SHE WAS A SMALL Mexican woman with a child and late at night sat so very alone on the hard plastic seats in the lobby of the airport in Austin. There was a kind of canvas-like bag in a seat near them. I had noticed her as I went into the bar by the lobby to have a nightcap.

When I came out she was still there, although the lobby was almost deserted. She seemed so very lost there with the child, a boy of about four or five. I decided to see if she needed any help, but we had difficulty communicating because she spoke very little English and my Spanish is bad and rusty.

"Excuse me, *señora,* but I am going into town and would be happy to give you a ride."

"No, but thank you," she said.

When I told her again that I would be glad to assist her I'm sure she thought I was some crazy gringo trying to hustle her.

"Well, the boy should be in bed. Is it your husband for whom you're waiting?"

"Yes."

"Then, have you waited long?"

"He will be here soon."

"The boy is tired."

"He sleeps easily. He sleeps anywhere. That is no problem."

I shrugged and walked out of the lobby to the car I had rented. Then I got to thinking that perhaps they didn't have any money, might even be hungry. I went back. She was staring straight ahead and had not moved an inch.

"Excuse me, *señora,* but could I take you to get something to eat . . . or perhaps bring you something?"

"Thank you, no."

"Your husband knows you are here now? He is very late."

"He sent us tickets to come to Austin. He has worked here for almost a year. We have come far, from Mexico to be with him. He is late but he will be here. Of this I am sure."

I nodded and went to the coffee shop which was closed. I walked to the car, drove to a short-order place, bought two hamburgers, coffee, and milk, and drove back to the terminal. The boy was asleep, leaning against her arm. She still just sat there, staring at nothing.

I handed her the food, the coffee, and milk.

"*Señora,* I hope you don't think I am too bold but, perhaps, I could make a phone call for you, to your husband. I know you have been waiting almost two hours and perhaps even longer."

"No. He will come soon."

"Sure. I'm sure he will. But . . . well, then goodnight."

I walked out of the terminal, got into the car, and drove to a motel in which I was staying on the Colorado River. I worried about the woman and the boy. I got out of the car, grabbed my bag, and started walking to the office to check in. Sometimes I wear worry and guilt like an albatross. I stopped, turned, went back to the car, and drove back to the airport. Perhaps there was a mistake. Perhaps her husband was somewhere else, maybe in San Antonio. Perhaps he had been in an accident and put into the hospital or maybe even killed. Perhaps, perhaps.

I parked and hurried back into the lobby. But the woman and boy were gone, and I never saw them again.

THE OLD FRAME building that housed the store was on a farm-to-market road, isolated and alone because the freeway had missed it by a mile or so. It was there, leaning a bit and with some boards loose, as though it had no place else to be.

Travelers seldom stopped at the old store because there were newer, more accessible places by the freeway, and even if they looked, they probably couldn't see the store, not even the old RC Cola sign, which hung high and crooked over the door.

Now the woman who runs the store had been standing on the porch with her two small children, watching my car as I drove down the road and stopped in front. When I got out, she went inside through the screened door, but the children lingered and then followed me inside.

I spoke to the children but they did not respond. The woman, who could have been twenty-eight or thirty-eight, wore a man's shirt and jeans and no makeup. She said, "Hello," and smiled, looking much younger and prettier when she did. It was about time for my breakfast-lunch, so I got a Pepsi out of the box and a candy bar, paid for them, and started to go.

"Uh, it looks like it might be going to get colder," she said. "Uh, if you want to take a load off your feet, just sit a spell in that chair yonder and enjoy your soda pop."

"Sure," I said. "Sure."

"Quiet around here," she said. "Not much to do. Uh, my husband he . . . we got this store here from his daddy and moved in about four years ago. He, uh, he works in town over yonder, and I run this place."

"I guess it's lonely, staying here."

"Uh, one time he took me to Dallas, you know. Oh, my, it was years ago. And we, uh, went dancin'. But we mostly just sat around because he wouldn't dance, you know.

"Uh, you can't tell it now but I used to be a pretty good dancer. My daddy he used to say I was the best dancer he knew of. My daddy he used to dance with me, swinging me all over the house, you know. Do you dance much? I bet you're a good dancer."

"The only thing I can dance to is 'By The Time I Get To Phoenix,' " I said. "If they don't play that, I can't dance very well, except sometimes when I've had too much to drink."

"Well, my oh my. Daddy used to have his beer sometimes I can tell you. He surely did. And . . . mister, you wouldn't believe this now but I used to be kinda pretty."

"You're pretty now. You've got very pretty blue eyes."

"Oh, I don't either (she blushed). I've put on some weight. You do that, you know, after you have babies. I, uh, well my daddy he used to say I was the prettiest thing he ever saw. But, uh, you don't see many people around here and there's no reason to fix up, you know."

"Hey, you look fine. I'm sorry you have to stay out here by yourself. Tell your husband you want to go dancing. Tell him to take you or you'll pack up and leave."

"Oh, he wouldn't take me out. Sometimes . . . some-times . . ."

"I know."

"He, my husband, he never says I'm pretty. He never does."

"That's the way things happen sometimes. He thinks you're pretty but just forgets to tell you. It's like, well, you keep cooking fine meals. You've done it so much for so long that it's just taken for granted and so nobody says, 'Hey, that was a fine meal.' It doesn't mean they don't think so."

"Uh, you want another soda? It's on the house."

"No thanks."

"You from Dallas, huh? I wished we lived in a big city. You know, there'd be more people to talk to and places to go. I like people, you know."

"It's odd, really. People who live in the city want to be in the country and people who live in the country want to be in the city. I don't know. I often wonder if they pass each other on the way."

"Yeah," she said, nervously. "Yeah, I sure do guess that's right. You got to go on, huh?"

"I'm supposed to meet somebody soon, but I enjoyed our talk. I think you're a fine woman and very pretty."

"Oh, come on, you don't either."

She started outside, through the screen door, the same time I was leaving. I opened the door to let her pass.

"Well, I'll be," she said. "You know an ol' country girl like me's not used to havin' the door opened for her."

She shivered and said again it was going to get cold.

I shrugged. Her eyes were watery and it scared me because I thought she was going to cry. I told her goodby and said, "Hi," again to the children, who still did not answer. But when I took off my sunglasses and looked at the children cross-eyed, they laughed.

I felt after I had left that the woman probably had gone into the back again and put on an old blue party dress, the one in which she once had gone dancing, and looked at herself in the mirror. God, I hoped the dress wasn't too tight.

Oh, SURE, I'VE seen a lot of kids like that, and you have, too. He was kind of tall, gangling, with a long nose and a Marine-looking haircut. He seemed a little at odds with his clothes, although it was obvious that they were new and that he was proud of them.

He had on a light blue, plaid, short-sleeve shirt and new store-bought jeans that looked as if they'd never been washed. I thought to myself, if they haven't been washed his legs will be blue when he takes off those jeans. And he wore new cowboy boots that seemed to screech a little when he walked. The boots had a flower-like design on them. He purposely pulled up his britches leg a little when he sat down because he was proud of those boots. They were the best $22.95 boots money could buy.

I figured he was seventeen or eighteen. When he said "hep" instead of "help," I felt a common bond with him because back in East Texas, where I grew up, we used to say, "Hep . . . I can't hep it."

He was a friendly kid and nodded a hello when he sat down near me at the counter of the cafe-bus stop. He was talking to the waitress, behind the counter, about a bus.

"Oh, about 3:30 this afternoon," she said. "You've got a little wait. But you go over there to that counter and get that ticket. This is the restaurant part."

"Well, thank you," he said. He put down a small suitcase, leaving it near the stool at the counter, and walked over to get his ticket. The large, sleepy man at the cash register in the cafe section walked across the room, got behind the bus counter, and sold him a ticket.

The kid came back, sat down, and ordered a Coke and a hamburger. The waitress asked him what kind of Coke he wanted.

"Well, a Coke. Just a Coke."

"You mean a Coca-Cola, a Pepsi, or a Dr Pepper?"

"A Coca-Cola, ma'm," he said. They both grinned.

A guy I took to be a trucker sat two stools down the counter, drinking coffee. "Son," he said to the kid, "you know those soda pops burn up your stomach." The kid looked at him, puzzled. The trucker continued, "Well, they sure do. You can take a piece of bacon, put it in a bottle of that stuff and it'll start sizzling."

The kid didn't know what to say. When his Coke came, he seemed almost embarrassed to drink it with the trucker watching him. But he wasn't embarrassed at all about eating the hamburger. He seemed very hungry.

The kid told the waitress his name was Dwayne. "Well, glad to meet you, Dwayne," she said. "My name is Barbara."

The kid finished his Coke and hamburger, and when Barbara came back and asked if he wanted any pie, he told her she was pretty. She blushed when he told her and, subconsciously, brushed back her hair in front and fluffed it a little in back.

He continued to talk to her in a low voice that was difficult to hear. I noticed, after she had disappeared for a while in back, that she came out with fresh lipstick. I don't know whether the kid was just being nice or hustling her a little, but it did her good. She looked seven or eight years younger after he began talking to her.

"You sure are pretty," the kid said again, louder.

"Well," the trucker said, joking, "I never noticed you were so pretty."

She gave the trucker a dirty look, and he said, "Hey, I'm just kidding. Okay."

The kid scratched the side of his head, although it didn't itch. The trucker got up, left some coins on the counter, took his check, and started to walk off. Then he looked back at the kid's boots. I hoped he wouldn't say anything, because the kid sure was proud of those boots, but I knew he would.

"Hey, boy, where'd you get those fancy boots?" asked the trucker, then laughed. "Those are some boots, all right. Ha-ha-ha-ha."

"Those ARE nice looking boots," I said, quickly. "They really are. I like that design."

The trucker shrugged and walked off. The waitress stared holes in him as he left. The kid sat there for a while, not saying much. Finally, he got up, and picked up his suitcase. He told Barbara, "It sure was nice meeting you." He nodded to me and walked outside to wait for the bus.

When the bus came the kid got on. He stayed in his seat, as did the other passengers, when the driver came in for a quick cup of coffee. When the bus left, Barbara watched it, seeming almost hypnotized. I think she was wishing, just for a moment, that she had gone with the kid.

I recall the yellow cotton dress, foaming like a wave around her knees; the birds like tender babies in your hands and old men playing checkers by the trees . . . — *Jimmy Webb,* MacArthur Park.

HIGHWAYS ARE all around Renner, racing God knows where but always racing and looking neither right nor left to see the countryside, which is shrinking into concrete. But despite the proximity of the highways, it is strangely quiet and peaceful in Renner.

The old schoolhouse burned down some years ago, but it wasn't being used that much anyway. There just aren't many children at all here, and the ones who remain go to school in the Dallas suburb of Richardson, a bordering city. Some four hundred people live here in about a four-square-mile area. There is only one small cluster of frame houses with a few outlying ones, and many houses, more and more, are being boarded up . . . closed and empty and forever keeping their own counsel, their own secrets.

But there still is action at the post office, or rather the room adjoining the post office, which is in an old house-like, frame building with gas pumps in front and a garage in the back. Rain and winters have long since taken the paint away, leaving only remnants of white around the door facings. If you enter to the left you go into the post office, which is squeezed in tight. If you enter to the right you go into the place where they play dominoes. A gas stove sits by one wall, midway, and three card tables with chairs are spread evenly around the room. A kind of ritual goes on here: Six days a week — Sundays are for church-going — a group of elderly men gather to play dominoes.

They are retired or semi-retired; some are farmers on days when the weather is suitable for farming. Maybe it is their age that brings them together. I don't know if their age puts them into people's way or if their habits, which have been built up for over fifty years, have become troublesome to the younger generation. I just know they come to Renner and play dominoes. They always do.

I always have loved the elderly and the secrets they hold from this life, although it often seems another life. I can remember my grandmother, who is over a hundred, telling stories about coming from Missouri to Oklahoma in a covered wagon and making friends with Indians they called the Black Hats. I could listen to her tell stories for hours and . . .

And two men were standing by the stove in the place where they play dominoes. "Oh, the rest'll be coming along in a minute," the shorter one said. He had on a hard-billed hat and freshly starched work clothes. His name was Elmer J. Smirl and he is retired, although he still helps young children cross the street before and after school.

"I used to be a cabinetmaker," he said, and I told him about my uncle who had been a carpenter and how when I was a kid I used to watch for hours as he worked.

Now the other man was backed up near the stove, with his hands behind him, palms up, warming. He smiled and said, "I'm W.R. Pond. You know, like a plain little old lake. Oh, I was in the engine rebuilding business before I retired."

"Yessir," said Elmer J. Smirl, "we play four-handed dominoes. The others will be here in a while. Oh, some come in about 10 or thereabouts."

"Yeah, there's always a game," said Pond.

"You see over there (he pointed out the window)," said Elmer J. Smirl. "Well, they're moving the post office over there, but Mr. Hartline owns this here place and he'll keep this domino parlor here. You know, this place here used to be owned by Mr. J.C. Wells."

"Yessir," said Pond, "he was mighty busy. This was a store in here, and the post office was on the other side. He was jumpin' round here mighty busy all the time."

"But I tell you one thing," said Elmer J. Smirl, "I never saw a time when he couldn't stop and play dominoes. J.C. Wells, yessir, he passed away not too long ago. He was a purty good domino player, that Mr. J.C. Wells was."

On the wall behind the stove they had the rules tacked up. They were simply:

No Spitting on the Floor.
No Cussing.
No Talking after Hand Starts.
No Gambling.
No Drinking.

"Them's pretty good rules," said Elmer J. Smirl, and Pond shook his head in agreement. "That's the way to play dominoes, by those rules."

"We all put up $15 a month for gas and lights," said Pond. "Sometimes that only comes to about a dollar each. It's a good deal." Smirl nodded agreement.

A man, wide and healthy looking and younger than the others, came in. He was wearing overalls and said, "Howdy," and sat down. He leaned his chair against the wall.

"That's my nephew," said Elmer J. Smirl. "Ed Smirl's the name."

"Glad to meet you," said Ed Smirl, who saw two coats hanging over a chair and laughed, "Those are mine. Left 'em here, one at a time."

I asked them who were the best players, and Elmer J. Smirl said, "Well, ol' Dub's hard to beat."

"So's Jackson," said Pond.

A pickup stopped outside, spewing gravel. "And that ol' boy coming here's hard to beat, too." said Elmer J. Smirl.

"Well, I be," said Pond. "He surely is. It's Mr. Elmer Adams."

Elmer Adams was a stocky, white-headed man with very mischievous eyes. He looks at you out of the corner of his eyes, and when I asked him what he did before retiring, he said, "Nothing! Just nothing." Everybody laughed. He added, "Aw, I used to have some oil interests, and other stuff like that."

We stood around the fire, warming, while Elmer Adams talked. "My grandfather," he said, "homesteaded in '98."

"Boy," said Pond, "you older than me. I can't remember back that far."

There was more laughter, and Pond said, "I can remember when there was hardly nothing west to Oklahoma. No bridges and we had to ford the river. I was born in November 1890. Yessir, it took us thirty-one days to go from Bowie to just across the Red River in a wagon. We took our milk cows, tying them to the back of the wagon.

"We got caught in a snowstorm and had to stay in the wagon yard a week. That was some snowstorm, I mean to tell you."

"Well, we got us four here now," said Pond. "Le's shake 'em up."

"Yeah," said Elmer J. Smirl, "you gonna talk all day. You 'fraid to sit down and play with us."

"Well I ain't exactly afraid," said Adams.

They sat around the table and shook 'em up. The dominoes sounded like a stampede, far, far away.

"Haw, haw. You in trouble to start with, boy."

"Well, if I'm in trouble then I just gonna come on outa it."

"Ohhhh. That ain't a lot of help. Whooooeeee."

And so they played dominoes as they do each morning except Sunday and laughed and kidded each other. They did not bother with, nor were they bothered by, what was going on around them.

Late at night lights flowed and danced across the Colorado River in Austin in a very dreamy way, although I thought as I walked that the new high-rise apartments on the other side looked obscene, taking the place of trees and brush which once had been there.

Perhaps a quarter of a mile away, just off the path along the river, I could make out what appeared to be an old pickup and a man holding something . . . perhaps a guitar . . . and sitting down by a small fire. When I got a little closer I could hear him play, or rather strum the strings, making music that he alone knew or could imagine. He was in his own key.

I went to where he was sitting, stood by the small fire, and told him I thought it was a fine night with the chill of fall just right for a fire. He was of Spanish descent, and I noticed the guitar had a missing string. I'm not sure whether he knew the string was missing or not, only that he did not care, that it made no difference.

"As you must know by now I cannot play the guitar properly. But when I am alone it matter not. It helps me to relax, you must know."

'Yes, I know. But don't stop playing. You sound fine to me. I like hearing what you're doing."

He shrugged, began to strum again.

"Do you come here often?"

"Well, no. Not too much, you know. But it is peaceful, is it not?"

"Yes, it's peaceful and restful, and I must go. I'm sorry if I bothered you, your thoughts."

"Ah, do not go. Stay here, *por favor*."

He handed me the wine bottle from which he had been drinking, and we began sipping, passing it back and forth. It was cheap, red wine but tasted strangely good, not too sweet. The wine, I suppose, also had a missing string.

And after we had stared at the river awhile he began talking. "You know, I had this girl. Grace Hernandez. But we broke up. I didn't want this, but she broke up with me. I am not sure what her reason was."

"Sometimes there is no good reason. It just happens."

"Well, you know, I work on this construction job and I have this boss of mine. I tell him Gracie doesn't want me around anymore, and he said, 'Ramon, you are just too shy. You do not talk enough.' Girls, he tells me, like for you to talk, to tell them the funny stories and dance all the dances with them. But, *señor,* I cannot do these things very well."

"Sometimes women don't like men to try to be too funny and talk a lot. Sometimes they like somebody who is quiet and shy."

"*Señor,* Gracie is not like that sometimes."

Ramon handed me the guitar with the missing string, and I, too, strummed it. He listened politely, fully understanding the key.

"El Rio Rancho Grandeeeee, el rio-rio-riooooo," I sang and he joined me, adding, "AIIIIIII-YIIIIIII-yi-yi!"

When we had finished our song, he said, "My boss he says, 'Ramon, you are lazy.' I do not know. Maybe Gracie stopped liking me because I am lazy."

"What is lazy?"

"Well, sometimes, you know, I dream with my eyes open when I should be working. It always has been this way. When I was a small boy I was lazy. My papa trimmed the trees and often would take me to help him. But he would have to make me get out of the truck.

"Do you see that pickup there? It is a '58. It was this same truck that my father had. When my father died, although I was not there when he passed away, I am sure his last words were, 'Ramon, he's a lazy boy, all right.'"

"I, too, was lazy," I said. "I am lazy, in fact, but when this is pointed out to me, I say I am deep in thought, meditating."

"Ahhh, meditating. You mean, like in the church?"

"No, like not in a church."

We looked at the river again, soft and velvet. I do not remember what I saw in the river, only that he saw Gracie Hernandez.

He took a deep breath and said, "That's me, Ramon. Shy. Lazy."

He took the guitar and sang, "Don't look so saaaad, I know it is overrrrrr." And I sang, "Forrrrr the goooood timeeeees."

Then we were silent again. "I know what we can do," I said finally, handing him the last swallow in the bottle. "Bring the guitar, let's get in the '58 pickup and go to the casa of Gracie Hernandez. We will give *gallo,* stand outside her window and play and sing to her."

"Hiiieeee! Would she ever be so shocked! But, no, I could not do this. I would drop dead from being so embarrassed."

We were silent for a long time, and when I got up to go, he said, "*Señor,* you do not have to go. Stay for a while."

"I'm going to my room back there in the motel and get another bottle of wine." I walked back up the path, over to the motel, and up to my room where I got the bottle. It was good wine that I had been saving to take back home, but it seemed appropriate to drink it then.

When I got back, Gracie Hernandez, we did not drink the wine shyly nor were we in the least bit lazy.

The sign on the lake house read, "For Sale."
Grass had grown high and the flowers by the porch needed watering.

THEY SAT ON the porch at night and looked out across the lake at the flickering lights of other houses, scattered among the distant trees. The sky was much larger out there, away from the city, and they also could hear the sounds of nature, which they could not hear in Dallas.

He was sixty-two and she was fifty-eight; they had been married thirty-five years and had reared four children, who were now grown and had begun their own families. Their children had moved away and seldom came to see them but phoned on Christmas and birthdays. The children, always were going to come to see them more, so they said, and certainly, it wasn't that much trouble to phone, and they were sorry they hadn't. It was no more trouble than, say, stopping to smell the flowers.

In their lives they hadn't done much of anything. They had worked, reared their family, and saved their money, gradually and sometimes painfully. They never had taken the trip to Europe they used to talk about, nor had they even been to Mexico, although they had talked about that, too. Most of the money they had saved went for the education of their children and for doctors and other things for which money must be spent.

So six months before they had sold their house and the second car and made a down payment on the lake house. It had been traumatic because the old house, the old neighborhood held memories of their life, good and bad and gray.

"This place here is too big for us now," she had said. "And the children are gone. I know. I know, you can't live in the past."

"Before the children came," he had said, "there was just us. Now there is just us again."

"I know," she said. "I know."

And so they had taken the furniture they valued most and moved into the lake house, which was smaller but more practical. At first the new place seemed so strange; they were disoriented. After a while they were not. They made friends with an elderly couple who lived just around the turn in the road and also had bought a lake house.

They found a stray dog, a wild one, and fed it and loved it, so the animal had stayed, making a home under the house. "Let's call him Dog," he had said. "But that's so impersonal," she had said. "Then," he had said, grinning, "let's call him Cat."

They found a cafe they liked in a small town near the lake and went two, maybe three, nights a week to eat there. He had picked up some jargon from their youngest son and rated things, as their son rated women, on a scale of one to ten. He liked to say the chicken fried steaks at the cafe were usually eights or nines, just excellent.

He got up very early and made coffee and read the newspaper. The morning paper came late to the lake house area, and so he saved the afternoon paper and read it the next morning because all his life he had read a paper early in the morning. It was a lifetime habit for him to have his coffee with his paper. One doesn't change lifetime habits, although one does adapt and alter them sometimes. Often he made her breakfast and took it to her, just as she was waking up. She giggled about the burned toast and he laughed, too.

During the day they read a lot, talked a lot, worked in the garden, watered the flowers, and spoiled the dog. Often in the afternoon, if it wasn't too hot, they walked down the tree-lined dirt road. And often they held hands as they walked. The time was good, punctuated by slow-moving dreams.

They finally had made it. But six and a half months after they moved into the lake house the woman suffered a stroke and died.

Further Adventures

THERE WAS NO way to keep the water from coming into the house. The wind was so high, blowing with such force, that it turned what had been rain cascading against the window into pounding, driving water that spewed through cracks around the window frame, the sill and door.

The storm had knocked out the electricity to the house and I could find no candle, but when the lightning came I could look out the window and, in flashes, see that the ocean, in its anger, had pushed across the sand and up to the porch of the beach house in which I was staying on South Padre Island.

When I had first gone outside earlier that day the wind had pushed me back against the house, making me feel like a puppet jerked by an invisible hand. I had had to hang onto the railing to make any progress along the porch. When I had looked at the nearby houses on the part of the beach where I was staying, most of the cars had been gone.

The day before I had taken my kids to the airport in Harlingen so they could fly back to Dallas. The beach then had been very crowded. But by the afternoon the storm hit, most everybody had left, crossing the causeway into

Port Isabel or perhaps going to Harlingen or Brownsville, as they do during storm warnings and storms.

I don't know why but I never thought about leaving. I have this fixation, fascination, about storms, and so when Amelia came I wanted to be where I was. As a small boy I loved to run into the tin-roofed barn near my grandmother's house when it rained. Rain, hitting the roof, was magnified in sound, and I would rest on the hay and listen for hours.

Actually, the storm that hit South Padre that day never really frightened me, but that probably was because of my ignorance about tropical storms. Winds of Amelia were said to be up to sixty miles per hour in the area, although at times they seemed higher, and a storm isn't officially a hurricane until the wind velocity reaches seventy-four miles per hour.

So when the storm came the winds had been high, causing blinding sand to sweep the beach, and there had been an oyster sky, although it was to get much darker. And then, suddenly, there had been a great calm late in the afternoon. It was as if everything had stopped. Then it had hit.

I watched the storm, whenever I could see through the window, until going to bed near midnight. It is an odd feeling, really, being inside a beach house during a storm without any outside contact. It is interesting, exciting, as though you are on some isolated island in a dreamy yet real world. You are there, really, and yet also almost observing yourself from afar. But I fell into a very sound sleep. And by the next morning the storm had passed. I mopped up the water that had come inside and cleaned off the porch.

The wreckage of a boat was scattered for miles along the shore. Debris, parts of speakers, doors, nets, the hull and cabin were scattered everywhere. I later found it was the wreckage of a shrimp boat, the *Margaret Webster,* which had been engulfed by a big wave and had broken up near the jetties. I got chillbumps when I saw the shoe of a sailor near part of the wreckage and I assumed everybody on board had been killed. They had not. The Coast

Guard had gotten the crew, all wearing life preservers, out of the water.

The hull of another, nameless, ship, crushed by the storm as though it were a toy, was down at the north end of the beach. People who had returned looked at it, walked past. But then one man went over and banged on the side with a plank. There was a soft banging from inside. He tried again. There was another response. Three men were inside. They'd been trapped there for eighteen hours.

The storm had swept the cabin and everything else off the deck and capsized the hull. Somehow, when the high winds had hit, the three men had been thrown into the hull, where they survived, getting air by forcing a hose to the outside. One said he believed he had gotten the message from his Maker and would not go out again. Another said he would immediately try to find another boat and sign on. The third said he was too shook up to know what he would do.

It didn't appear anybody was going to clean up the wreckage on the beach. Nails were turned up in splintered boards. I went to the City Hall and told the officials that if they didn't clean up the beach somebody was going to get hurt. A spokesman there said they just weren't sure whether it was their responsibility or that of the county's. I repeated that the beach was an awful mess and hinted that I might write a story saying that the city had no idea whether it was responsible for cleaning up the beach or not.

The next day they began cleaning up the beach. It had taken seconds for the storm to wreck the boat and a week to clean up the remnants. That is the nature of things.

I LOVE EAST TEXAS most in autumn. I'm talking about the section east of Mt. Vernon, where the land is sandy dune and the leaves on the trees turn gold and red in the timeless process of nature and clash so beautifully with the green pines.

Pine trees endure. My friend, the late Forrest Carter, author of books such as *Gone To Texas* (from which the movie *The Outlaw Josey Wales* was made), *The Education Of Little Tree,* and *Watch For Me On The Mountain,* was Cherokee, his Indian name actually being Little Tree. He used to tell me that when you are alone in the woods pine trees tell you things, talk to you, just as do streams and birds. He said the Indians always had known this and that I should go back in the woods, be alone, and find out for myself. He also said pine trees were medicinal, especially for the mind, and that if you sit quietly among them you'll feel an inner peace.

I have built a house on a hill covered with cotton woods, oaks, and pine trees in the woods not far from Cypress Springs Lake. A road near the house is not yet paved and cars do not pass, unless somebody gets lost. So you can be so very alone.

When you're alone in a house in the woods you begin to hear sounds you haven't heard and see things you haven't noticed before. You find the tracks of deer along paths that snake through the woods and see the animal, little more than a stick-like shadow, go across the road in a kind of natural ballet. Gradually, the tracks, sounds, wild flowers come to have names, and you can better enjoy the ever-so-soothing sound of the wind rustling through the trees. At first there are some unsettling noises, such as the cry of a wildcat, which sounds like the loud whining of a baby, or movement in dry leaves near where you're walking, but you soon get used to these.

I had never paid much attention to birds before but fell in love that summer with the hummingbirds that came to the house to drink water, mixed with sugar and coloring, in a container hanging from the porch.

When the house was first finished, I stayed there alone for a week or so and became friends with a large redbird. The first morning about 7, I was awakened by a kind of pecking sound. I got up, looked around, and couldn't figure out from where the sound was coming. I went to the door, thinking somebody might be knocking. Then I tracked it to the glass front on the balcony upstairs.

It was a redbird, just pecking away at the glass. Then he flew away.

He woke me up at the same time with the same sound for the next five days. I began to think all sorts of things, about reincarnation, this and that. I found myself wondering what person the bird might have been in another life and if it had been someone I had known. Then I thought how silly it was to think that at all. But I began to leave bird seed and a small dish of water on the balcony.

I left, came back to Dallas for a week, and then went back to the house in the woods in East Texas. Sure enough, the bird pecked on the glass around 7, waking me up once again. I began telling it good morning and looking forward to seeing it. But each time I would approach the balcony it would fly away.

When I left again and came back two weeks later, the bird was gone and has not been back, but I keep hoping it will. It gave me a certain feeling that is difficult to explain and I was sorry I didn't know the language that Forrest knew.

WE WERE TREADING water in the very cold Pacific Ocean about thirty yards off Zuma Beach, waiting for The Big Wave. We had driven over from Thousand Oaks, California, where the Dallas Cowboys train before the season, and I had just shown Frank Luksa, Jr., of the *Dallas Times Herald* my famous windmill body-surfing technique. Using this technique, I miss the crest of a wave and thus am sent banging 180 degrees to the ocean floor, my feet momentarily sticking up out of the water like two periscopes.

We had been talking all afternoon about the Great White Shark or Carcharodon Carcharias. The Great White craze, at that time, had been sweeping the country because of Peter Benchley's book *Jaws* and the movie of the same name. Perhaps, as experts tell us, such a craze is only a fad; nonetheless, the obsession with sharks was very prominent around the beaches in California. Since the

Cowboys had opened training camp two shark attacks had been reported and three Great Whites harpooned along the California coastline.

"There have been two shark attacks and three Great Whites harpooned along the California coastline," I told Luksa as we waited for another Big Wave. The sun came out of the smog, reflecting on the water and distorting my vision momentarily. I blinked, then saw something move slowly in our direction.

"Look," I said, "maybe that's a Great White."

Luksa looked up out of the water, the fear that crossed his face quickly changing into a smile. "Fool, that's a boat," he said.

"Yeah," I said, "a boat looking for Great Whites so they can warn helpless swimmers and surfers or harpoon the creatures before they attack."

"If it bit off your nose it wouldn't have to eat again for a month," said Luksa.

We caught The Big Wave and rode it a foot or two toward the shore, then went back and waited for another one. Something went past us, just below the water surface. "Hey, what's that?" I said.

"Will you shut up," he said. "It looked like a piece of paper or something."

Neither of us talked for while, but I was ten to fifteen feet away from Frank Luksa, Jr., and could see him not only waiting for The Big Wave but also scanning the horizon for any sign of danger, like a fin for instance. I don't know what made me do it — I know it wasn't funny — but I made my way around behind him, dove under the water, and started toward him. Then, with all the power and force I could muster, I grabbed his lower leg, clamping with my fingers.

"AIIIIEEEEEEEEEEEE!" he yelled, leaping five or six feet out of the water and flattening out in mid-air as he searched for the foot he thought the shark had taken.

I surfaced, laughing hysterically, and said, "Ha, bet you thought it was a Great White, didn't you?"

His wet hair stood straight up and he screamed, "I'LL KILL YOU FOR THAT! I'LL KILL YOU!" He swam toward me, his eyes saucers, and I took off for the beach. He yelled, "I HOPE A SHARK GETS YOU AND BITES OFF YOUR . . .!''

There had been twenty-nine shark attacks along the California coastline since 1950, although only four fatalities are listed. But you wonder how many weren't reported because the victims were eaten. The experts tell us not to worry, to go to Zuma or Malibu and enjoy the ocean as usual. Marine biologist John E. McCosker even noted in the newspaper the other day, "We've eaten a lot more sharks than have eaten us.''

One theory is that the ocean is becoming so polluted that the Great White is looking closer to shore for food. Another is that you just hear more about the Great White because it's become such a celebrity now. They say commercial and sport fishermen used to sight and catch just as many Great Whites but just tossed them overboard or cut them up for bait. With the current interest, they're now bringing them in to sell.

Still, four sightings and two attacks. That's a little much. By the way, the attack on Frank Luksa, Jr., was not reported.

A GROUP OF US were aboard the 3T's charter about a mile and a half offshore from Fort Lauderdale, with a fair wind, you might say, in our faces. Frank Luksa, Jr., of the *Dallas Times Herald,* determined to catch the dreaded two-foot Bonita, much as Captain Ahab had wanted Moby Dick, had arranged for us to charter the boat one afternoon of Super Bowl week when the game was held in Miami. The sky was overcast, the water choppy, the deck rolling. But that was all right because after the party we had attended the previous night we also were overcast, choppy, rocking.

Our instinct, prompted by crewman Rick Matt, told us it was time to assume our fishing stances. So radioman Mark Oristano deftly found the nearest bunk and went to sleep. Luksa and I took the fishing chairs at the stern with Jim Dent of the *Fort Worth Star-Telegram* and Denne H.

Freeman of the *Associated Press* behind us. Luksa, his face grim, foreboding, leaned slightly forward, scanning the waters.

Dent kept asking when we were going to catch the Great White Shark and swigging beer. Freeman, a veteran of many catfish stories, real and imagined, tried to crush a beer can in his hand and, failing to do so, stomped it with his foot. "I feel strong, soooo strong," he said. I turned my baseball hat around backwards, draped one leg over the arm of the chair, leaned back, and tried to take a nap.

Luksa, suited out in the best of fishing clothes, told me, "You look ridiculous. It's embarrassing to be on a boat with you. Why don't you get one of those little propellers and put it on top of your hat. But you'll probably catch something, the way this week has gone."

Dent, getting another beer, stood up and said, "This business of the bulls is a serious business."

"Fish," snapped Freeman, "fish, not bulls."

"Just like I was saying," Oristano said, sitting up momentarily and then falling back to sleep.

Tension was thick. "My goodness, the pressure is getting to me," said Dent. "Where's the twenty-five-foot Great White Shark?"

"You danced with it last night at the party," I told him.

"Shut up and fish," said Luksa. "Shut up and fish or get off the boat. I've been fishing with this fool (he nods toward me) three times and the only thing we've ever caught was a three-and-a-half-foot hammerhead shark. And he caught that! He just sat there with his thumb in his ear and caught it."

"Hum. I think I danced with it last night," said Dent.

Our lines were on a mullet kite, hanging far behind the boat. I was about to doze off when the fish hit, feeling somewhat like it was going to jerk off an arm and a leg. I saw it jump once, grabbed the pole and started reeling.

"It looks pretty big," said Matt. "Maybe a five-foot sailfish."

"You're tired. Want me to take over, Bob?" said Luksa.

"It's a Great White Shark," said Dent.

"Reeeeeeel. Reeelllllllll!" yelled Captain Timms. "You'll lose it."

"Why, you can hardly turn the reel," snapped Freeman. "I've caught catfish bigger than that. You're weak. Your face is red, getting redder."

"Sure you don't want me to take over," said Luksa.

The fish jumped three more times and everybody got excited, including Matt and Captain Timms. I was just sorry I didn't see the other jumps but I was struggling too hard to look up.

"My gosh, I wish we had a camera to take some pictures," said Freeman.

"At the rate he's bringing it in," snapped Captain Timms, "you could paint it in oils."

"I've got the impression," I gasped, "that this fish is reeling me in, not me it."

"Reeeeeeelllllll!" yelled Captain Timms.

"It's a marlin," said Matt. "A big one. A really big one."

"I told you to get up and let me bring it in!" yelled Luksa.

"Look at it!" said Dent. "We . . . we need a bigger boat!"

Everybody got very excited when I'd brought the fish near the boat and Matt prepared to hook it. Even Oristano raised up, glanced over the side of the boat, then up at the sky, and said, "Under a low-hanging oyster sky . . ." Then he fell back down on the bunk.

"I need help getting it in," said Matt, putting a hook into the fish. Freeman, Dent, and Luksa obliged. Freeman cut his hand on the bill; Luksa wrenched his back; and the fish was dropped on Dent's foot.

"There's no justice," screamed Luksa. "You land this marlin without knowing what in the hell you're doing and everybody gets hurt but you."

"Just like I said this morning before we left, I'm going out there and catch a white marlin," I told him.

They said that the fish, which weighed 111 pounds and was just over nine feet long, was the biggest white marlin ever caught off Fort Lauderdale's coast, that it broke some records and that I'd be up for a trophy, etc.

Oristano got up, looked at the fish, looked at me, and said, "You have made these shores safe again, my son. Bless you." And then he went back to sleep.

"I'd like to take this moment to issue a formal apology to all the fishermen of the world," I said. "And to you fish, I know how ridiculous you must feel."

We had two hours left on the charter but I suggested, "Let's go back in, I'm tired." Luksa stared at me, coldly. Dent caught a two-foot dolphin, claimed it was a Great White, and then we started taking the lines out of the water for the trip back.

Luksa, whose line was the last to be pulled in, said, "I think I'll kill you for catching that fish."

About that time a big sailfish hit his line. In what seemed about fifteen hours he brought it in. The fish was seven-feet long. I shrugged when I saw it. "It's too small," I noted. "Toss it back." Everybody laughed but Luksa.

THE HOUSE IN which the cocktail party was held was done in modern people. They were dressed in the style of the times, which had nothing to do with tomorrow, and were seated on the floor, against the wall, in chairs. And they were in between. They sipped drinks.

I stood next to a post because I felt we had something in common. It was difficult to miss the woman in the silk dress, split just enough up one leg. She kind of slithered around the room, almost snail-like. She introduced herself and I, in turn, introduced her to my friend the post, and she said the book I had written was just wonderful.

"Thank you very much," I said. "I appreciate it."

"Well, you deserve it," she said. "It was wonderful."

"Can I buy you a drink? Would you like to dance?"

She laughed, and when I asked her why she liked the book she said, "Oh, I must confess I haven't read it yet but I just know it's wonderful. Just wonderful."

We talked silly talk for a while and then she said, "I'm going to do a book one of these days. I've lived a very interesting life. I just know it'll make a great book."

(Oh no, I thought, she's going to tell me about her entire life.) Hitting only the high spots, she told me about her life. "You see," she said, "it would make a great book and a movie."

"You could start on it first thing in the morning," I said.

We had been playing basketball and, exhausted, sat on the floor in the corner of the gym, drinking soda pop. It was the best soda pop I ever had. My friend said he hadn't gotten my book yet, but planned to do so.

He paused and added, "I've aways wanted to write a book. Gosh, you see everybody writing books these days and having great success. I'd like to get into sports, the inside story, tell things like they really are. Expose the phoniness, the crookedness. I've had it in my mind for a long time. Now, let me tell you the basic situation, if you've got a minute."

(Oh no, I thought, he's going to tell me all about the basic situations in the book he's going to do.) It took him forty-five minutes.

"Well," he said. "What do you think?"

"Great," I said. "You ought to start on it first thing in the morning."

Three of us sat around the table at the bar, having a late-afternoon-going-home-Friday-beer. They said they had seen my latest book in different stores around town.

"I've got this great plot for a book I'm going to write," said the insurance man. "I haven't decided whether to do it in novel form or not. The real inside, you know, on the insurance business. Insurance involves everybody, right. I think it'd sell like crazy. I've been tossing it around in my mind for years now."

"I've always wanted to write a mystery," said the other man. "I used to read mysteries like crazy and sometimes I'd think, hey, I could do better than that. I think I should have been a writer, always wanted to be. But I just got sidetracked. But I'm going to do that book, that mystery. How do you go about it?"

"Philosophically or physically?"

"Both."

"Well, the way you finish a book, the way you gain the discipline to finish a book, is to first take an advance from the publisher, then spend it as fast as you can. If you don't finish the book by a certain date, you, theoretically, have to give the money back. You no longer have the money because you've spent it. So, you finish the book."

"Oh," said the insurance man, "I don't think I'd have any trouble finishing, once I got started."

"You ought to start it first thing in the morning," I said.

The doctor said he heard my book was doing well. Then, of course, he said he had a great idea for a book. "I think," he said, "I've always wanted to be a writer. I envy people who write."

"I envy people who make the money you make," I said, grinning.

"I'd like to do a book and tell what the medical profession is really like," he said. "Maybe in novel form. Follow a young student from the early days until he starts his practice."

"Arrowsmith. As in Sinclair Lewis."

"More modern. I've had it in the back of my mind for a long time."

He told me the basic plot. "You could start on it first thing in the morning," I said.

A woman I do not know very well phoned me at home and said she'd like me to sign my book so she could give it to her father for Christmas. I told her I'd be delighted.

"It cost me $9 and some cents," she said. "They had some at the book store you'd already signed, but I wanted a personal thing."

"You should have gotten one of those I'd signed," I said. "They sell those $2 cheaper."

"Oh, silly. Uh, listen have you read *Marry Me* by John Updike?"

"Yes. And *Couples* and about everything else he's written."

"I think," she continued, "I'd like to do a novel about marriage on the rocks, about the pressures you face in suburbia. I've had a book in my mind for a long time. I think it'd be good and might turn into a movie. I've always been encouraged to write but have just never done it. But now everybody does it these days. If you have a minute I'd like to tell you about what I have in mind."

"Could you tell me first thing in the morning?"

It's not that you're getting older, it's just that the world is going by faster. —*Larry Gardner,* physical therapist.

T HIS IS A COLUMN for the Great Pumpkins out there and, if you are not one, don't bother reading any further because you won't understand. It is meant, then, for those who attempt to continue their athletic careers into severe adulthood without rhyme, reason or, realistically, the logical pursuit of happiness. It is meant for the heavy ladened.

For the life of me I cannot grow up, so I am cursed by the Gods of Faded Athletic Careers (GFAC), compelled, as it were, to continue along those pursuits like an old, blind, crippled bird.

I've tried to quit. God knows I've tried. Why, two years ago when I was a forty-year old teenager, still partially sound of mind and body, I decided, as they say in the sports vernacular, to hang 'em up. I worked for the *Dallas News* sports department then and it occurred to me that the time had come when Dallas Cowboy assistant coach Danny Reeves, who has two awful knees and sometimes can hardly walk, not only outran me in a 30-yard dash but actually, as he reached the finish line, glanced back over his shoulder and waved at me.

I thought about my future, considered my family, and reached a decision. I mean for the rest of your life you can't run races, play one-on-one, two-on-two, three-on-three basketball, touch football and have kids on your junior league baseball team hit you ground balls at third base in order to relive the great mediocre moments of a former baseball career.

I felt Tom Landry should be the first to know. He had watched from afar as I continually had gotten hurt in pickup games during Dallas Cowboy training camps. And he had continued to tell me, "St. John, I'm glad you're not my responsibility."

One year I had been in training camp for five weeks, and as my wife met me at the airport in Dallas on my return, I greeted her with a black eye and cast over a broken foot. She didn't even flinch. The first time we'd met we went to a party in a house with an old porch, surrounded by hedges. When we left I claimed I not only could clear the hedge with one gigantic leap but, by taking a running jump off the porch, could clear the hedges and land on my feet. I would have made it, too, but one foot caught in the hedge, causing me to fall on the side of my head. I suffered a slight concussion and sprained my neck.

Anyway, I told Landry it was time to quit. "Tom, I'm through," I said. "No more sports. When you reach a certain age your quickness goes fast."

"Especially," he said, never looking up from his clipboard, "when you've never had any."

But I tried a comeback. In early December I was showing my son, Todd, 12, how to throw a right cross. It was okay that he accidentally bloodied my nose with a counterpunch. Those things happen. But then we got to horsing around. He was Kung Fu and I was a bad cowboy, giving him a hard time. I think I've always been a frustrated stunt man, so we were falling over chairs, all that stuff. Finally, in a *coup de grace,* I accidentally put my eye on one of his fingernails, which took a hunk out of the blue part.

I had to go to the emergency room of the nearest hospital and they put an awful patch on it. I had thought I might get one of those sexy black patches but they just put on a white bandage. So I took it off the next day.

I was working out on weights with my son Scott, 15, the day before Christmas. I don't know whether it was because there was a full moon or what but I felt very strong. So I decided if Scott would spot me, I would bench press 250 pounds. Now, I weigh about 175 and cannot bench press 250 pounds, but I thought I could.

"You can't do 250," said Scott. "The most you've ever done is 215."

"Son, want-to will allow me to do it. Want-to is what made this country great. Now man your station while I break the barrier."

When you spot somebody, you stand up over the bench press and ease the bar with the weight off its holder onto the outstretched arms of the person doing the bench press. We did not communicate well. He thought I was ready to take the bar and I wasn't. So he eased it off . . . and it fell on me. I thought it had crushed my chest, killed me. We got it off and I rolled on the ground for five minutes, yelling I'd been killed.

Then, realizing I was making a scene, I calmly got up and announced that it didn't even hurt me. I finished the workout, excluding the bench press. I willed myself not to be hurt. If you have the will, you will not be hurt. But four days later I phoned Dr. Pat Evans at the Sports Medical Clinic of North Texas. He says it has become such a habit hearing from me weekly that it makes him feel odd if he doesn't.

I described how I felt and he said, "It sounds like you've fractured your sternum."

"I have not!" I said.

Three days later I went to see him to get a shot in my back, which I first injured during my baseball career when I crashed into a fence chasing a foul ball. That particular accident also caused me to suffer a badly broken leg but I did make the catch. Anyway, in the process of giving me a shot in my back, he urged me to get my chest x-rayed.

"I still think you might have a fractured sternum," he said.

"I do not but just to show you, I'll get the x-ray."

They took x-rays and I had a fractured sternum.

"That's it," I said. "I quit. No more workouts. No more athletics. That's it." I smiled, jokingly said, "I'll take up knitting."

"You'd just swallow the needle or something," he said.

"It's not easy still being a kid," I said. "It's not easy being me."

When I left his office the nurse, Sharon (Sissy) Sisler, told me I'd been a good boy and gave me a balloon and a sucker.

From the Children's Room

ONE OF THE sweetest kids I ever met was Kevin Moody. Now Kevin was a very, very avid Dallas Cowboy fan and used to go to the games or listen to them over the radio and he had his heroes and dreams. Kids always have heroes and dreams and they are made for each other.

Oh, he wanted to be like Mr. Bob Lilly or Mr. Bobby Hayes and when he'd listen to or see the games it was Kevin Moody who would be running under a bomb from Mr. Roger Staubach or Mr. Craig Morton. And he'd catch the pass behind some grasping cornerback and run into the end zone and spike the ball and the fans in Texas Stadium would stand up and go wild. Kids are like that. Dreams are like that.

Right . . . Like that. Kevin played a lot of catch with his brothers. One day he was having trouble catching the ball, and his father noticed that Kevin seemed to lose its flight and the ball would bounce off his chest. Perhaps he needed glasses. But they checked Kevin Moody's eyes and checked them again and he didn't need glasses. He was nine years old and doctors determined he had a brain tumor . . . And he was nine years old.

Kevin underwent surgery for the tumor in March but they didn't get it all out. They got so far but had to stop because going further might have killed him. So he had to quit playing catch, but I imagine he kept dreaming and heard cheers because I know kids are like that.

He underwent surgery again in July but the tumor was still there, lodged crucially between life and death. By that time Kevin was legally blind, although he could see shapes of things and people in shadows. If they got very close he could tell who the people were.

I met him a couple of months ago and he was pale and the hair had started to grow back over the scars on his head but he wasn't concerned about anything like that. He was very polite and amazingly bright, although he sometimes would lose his train of thought and forget what he had said or had been said.

Well, the doctors decided to operate again and said Kevin had a 50-50 chance. The thing Kevin most wanted to do was meet some of his heroes, who always had been, sure, bigger than life but also life to him. So I met Kevin and his dad at the Dallas Cowboy practice field a week ago Saturday morning.

Now he tired easily and became flushed in the morning sun he hadn't seen clearly in months. He had trouble keeping things straight in his mind at times and could barely see, but he knew where he was and what he was doing and he smiled a lot and was very excited and happy.

Kevin sat on the blocking sled and saw forms moving around the field. Soon a large form started walking toward him and he looked around in apprehension. It was Bob Lilly, who bent over and shook his hand.

"Hi, Kevin, I'm Bob Lilly." Kevin looked at Mr. Bob Lilly, blinked and his breath became short. He smiled but he just wasn't sure. He leaned over to me and said, "Is that really him? Is that really Bob Lilly? Is it . . . Oh, is it really." I told him it was and he looked as if the happiness would make him burst.

Bob had on a practice jersey with No. 78 on it, instead of his usual No. 74. Kevin knew the number was wrong. The jersey was old and had holes in it, and Bob laughed and said, "You see how I rate, Kevin. They won't give me a decent shirt." Now Kevin felt it was the man, Mr. Bob

Lilly, and he wanted to touch him and make sure it wasn't a dream, that he really was there. Lilly bent over and Kevin reached out and ran his fingers along the nose guard on Bob's helmet.

"My goodness," Kevin said when Lilly had shaken his hand and left. "Oh . . . Oh, my goodness. Mr. Bob Lilly. The Great Mr. Bob Lilly. Oh . . . Oh, my goodness."

Kevin tired sitting on the blocking sled and we walked over to the exercise area adjacent to the practice field, where he could lie down on one of the tables and rest. He would be very still for a while and then sit up and look around as though he wanted to make sure he was not dreaming, that he really was there.

Toni Fritsch, who was standing nearby, asked about Kevin and then walked over to where he was resting and shook his hand. Toni has a little boy and kept kidding Kevin, who smiled brightly again. "You see des leg," said Toni. "Es de strongest leg in all de world."

Kevin looked around. "Really," he said. "Really. Oh, my goodness, the strongest leg in all the world."

"You like to be keeker?"

"Oh, yes," said Kevin, and then he thought about what he had said for a second and added, "I mean, yessir."

And Kevin met Bobby Hayes and was very excited again and remembered, "The fastest man in the world. Oh, he's the fastest man in all the world."

John Niland saw Kevin resting and came over and picked him up and carried him into the dressing room. "This is my friend," John told everybody and Kevin was so very happy. So very happy.

Somehow, someway, a scene, came into Kevin's mind ever so briefly and then it was gone. He had been there, in the Cotton Bowl, and seen Craig Morton. And when Kevin saw Morton in the players' lounge he was there again in the Cotton Bowl. And Morton shook his hand and said, "Hi, big fellow." Kevin Moody was smiling so hard he almost was laughing out loud.

Roger Staubach talked to Kevin and wanted him to come to the Cowboy game. He got Kevin a Cowboy T-shirt. Like the rest of us there he wanted to do something. Anything. Just anything. Jean Fugett watched from a nearby locker and walked over and bent down and talked to Kevin for a long time. Jean was very kind and patient with Kevin and was in no hurry to get through.

I guess Kevin shook hands with most all the players, and some would say they wanted him to come to the game, that they'd leave him a ticket. But Kevin's father, Grayson Moody, would shake his head slowly and whisper that Kevin would be preparing for surgery on Monday and would not be able to come. Grayson then would whisper to Kevin that perhaps he would be able to come to another game. There were always other games.

Kevin told the players goodby and took my hand as we walked out to the car. It was the smallest, most innocent hand I've ever held and I thought about what he was facing and could find no way in my mind that it was fair. It just wasn't fair.

But as Kevin got into his father's car to leave the color was back in his face and he was smiling and I wondered if he was hearing the cheers again. He was so very polite and thanking everybody and told me so shyly, "Thank you." Then he seemed puzzled and added, "I mean, thank you sir." He was in the backseat of the car holding the Cowboy T-shirt and a football, which the players had signed, and he was so happy as he was driven off . . .

When they took Kevin Moody into surgery Tuesday a nurse came in and gave him a shot. When she had finished he called the nurse back and motioned for her to bend over. Then he kissed her and thanked her for giving him the shot. This time the doctors had to go all the way to try to remove the tumor on his brain because if they didn't he wouldn't live another year. It was as big as a golf ball.

They got it out this time and Kevin Moody, age nine, died on Wednesday. He never regained consciousness. Time, I thought, slips away, and we don't know how precious it is unless it is slipping away and never coming back again. I guess he knew it was slipping away. I guess he did.

And I guess the reason I have written this column is that I want you to stop rushing by so fast and know about Kevin Moody, who wanted to grow up to be like Bob Lilly or Bobby Hayes or . . . And if you have a son who is nine years old I want you to look at him and know that you are very lucky.

WILLIE AND TAG really were the odd couple. Willie was a white, furry, round, pint-sized poodle-cocker and Tag a large mean-looking black dog whose father was a German shepherd and mother a collie. Tag was very real with a loud bark and, when riled, presented a threatening countenance. But Willie never seemed that real. He was just too cute, toy-like, as he bounced around with his hair almost hiding his eyes.

Tag was an old man and Willie was about eighteen months old, full of mischief. Many times when Tag was trying to sleep, Willie would charge over and start barking at him and nipping at his ears. It always seemed odd, but Tag never hurt Willie. He just tolerated him, brushing him away when he was bothersome.

The big dog had a mean streak. Before Willie came, Tag often tore up our back fence. The fence was wooden, seven feet high, surrounding a large yard. But dogs don't like to be cooped up, so Tag continually got out . . . and I continually had to go to the pound and bail him out. He could jump as high as the fence but insisted on escaping by tearing up the gate. He'd literally demolish the wooden gate, biting into it and jerking it apart.

Sometimes when he got out he chased people on bikes, scaring their feathers off. Once a man rode by on a bike, and Tag ran after him and nipped him on the tail. The man yelled, came charging to the door, his hair standing up. I tried to hide, but he saw me in the window and so I went to the door.

"He bit me! He bit me!" he yelled, over and over, rubbing the spot. Tag stood nearby, his head hanging low, his eyes on the ground. He knew what he had done, but I guess the devil made him do it. I know it hurt the man, but I couldn't help snickering and, before I could calm him down, I thought he was going to sue me.

When we got Willie, Tag calmed down a lot. At first he just tolerated Willie, but then they became great friends and played games. Willie belonged to my son Todd. I guess Todd and Tag knew Willie best until the last couple of weeks when we all spent a lot of time with him. We were on vacation at our house by Lake Cypress Springs in East Texas and so we had a lot of time for things, including Willie.

The dogs loved the freedom we gave them at the lake. There were no fences and they romped off down the dirt road, looking so weird together. One night they stayed out. When they showed up the next morning, they were covered with brush and stickers. Willie was bouncing around and happy, and Tag looked like he'd been on a week's drunk.

The second night after we'd gotten back from our vacation to our home in Richardson the dogs got out the gate and we couldn't find them. Todd already was asleep and I didn't wake him because he wouldn't have been able to sleep until the dogs came back. Finally, about 10 P.M. Tag came home, but his tail wasn't wagging. Willie was not with him. I was afraid something had happened to Willie. I drove all over the place but couldn't find him. Just after I'd gotten back home the phone rang.

"Do you have a little white poodle missing?" the woman said.

"Yes."

"Well, I'm sorry to tell you he's been hit by a car."

"He's dead?"

"Yessir."

I remember when I was Todd's age how I'd found this stray dog and become very attached to it. The dog was just a lazy, old hound but became my buddy, a great constant in my life. All he demanded was food, water, and a pat on the back, and he'd be a friend for life. One day a neighbor poisoned the dog because it had gotten into her flowers. I still remembered the awful, gnawing sadness I had felt and hated so much for Todd to go through it. This sounds stupid, but I think I'd have given five years of my life if Willie hadn't been hit by the car, if Todd hadn't had to go through the hurt and sadness. But he's going through it now and, as they say, I suppose it's a part of growing up.

For days now Tag has made this awful, wailing noise. There's really not much you can do except pay more attention to him. He just misses his buddy a lot. We all learned something I had forgotten. Dogs really are people too.

EVERYBODY WAS always talking about the influence of peer groups but my friend said he'd reached the point where he no longer was sure whether his kid was influencing a peer group or it was influencing him. My friend said he just didn't know anymore.

He said when his boy was twelve that the kid had missed a lot of school, hanging around a nearby 7-Eleven, talking and smoking cigarettes. When he and his wife found out the boy had been missing school they put a stop to the smoking sessions at 7-Eleven. Well, at least they tried, but 24-hour surveillance was difficult.

At thirteen the kid stole his mother's car keys. He sneaked out of the house, got the car, picked up some friends, and rode around town, just having a little fun. My friend said he got a call at 3 A.M. from the police who said they had his son and some of his son's friends. He told them that was impossible, that his kid was sound asleep in his room. He went to the police station and got his kid. He couldn't get the car because the kid had crashed into another car and injured a woman. The accident had hurt the woman's back. My friend said this all cost him a lot money and worry.

"I don't know where we went wrong," he said. "We both look back and try to see what we did wrong. We didn't mistreat the boy. We gave him things we didn't have. That sounds like a cliche, I know, but I don't think we gave him too much. So many times we had talks, and he seemed to understand. He seemed fine. Well, he did and he didn't. His teachers told us kids nowadays have a lot of peer pressure."

They got the kid professional counseling, but the boy didn't particularly like the woman with whom he was conferring. He said she was all right but didn't understand. Nobody understands, the kid said.

But my friend said things went all right for a while. The boy passed his grades in the fall. In the spring when the boy was fifteen the police called and said they had him and two of his friends. They had been to Oklahoma and drugs were found in their possession. This time he didn't tell the policeman the kid was upstairs, sound asleep in his room. My friend said he'd gone to get the boy. He said he was very mad, but the kid cried and said he was sorry. He said the kid told him, "I can't stand the pressures . . . the peer pressures."

Then they'd taken the kid to a psychiatrist. The boy said he liked the psychiatrist just fine and went for a number of sessions. But that summer the boy disappeared for two weeks. Finally, they got a call from North Carolina. The kid said he'd hitchhiked there. He started crying over the phone and said he wanted to come home. His mother cried. My friend said he cried, too. They wired money to the boy to buy a plane ticket back home. The reunion was loving, tender, he recalled. They all cried again, and my friend said he believed the boy had finally been reached. He said the boy seemed to understand them better and that they, in turn, understood him.

"I believed we'd finally seen his viewpoint," said my friend. "I felt we'd learned to accept him, love him for what he was, not for what we wanted him to be."

There were a few other episodes, mostly minor. The boy would take things that didn't belong to him around the house. The boy would say somebody else must have done it. My friend said he kept thinking that somebody else might have done it.

When the boy was sixteen, he disappeared again. A week later my friend got a call at his office. He said the boy had phoned him from a motel in California. He said the boy told him he'd gone to California with some friends, but they had disappeared. The boy said he was alone, sorry for what he had done, but that peer pressures were getting to him. He said he felt he had to leave for a while. He said he was sorry he didn't call but you know how that goes. The boy was crying and asked my friend to please send money so he could fly home. He wanted to come home.

"I was silent for a while," my friend said. "Then I said, 'No.' My son said, 'You don't understand. I'm stranded. No money. Please.'

"So I told him, 'You got there. You get back.' Then I hung up."

HE WAS STANDING on the highway about thirty miles this side of Austin and didn't seem to be overly concerned about getting a ride. As I drove past him I thought about how when I was younger I often picked up hitchhikers but had had a bad experience and decided not to do it again. That time I had stopped for gas en route to Fort Worth and two guys approached me. They said they were broke and would appreciate a lift to Fort Worth. I told them to get in. One got into the backseat and the other in the front.

I remember feeling uneasy with the guy behind me, but I had met many interesting people in the process of picking up strangers. When we got to Fort Worth they said they had decided I'd take them on to the next town. I told them I would not. They insisted and even then, I knew the better part of valor and said, "I've decided I'll take you on to the next town."

Terrible things went through my mind. I remembered stories I'd heard about people being murdered and their cars stolen. I cursed myself for being so stupid, which I sometimes think is one of the consistencies of my life. There was an old machete under the driver's seat, and as we stopped at a red light, I grabbed it, opened the door, jumped out, and threatened them. They said they were just kidding, not to get excited. They got out and started walking again. To tell you the truth I had felt pretty good about myself, scaring off those guys, but had known in my heart that if I'd been challenged I'd probably have cut off my hand wielding the machete.

But I felt bad about the guy on the highway to Austin and turned around to go get him. He looked so small, helpless, standing out there. He had on a poncho, dirty jeans, tennis shoes, and a stocking cap. He carried a small bag and a guitar, thrown over his shoulder. Two strings on the guitar were very loose, meaning there was not way it was in tune.

"It don't matter," he said. "I just strum. I just play it for myself."

I had thought he was older but when I looked at his face he appeared to be about eighteen or nineteen. When I asked him his name, he said Fred.

"What's your last name?"

"Just Fred."

"Well, Fred-Fred, where are you headed?"

"Oh, nowhere."

"I've been there many times."

He smiled. But for a long time he only would mumble, answering only yessir and nosir when I'd try to talk to him. This is the equivalent of nodding or not nodding. Finally, he started calling me Bob-Bob, and I felt if he were playing the game he might start talking about himself. And he did.

"I just left about two years ago. My parents always were hassling me, you know. Do this. Do that. Why don't you do this. Why don't you do that. You know?"

"Having been somewhat of a hassler myself, I know."

"Well, I've just been movin' around for a while, you know, letting things happen."

He said he'd left school when he was sixteen because the teachers were hassling him. "My dad said if I quit, that was it. (He laughed.) Well, I never figured out what *it* was, you know. But I just left. Went back home six months ago. They were glad to see me, and then they started hassling me again, you know.

"I've had lots of jobs but not the right thing. My bosses always give me trouble."

"They hassle you."

"Yeah, and this one guy ripped me off. I worked like sixty hours, you know, and he paid me for forty. He said I was too young and he didn't have to pay me overtime.

What a rip off! But I'm going to get me this good job one of these days.''

"Well, even though you left school, you could get this great job sweeping or loading trucks or . . .''

"You hassling me, too? Figures. What do you do anyway?''

"Well, I try to write. I work for a newspaper and do a book every once in a while and some magazine stuff. Then sometimes I try to figure out what I want to be when I grow up.''

"I might like being a writer. That sounds interesting.''

"Maybe I'll be a hitchhiker going nowhere.''

"Well, you don't understand, man.''

"I do for the most part, or at least understand that I don't understand. Moving is fine to a point. A guy named Billy Joe Shaver once wrote something cool about Willie Nelson. It was in a song called 'Willie the Wondering Gypsy and Me.' A line was, 'Willie he tells me that doers and thinkers say movin's the closest thing to being free.' But sooner or later everybody has to be somewhere.''

I started to preach about going back to school, about understanding, about cabbages and kings, but found myself sounding like a recording. It was frustrating, perhaps as frustrating as being hassled. I gave him $20 when he got out of the car in Austin and told him it was for promising to phone his parents. He said he would. I figured it wouldn't make a lot of difference what I said to him, anyway, as long as he wasn't saying it to himself. But I just knew, just knew that if he ever took time to look inside himself he would find Fred in there.

THE MAN IN THE Air Force uniform sat just to my right, a row down, in the bleachers at the ninth-grade football game in Richardson during mid-afternoon on a Thursday in autumn. Another man, very chubby, sat on the top row. He had been screaming at the officials for a long time. A long time.

I would have to reach deep into my psyche to know why, but I kept imagining the chubby man as having a pumpkin head, with the eyes and mouth cut out for Halloween.

"Start the clock!" he yelled. "You fools! Don't you know the rules! Start the damn clock!" He would yell things such as that, over and over, between the plays, and the man in the Air Force uniform would look up at him and smile. Once the man with the pumpkin head looked down at the man in the Air Force uniform and said, "The idiots don't know the rules." The man in the Air Force uniform said they sure didn't. He yelled, too, but seemed more in control.

My son Scott plays for West, but I sat on the borderline between the Bronco fans and those for the opposition because it was the only place I could find a seat. All of us concerned with West are very proud of the team. When the current ninth graders were in the seventh grade they didn't win a game, nor did they win one in the eighth grade. But now in the ninth grade they're 3–3–1. There is such a big difference in the way they play because you can see the pride. Their coaches have done a fine job. So have they.

But, generally, you get to feeling good about their opponents, too, and all the other junior high kids because it is such a great time in their lives. It's an age when you begin to indulge more in the present and start to feel physical and mental potentials, realizing that you are pretty, smart, sensitive, that you can be a hero, can be this or that and, perhaps, beginning to sense that even the simplest of things can by lyrical.

Anyway, this particular game wasn't one of the times that things were working out for West. They were getting it put on them by the other team, although they never stopped trying. Their chance for victory had long ago ridden over the sunset, but the man with the pumpkin head on the backrow wanted more and so did the man in the Air Force uniform.

Late in the final period when one of the West linemen jumped offside the defensive player just reached over and nudged him as the flag dropped. Now you have seen Harvey Martin or Randy White knock a blocker into the nickel seats when he jumped offside. I didn't particularly care if the defensive player had belted the West blocker, but the man in the Air Force uniform jumped up and began to scream, "Hey, when he does that, blast him! Kill him! Knock his head off, kid!"

And then after the next play he began to yell as loudly as the pumpkin about the officials. "Idiots!" he said. "Damn idiots!" I stared at him for a while and finally couldn't stand it any longer. "Hey," I said, "let's charge out of the stands, tear down the restraining fence. Let's do. Let's rush onto the field and grab the officials. Let's tear them apart and then stomp them into the ground. Jump up and down and mash them to pulp."

He looked at me, blankly. Then he turned to the person sitting next to him and said something. I'm sure he was talking about the Crazy sitting near him.

At another game on a recent autumn afternoon, a ninth grader was having a fine day. He scored a touchdown and made another outstanding run. Suddenly, a short man with glasses stood up and started screaming his head off. "Loooookeeeee!" he said. "Did you see that? Ho, boy! Who was that? It was the kid, my kid!" He stood up for a long time and held up his hand, signifying No. 1.

When the kid made another nice play the man turned to a ninth grader sitting in the stands nearby and said, so we all could hear, "Put it on me! Gimme five! Who's that? That's your neighbor! Be proudddddddd! He's something elseeeeee!" He held up the sign of No. 1 again. It was fine that he was so proud of his boy. It was just that I couldn't decide if the No. 1 sign was for his son, the team, or himself. I'm not sure he knew either.

The more I go to junior high games, the more I realize what a fine time it is for all the kids, the players, the students, cheerleaders, pep squads, bands, etc. I just wish adults would help keep it that way.

I ALWAYS HAVE believed that the greatest benefit of organized summer baseball programs for kids is that they keep adults off the streets. Otherwise, I have mixed emotions as to their worth and have griped a great deal about coaches and parents stressing to kids in the 8- to 12-year-old range that winning and losing is life and death.

Now I have seen many fine coaches who care about kids and do not take out old frustrations of past personal failures in athletics on them. And I have seen many fine parents who allow their children to play the game for fun. But I also have seen coaches of small boys charge onto the field and browbeat teenage umpires. I have seen one coach try to bat his best hitter out of order to try to win a particular game. I have seen one mother yell at her son, who had just struck out, "You just wait until I get you home!"

One coach with whom I came in contact had a son who played first base. After a particular game he told his son before the entire team, "You ought to apologize to your teammates. Your error lost this game and hurt everybody on this team. I hope you're ashamed."

So a few years ago when my son Todd was ready to play organized baseball I decided I would coach, using a very low-key, non-pressure approach and trying to teach the kids some proper fundamentals that I should have learned in the many years I played baseball . . . even if I didn't.

We certainly didn't set the league on fire, but I got to know and love a lot of kids and to dislike a lot of parents. I'm sure the feeling was mutual. So, I admit our record wasn't too good, but that was because we just couldn't win the close ones, such as 10–2, 11–3, 15–4. But, generally, we managed to hang in there fairly well if we could keep the other team from getting ten quick ones on us. I had a lot of help. The father of one boy on my team actually charged out of the stands to argue with an umpire. I don't think he realized what he was doing until I pointed out to him that he should get his tail off the field. Another father was giving steal signals to his son from the stands but I also was able to cope with that.

I angered some adults when I kept after the kids to swing at the ball if it were close enough, if they could reach it, whether it was in the strike zone or not. When you are of the fifth or sixth grade age, seldom do pitchers consistently get the ball in the strike zone. So many times I had watched kids go up to the plate to walk and walk and walk. For the life of me I never could figure out how you learned to hit the ball when you were told to try to walk. So you might say we were mostly a swinging team, often beaten by a walking team. I became controversial.

The best time for me to have workouts was about 3 P.M. Then I realized that it was difficult for parents who were working to bring their children to practice in mid-afternoon. Once I tried to make it easier by scheduling an early Saturday morning practice, although most of my life I have been a late Saturday sleeper. One mother phoned me and really let me have it. "I get two days off a week and Saturday is one of them," she said. "Now, you've messed that up. Now I've got to get up early to take him to practice. You have no consideration. I hope this makes you happy, making me work on my day off."

"I know how you feel," I told her. "It's my day off, too."

She slammed down the receiver. All my life I've wanted to be the first to hang up on somebody, but people always beat me to it.

To tell you the truth I became so involved with many of the boys that I spent many sleepless nights worrying about their lives. Sometimes I also have a knack of thinking the right thing and doing the wrong thing, so I was afraid I might not be fair or say the wrong thing at the wrong time.

One kid on my team obviously was getting a lot of pressure from home and continually would beg to play third base, which two other kids played better. I would start one of the other kids and he would tell me, "You hate me, don't you. You just don't like me." His big problem as a player was that he used his foot to stop ground balls instead of his glove. I told him I didn't hate him, that I liked him very much, but that if he broke his foot he would hate me, his parents would hate me, and I would hate myself. One of the few times I remember him laughing was once when he fielded a ground ball with his glove and threw a kid out at first base. He came into the dugout with a big grin on his face and I said, "You hate me, don't you. You just don't like me." He laughed and I told him to stick out his foot next time they hit the ball at him.

I was an awful coach but God knows I tried. In one of our first games my rookie year coaching we had kids on first and third base with two outs and our best hitter at the plate. I was coaching third base, next to the opposing team's dugout. I told the kid on third to listen to me carefully and I'd tell him how much to lead off and when to get back to the base. He looked up at me with trusting eyes. The opposing coach, a veteran of many wars, came out of the third base dugout and started talking to me. He was very nice, sympathizing with my problems. I am vain and he got my undivided attention when he said he read my column, that I was his favorite writer. As I chatted with him his catcher picked off my kid at third base.

In spite of what I felt inside (those of you who also have Irish blood will understand), I wanted my kids to see how cool I could be, so I controlled myself to the point that I only dropped to my knees and put my hands over my face. I got up, looked angrily at the rival coach, who grinned, shrugged and walked away. But I admit that as I walked back to the dugout I put my hand behind my back, giving him a universal sign which kids from one to ninety-three understand. The kid who got picked off third wouldn't lead off the base the rest of the summer. I understood how he felt.

I got great satisfaction out of the smallest kid on the team. We had two main pitchers, one part-time pitcher, and the smallest kid on the team was our tenth player in line to pitch. He begged to pitch for a long time but finally gave up, hating me I suppose. Near the end of the season we were behind a couple of dozen runs but I knew, with a good strong rally, we might pull it out.

The smallest kid who always wanted to pitch sat alone at the end of the dugout, cobwebs hanging from his nose. I went over to him and asked if he believed in magic.

No, he said, why. "Wellllll, hocus-pocus," I said. "You're a pitcher. So get out there and pitch." His teammates got mad at me for letting him pitch, but he only walked the first nine hitters he faced.

Another boy was afraid to play. He'd work out during the week but when I tried to put him into the game he'd say he was sick or had a sprained ankle or somesuch. He obviously was scared but eventually consented to go into a game. Anyway, he got a hit and it made us both feel about as good as we did all summer.

Every year I tell myself I won't coach again, that I don't have the time nor energy but I end up doing it anyway. I just like to watch kids develop . . . and hope their parents do.

THERE ARE SOFT memories of childhood which come and go and pale and cloud but they always are there somewhere. Oh, they are memories of girls with freckles, the smells of honeysuckle, and a haunted house where you ran and touched the door on a dare and then split your pants on a sticker bush trying to get away before something terrible and awful opened the door and got you.

And to this day I remember a time when I was about nine and met a minor league baseball player named George Sprys, who was in the outfield for the Paris Red Peppers. One night after he hit a home run to beat the Sherman-Denison Twins he actually talked to a bunch of us snot-nosed kids and bought us some ice cream. God, I couldn't believe it. Just couldn't believe it. It was the best of times.

What I am getting around to is that I have a son named Todd, who is the World's Greatest Toby Harrah and Texas Ranger fan, in that order. Todd believes in his heart that if he lives a good life, brushes his teeth, etc., he one day will die and go to Toby Harrah. Now his name could be John Smith or Johnny Jones or Larry Stephens but it is Todd. So with the help of *Dallas News* baseball writer

Randy Galloway and some nice people with the Texas Rangers Todd actually got to meet Toby Harrah Friday night. Time stopped for him. It always will have.

I suppose the magnitude of the situation can better be appreciated if I tell you more. Todd listens on the radio to ninety percent of the Texas Ranger games he does not see. He keeps a notebook in which the details of each game are taken down. His mood, his daily life is predicated on how Harrah and the Rangers do. Again, it is in that order. I can not get his attention on much else. He has turned down offers of movies, ice cream . . . and to meet freckled-faced girls in order to listen to the Ranger games.

I try to take him each summer to South Padre Island because it is the last beach I know where you can walk with your eyes closed and step on sand, not people. I have been most anxious for Todd to learn about the sea, what it means, what it is, and, hopefully, to appreciate the relaxing, almost magnetic effect it can have on a person. I like to walk early or late when people aren't there much at all. One night Todd was walking with me and you could see the lights of faraway boats in the darkness, and I wanted him to look at them, wonder where they had been and where they were going.

He seemed very nervous and when I asked him what was the matter he said, "Dad, the Rangers are on late tonight. They're playing in California and the game is about to start. I think I'll go on in. I have this great feeling Toby is going to hit one out tonight. Why don't you just stay out here and watch the boats. Okay?"

Okay.

The Texas Rangers were with us every minute last summer during the weeks we spent by the sea. And when we played games of "pepper" on the sand Todd was always Toby Harrah. We finally made a deal where he would go into one of the bedrooms of the beach house I rent to listen to the ballgame and I would go into the other bedroom to read. This worked out for about a minute at a time until Todd began yelling or slamming down things when Toby failed to get a hit. And each time Toby would come to the plate Todd would open the door and give me a pitch-by-pitch account in his best Ranger broadcasting voice. I gave up trying to read during Ranger broadcasts.

On the night Todd was to meet Toby Harrah he was very nervous as we drove to the game. I told him Toby was just a regular guy, had actually once been a kid, too.

"But you don't understand," he said. "He's . . . he's Toby Harrah."

After a moment of silence, I said, "Toby Who?" He gave me this hard look, and then we both started laughing. Before we got to Arlington Stadium Todd combed his hair four times and tucked his shirt tail in three. It was out again when we got there. He didn't say much as we walked through the dugout to the Ranger dressing room because it was very difficult to talk with his heart in his throat.

In the dressing room Toby walked over to us, bent over, and shook Todd's hand. I thought Todd would wet his pants. I know I would have. "Todd," said Toby, "I'm glad to meet you." Todd said, gulp. "Would you be my pal?" said Toby.

"Oh yes," said Todd, grinning from ear to ear. "Oh yes."

Toby got a baseball and signed it, "To my pal, Todd, Toby Harrah." He talked to Todd for a while and then reached into the rack and got out a bat he had slightly cracked. "Here," he said, "this is for you."

"Thank you," said Todd, who looked at me with his I-don't-believe-this-face.

"Heck," said Toby, "let me find you a new bat. Here's one. Take it, too."

Toby told him if he actually planned to use the bat, which was about as tall as he was, he should choke up to a certain spot. "When I was your age," said Toby, "I choked up to right here."

They talked for a while and Todd floated out of the dressing room, thanking everybody for their trouble, including the dugout posts. He choked up on the bat as Toby had shown him and hit a grand-slam home run in the bottom of the ninth as we walked back to the stands. During the game he kept saying, "I can't believe this. I can't believe this. He talked to me. Can you believe that? And he was so nice. He was so nice. Do you think he really wants me to be his pal?''

"Sure, Toby Harrah wouldn't have said a thing like that if he didn't mean it.''

"Can you imagine? He talked to a little kid like me.''

"A little snot-nosed kid like you. Take a napkin and wipe your nose.''

"Well, I saw you wipe your nose on your sleeve once, too.''

"When you get as big and old as me you can wipe your nose on your sleeve, too, but not now. It isn't . . . polite.''

"I can't believe Toby Harrah talked to me.''

On the drive back from the game Todd had two baseballs, two bats, a rain jacket, and a Texas Ranger baseball cap, and he had talked to Dick Risenhoover, the voice of the Rangers, over the radio. And he had become Toby Harrah's pal. He became very quiet, and when I asked him if he were sleepy, he said, "I'm about to have a heart attack. Get an ambulance.''

"A heart attack?''

"Yessir, I'm so happy I'm about to bust in my heart. It was like a birthday and Christmas all in one. I mean I'm going to sit right here and die in this car I'm so happy.''

"Could you wait until you get home and die because I don't want to have to stop and let you out.''

"Oh, Dad, really, this is the greatest day of my life. The greatest.''

"Mine, too.''

Summers, real and in spirit, fade with final games but for Todd this one became a kind of snapshot that he will always see, will always have in the photo album that we keep in our minds. When I left him that night he had gone to bed, wearing his Texas Ranger hat and holding Toby Harrah's bat. He got a lot of hits with Toby Harrah's bat that night. Oh yes, Toby was 0–3 in the game. Not really. He got a lot of hits, too.

Faces, Out of a Crowd

SANDRA WAS LIKE too many people who linger in my mind because, I suppose, their lives are too true to be good. They seem sharp, sensitive, have some talent, but their lives have been a kind of cartwheel which has left them too tired, too exhausted, or too pinched in to do the things that they might have done.

Whatever. The first time I ever saw Sandra she was leaning against the counter of her station as barmaid in a local establishment of higher drinking and waiting for the bartender to bring her the next round, which she'd distribute to various tables, according to needs, real and imagined.

Oh, she probably was thirty-six, more wrinkled than she should have been, but I suppose that happens if you wait too long for the cards to be dealt, rather than dealing some of them yourself. She was about five feet six, far too skinny, and her hair was stringy. Sometimes you could tell she'd been trying to fix it up but it still looked stringy.

You'd see her there, speak, and she'd smile. I'd never talked to her that much. But late one afternoon there were heavy rains in the area, causing traffic to crawl out North Central, and I'd stopped for a beer. The place was almost empty, with only two, three people scattered at tables. I sat at the bar, next to her station, and we started talking.

She had a strong twang and some of her vernacular meant she either was from far West or East Texas. She knew I dabbled in writing, and all of a sudden, she began talking about books. She'd read just about everything she could get her hads on concerning F. Scott and Zelda Fitzgerald, also some of John Steinbeck. She said Scott was weak, Zelda was a (deleted) and that she liked the book Steinbeck did when he traveled around the country with his dog (*Travels With Charley*). I hadn't expected that she was so well read and just sat there and listened. She also mentioned that she'd just read a book by John Updike, called *Marry Me*. I later found out she'd overheard me talking about the book and decided she'd read it.

"Updike confuses me at times," she said, "but the conversation he had in the book sure hit home a lot. It sounded like people really talk, you know, a couple when they're having trouble. You know, marriage on the rocks."

I told her I'd read the books she was talking about. I agreed with what she'd said about the conversation in *Marry Me,* and told her I very much enjoyed *Gatsby* and *Tender Is the Night* and wished Zelda had run off and joined the circus when she was fifteen and never met Scott.

I asked her about herself and she said she had a couple of kids and was living with this guy who didn't always treat her very well. She said sometimes he'd get drunk and slap her around. And she said when he didn't get drunk, or wasn't working, he'd just go fishing, talk about baseball or football, and sleep.

"It's like, you know," she said, "being two different people. I don't like either one of them. One's mean as hell and the other one, although I swear I can hear him breathing, is dead as a doornail."

"Dead as a doornail?" I said. "You've got to be from East Texas. I lived there as a kid and can remember people saying, dead as a doornail. That dog in the street is dead as a doornail."

She said she was, matter of fact, from this small community in East Texas. "Oh, you know, he's good to my kids, I suppose, but one of these days when he comes in and pushes me around I'm gonna grab a baseball bat and bash him and he'll be seeing stars the rest of his life.

"Shoot, it don't matter. At least I've got somebody. You look like me and you'd better keep what you've got. You might have observed (she starts speaking very clearly and properly) that the gentlemen who come in here don't exactly chase me around the tables trying to gain my favors. Now, if I looked like her (she nods toward the barmaid on the other side) I just might go into business for myself." When she made the last statement she sucked in her stomach, pushed out her chest, and closed her mouth, giving it a pouting look.

"Yeah," I said, "she is cute but I bet she thinks Scott and Zelda are people who come in here to drink and eat a hamburger on Saturday night."

Sandra delivered drinks, then came back and stood, waiting. "I paint some pictures," she said. "I bet you didn't figure that one, did you? You just looked at me and said, 'Well, all she's ever done is wash and iron.' Well, when I was little I was very good with watercolor paintings. People used to brag how good I was. I could do landscapes and flowers and my aunt said I would be a famous artist someday."

"Watercolors are the most difficult to use," I told her. "You can't wipe out or make up a mistake in watercolors. In oils you can. I admire that. I wish I could use watercolors. The only thing I could ever paint or draw was airplanes, those warplanes with their guns blazing red."

"Well, you know, we got this wallpaper at home with flowers on it. What I've been doing lately is painting those flowers that are on the wall. I've got them down good. Sometime I'm going to do some pictures of those flowers, go out into the country and paint them into a landscape or something. I'd like for you to see what I've done except you'd laugh. You'd say it was good, even if it wasn't, so's you wouldn't hurt my feelings."

"No," I lied. "I wouldn't say it was good if it wasn't. I'd really like to see what you've done. I wouldn't say it was good if it wasn't."

"Oh, you'd tell me they were good anyway. You'd lie. What would you say if you didn't like them, 'They stink?' No, you'd lie."

"No, if I thought they were bad, I'd say, 'Hey, why don't you start doing warplanes with blazing red guns.'"

"I really do like flowers," she said.

A few weeks later when I went back she came up to me and said, proudly, "I got my high school diploma. I really did, after all these years."

I told her that was great, that I was very proud of her, and she said, "Oh, I guess, you know, it's like getting a degree from Sears and Roebuck. But I took it through the mail. I made up my mind, you know, that I was going to better myself and I did. No, I forgot to bring those paintings but I will. And you got to tell me the truth about them, okay."

That day she told me she'd gotten married when she was seventeen and that she really wasn't bad looking then. She said she'd had two kids, "lickity-split," and had had to run her husband off because he was seeing other girls. She said at least the guy with whom she was living now didn't see other girls.

"If he wadn't drunk," she said, "I'd have to wake him up so he could go mess around. And he'd probably fall asleep on the way to run around. What? No, he hadn't been drunk and hit me lately."

I told her if she insisted on staying with him she should protect herself. Frankly, I haven't particularly been a person to turn the other cheek and suggested if he hit her again she should get a baseball bat. She said she had just been kidding about the baseball bat and wouldn't have the nerve to use it.

She asked me about some books I thought she should read and I wrote a list down on a napkin. She put the napkin in her purse, behind the counter. She said she'd get the books out of the library and that maybe we could talk about them later. "Sure, I'd like that," I said.

Two weeks later I came back, but she was gone. They said she'd been drinking on the job and that they'd had to fire her. I haven't been back to that place again.

JOSEPH BRUNNEL, a bearded, somewhat rugged looking man in his mid-thirties, slowly made his way to the microphone on the mini-stage in the Veranda Bar in the old Faust Hotel, one of those fine old inns which has been renovated and reopened to link the past with the present. People operating the Faust, which is in New Braunfels, would like to make the Veranda Bar a habit, and so they hired Joseph Brunnel. For him it was another bar in another town before an audience which so often watches with opaque eyes.

He looked at the microphone about as blankly as it looked at him. And then he told the dozen people in the bar, "Hello, my name is Joseph Brunnel and I'm from Midland, Texas, and I just got here . . . yesterday."

He picked a little on his guitar, sounding very good, and sang a little in a voice which was a little remindful of Kenny Rogers. Then he said, "I went to the Kerrville Song Festival and was lucky enough to be one of the winners in the song-writing contest. They gave six places. I was sixth with a song I wrote called 'White Cloud.'"

He reached over and picked up a record, a single. "Here's my first record, and if you're interested, you can purchase one for $2. Well (he holds the record out and stares at it), it must be a record. It has two sides, is round and has a hole in it." He financed the record himself, with money he made singing in bars, so the $2 was important.

"Frankly, I wrote 'White Cloud' when I was about half drunk," he said. "I was coming home early one morning, looked out the window of my car and saw these clouds floating in the darkness. Well, anyway, here it is . . ."

White cloud floating in the sky
Can you hear me wishing I could fly . . .

It was a good, somewhat lamenting, somewhat dreamy song, and when he had finished, about five of the dozen people sitting in the bar clapped. One couple clapped and so did two guys sitting at the bar. One wore a golf hat and the other, his hair very long, had an Indian band around his head. Finally, another couple, hearing the applause, clapped, too, although they had no idea why. But the cocktail waitress clapped louder than anybody.

Brunnel is one of those faceless entertainers who tour the bars and pick and sing their guts out for anything, from nothing, called exposure, to $300 a gig. They are here three nights, there two nights, playing for an infinity of drunks, semi-drunks, and some good listeners. The good listeners recognize their talent and know that they, although luckless, are as good if not better than some known entertainers. They have an endless repertoire and can play their own songs or "Melancholy Baby."

They have to be awfully lucky to get discovered. It all becomes terribly frustrating. Once a man in the crowd stepped up and told Joseph he was so-and-so, a known entertainment figure. Joseph knew better but played along. The guy invited him over to his place and went through all the motions, even picking up the phone and pretending he was talking to, first, Waylon Jennings, and, second, Willie Nelson. The guy said things really looked promising and that he'd be back in touch. But, of course, the guy was just living out his own fantasies. Brunnel shrugged. He'd been through such things so much the incident wasn't even another wrinkle in his face.

The other night before his set ended at the Veranda, a group of young females, looking just old enough to drink, walked in. They giggled a little, sat at a long table. They ordered tall, colorful-looking drinks, which appeared to have come more from a poster than behind the bar. They seemed to pick up on Joseph. He seemed to have his camp followers. When he finished a number they clapped as loudly as they could, although not as loudly as the cocktail waitress.

Joseph did an instrumental in which he played both the guitar and harmonica. When he'd finished, he said,

"That was Joseph Brunnel on the guitar, Joseph Brunnel on the harmonica, and (motioning over to the bar) Mary on the blender."

He really had an easy, comfortable, philosophical manner. Outside. But during the break between sets he said the life of a bar and small club entertainer "can be a low, long trip to nowhere. It does play on your psyche. To tell you the truth, I think when I first started bar singers were more appreciated. Now, you're kind of like the decorations. You know, a guided tour of the bar . . . Ladies and gentlemen, over here we have this fine brass rail. And there, right over there, is a fine painting. And then, ladies and gentlemen, over here we have, in the lounge area, a fine antique couch. And in the corner, over there, is our folk singer."

Brunnel went to high school in Midland, where his parents still live in retirement. He likes to keep his base there, because at their age his parents might need him. He finished high school, hung around college for a while but wasn't particularly interested. What he'd always liked was music. He used to dream of making records, writing songs. He said he couldn't find anybody to teach him guitar so he, mostly, taught himself.

"I was terrible until about 1975 when I started getting pretty good," he said. "I worked hard. Sometimes you make just enough doing the bars to get hooked. And every once in a while things go just right, the audience will be just right and it's very satisfying. But you know it leads to nowhere."

He wants to do records, instrumental arrangements for television, movies. He also writes a little poetry and would like to do a book on people he sees in bars. With Joseph Brunnel, bars are a two-way mirror. It's just that nobody has particularly asked him to be discovered and become famous, and so he has to hustle money to put out his own records. "Golfers, people like that, get sponsors," he said. "But we don't."

Some of the girls at the long table looked over at him and he nodded back at them. Some of the girls at the long table giggled. He said people have a misconception about bar singers getting propositioned a lot. "But," he added, "the opposite is true. It's not the thing to do now. I mean, pick up or let yourself get picked up by girls."

He was five minutes late starting the next set and the girls at the long table had finished their tall, sweet poster drinks and left. Our conversation had been the cause of him being late and I felt bad. But someone who knew the girls said, "Oh, they were leaving anyway. The picture show started at 8 and they had to hurry to get there on time."

When he did the first song on the last set only three people remained in the bar. But they all clapped, although not as loudly as the cocktail waitress.

NOBODY KNEW FOR sure because none of them just came out and said anything. But they sure did seem to be applying a little pressure here, a little there and, ever so slowly, stripping away his pride. You take away a man's pride and nothing's left but a blank. But nobody knew for sure.

He was in his sixties, had been at the oil refining plant well over twenty years and was so close to retirement that it was like . . . like, well, he could almost reach out and touch it. He had spent all those years working in the dusty, dry-hole desert town, hardly more than a dot on the road, except for the plant and telephone poles. But the company had made a much better retirement plan an enticement to get people to work in the nowhere place and so he had.

He hated the place and so did his wife, but they'd made the best of it, you understand, as people have to do sometimes. Sure, there was talk around the plant that a couple of guys in another section had been forced out before they reached retirement, but he hadn't know that for a fact. And you know how people talk.

There had been good years, bad years, slow years, and fast years but it was just about over. He'd worked his way up from small, unimportant jobs to foreman of one of the most important sections of the plant. He was proud of what he had accomplished. Whispers were that he was getting too old for the job, but nobody really came out and said anything. Finally, he was called into the executive offices and his boss said, in a nice way, that he wanted to relieve him of some of his duties, some pressures so his final year at the plant might be more pleasant. His boss said they were bringing in a younger man to be foreman, but that he'd have the same salary and be assistant foreman. That bothered him but he understood.

He talked a lot with his wife about the plans they had for after his retirement. They were going to buy a trailer and head into the mountains, where the streams were clear and the fish never stopped biting. His wife was a tall woman, a couple of inches taller than he was, and she had fiery red hair. You know what they say about redheads and how stubborn they are and what bad tempers they have.

One day he came to work and they called him into the executive offices again and said they had another job for him to do. What it amounted to was that he was going to do the job that people who worked under him were doing. That hurt, worried him a lot. And after a while they called him in again and one of the executives said he wanted him to start handling the cleanup duties around the plant. "You know," the boss said, "it's hard to get good help these days. We know you can handle the job. People leave things out and somebody might get hurt. So if you'll just see things are picked up."

Some of his friends around the plant didn't like what was happening. They said they were going to protest. But some also said a warning had been issued that if anybody caused any trouble they could start looking for another job. You know how talk is.

Finally, one of the executives called him in and suggested it might be a good idea for him to start seeing that his office was clean. You know, take out the trash, dust and sweep. He left the boss' office and sat for a long time by himself, his hands over his face.

His friends said he really was getting a dirty deal and that somebody ought to do something about it. But, of course, nobody did. Sometimes when he'd come around them, they'd be cordial, hello-how-are-you-doing-how's-the-wife, but then they'd say they best had be getting back to work.

He'd always slept well but had trouble sleeping now. He'd hear people who were not even there whispering about him. His shoulders stooped more than ever. "Hold up your shoulders!" his wife kept telling him. She knew what was going on and said she ought to go right down there to the plant and tell them what she thought. And she would have, too, but he stopped her. He told her she just couldn't do that, so she just simmered. You know how redheads are. Besides, they had only about six months to go to retirement. All he had to do was hang on.

They talked briefly after he got home from work one day. He was especially tired. Especially dragging. She went into the next room and heard this terrible explosion cut through the silence of the dry-hole town and her heart. He had taken a shotgun, put the barrel to his head and pulled the trigger. She screamed when she saw him, then cried, "Oh no! Oh God no!" But nobody heard her for a long time.

The laws of the time didn't help much. He got only partial retirement. His insurance was no good because he'd committed suicide. Everybody said what a fine man he was and the executives at the plant noted he was one of the hardest working employees they'd had.

Well, a lot of people turned out for the funeral in the small church on a gray day. His relatives and friends were there and so were four executives from the company. They sat on the front row, their faces masks of grief. And flowers . . . nobody had seen so many flowers and wreaths. And one of the wreaths was huge, larger than all the others. It must have been four, five feet tall and almost as wide. The company had had it made special. The organist played and the choir sang and then the preacher stood up and said what a fine man the deceased had been.

"It's just a shame that his family and all his friends I see out there had to be drawn together on such a sad occasion," said the preacher. "Oh yes, really, it's just a shame . . ."

"Stop! Wait a minute!" There was silence as people turned toward the voice. It was her, the redhead. She stood up. Her face was almost as red her hair. "I don't think we're quite ready for the services to start," she said, walking slowly but very determinedly toward the flower display. Her head was held high and it was as though she were marching.

She picked up the largest flower display and marched to the door. She set it down, opened the door. Then she picked it up and threw it outside. Two of the executives got up and hurried out the door. The others sat there, transfixed, as if impaled by some invisible spear. Calmly, she went back to her seat and said, "Now I think we're ready to begin."

But you know how redheads are.

> My memories of an early morn
> On a small and sandy farm
> Are like this
> A rooster crowing
> Cattle lowing
> Daddy at the back gate whistlin' softly
> Dishes rattling
> a churn a-paddling
> And the smell of bacon frying
> Mama standing at my door calling
> Hugh, the sun is rising.
> —*Pat Minter,*
>   "Hugh, The Sun is Rising"

ON A SENSELESS day in March, 1970, Doyce Miller slowly moved with his Marine patrol into what was said to be, felt to be, an enemy fortified area in Vietnam, that small country in Southeast Asia, which was so far away and became so near. But the place seemed deserted and they moved inside the area. Suddenly, a faceless man called a Viet Cong sprung the trap, igniting an arc of land mines, catching Doyce and the other Marines in a man-made hell. Some survived. Some were killed, others maimed. A man died. Another a foot away lived.

Doyce Miller, twenty years of age . . . Doyce Miller, who unlike so many was there fighting because he believed it was the right thing, the moral thing to do . . . Doyce Miller, who so much liked the sandy loam area and pine trees of his East Texas and who wanted to be an artist, was dead, far, far across the world . . .

Nubbin Miller is a small, kindly woman who hates to be called by her real name, Willie Mae. So her husband Delbert nicknamed her Nubbin. The other day she was passing through the kitchen and saw a note on a burner of the stove. She stopped, her heart beat increased. Chill-bumps came. Doyce always used to leave her notes on the burner, but of course he was gone and the note had been left by one of her two daughters. But for a minute, just for a minute.

It has been more than eleven years since that awful, numbing news came that her son had been killed in Vietnam, but she said, "My goodness, there's not a day goes by that I don't think about him. My goodness."

Nubbin and Delbert work hard, have worked hard all their lives. They have a small place in Tyler, two grown daughters and another grown son, older than Doyce, who would have been thirty-one now and, perhaps, married with children of his own and a career as an artist.

"Oh," she said, "He so loved to draw. He always was drawing, sketching. He so much liked to go down to his grandaddy's farm (near Pickton) and fish and hunt. Why, he'd just get this ol' cane pole, maybe take a sandwich and go fishing. He also liked so much to hunt. One time he took me hunting with him. He gave me a gun but wouldn't let me have any bullets because I guess he was afraid I'd hurt myself. Oh my, he was probably right."

Now my memory takes me back
To a running brook, a paper sack
I'm carrying
No trouble, sorrow, death or hate
Or swearing

A cool shade, a short nap
My lunch is resting in my lap, it's heaven
Waiting for another dawn
On Daddy's small and sandy farm and
Hugh, the sun is rising.

When Doyce visited his grandparents he often stopped by to see Pat Minter, a friend who is now a singer-entertainer-songwriter but was then cutting hair. "He'd come in and get his hair cut or sometimes he'd show up just to talk, visit," said Pat. "He was a real nice, clean-cut kid. He was easygoing. Such a nice kid."

"Oh, he was always so loyal, a loyal type person, you know," said Nubbin Miller. "In school at Lee in Tyler, he played football and was all full of school spirit. Just full of spirit. And, and, and so patriotic. So very patriotic. Well, his father had been a scout sniper for the Marines in World War II. Doyce always said he sure didn't want to be in the Marines, that it would be too tough. (She laughs.) He used to tell his father that a lot."

After the official, unofficial war had begun in Vietnam, one afternoon Doyce was driving his mother to the store. She remarked, "Doyce, I so wish we would get out of Vietnam and get all those boys home before they get hurt or killed."

"Mama," he said, "don't ever let me hear you say that again. If we pull out, the North Vietnamese would come down and massacre those people in the South. We can't let that happen. We just can't."

So Doyce Miller, who had studied art for a year at Tyler Junior College, joined the Marines, just as his father had done. "He was already gone before I knew about it," said Pat Minter. "It was like he was here, and then he wasn't. He never came back."

A sweetheart that I left behind
A buddy dead from a land mine
It's awful
The broken bodies on the ground
It's frightening

A sharp command, a bugle's blow
A voice from the bunk below saying
Hugh, the sun is rising.

"Then, of course, he was killed," said Nubbin. "It was an awful, disturbing time. We were here sitting around the living room with the preacher and a singer at the church. Everybody was talking about the person we'd get to sing at Doyce's funeral.

"Suddenly, I saw the name Pat Minter. I didn't know Pat, had never met him, and didn't even know he was a singer. But the name just came to me so strong. So I turned to Delbert and the preacher and told them, 'Pat Minter will sing at the funeral. Doyce has picked him.' So we got in touch with Pat and he did a beautiful job."

Minter was very affected by Doyce's death. When the funeral was over, he went home and sat up much of the night. He thought about Doyce, the boys from his part of East Texas who had been killed in Vietnam. Then he wrote about them, but mostly about Doyce, in a song called, "Hugh, the Sun is Rising."

"Oh, it was such a beautiful tribute to Doyce," said Nubbin. "But Doyce wanted to get Pat to sing. I know he did."

"People say to me it was such a shame you didn't have him any longer than you did. But we were so very close. We spent so much time together. So many parents are not close to their children and don't spend much time with them. The way I look at it I had him for twenty years and we were together more during that time than most parents spend with their children in a lifetime."

She got quiet, then blushed. "Oh, Doyce always used to say his mama was the prettiest girl he knew. He always said that. Of course, you know it wasn't true, but it was nice of him to say it."

"He was right," I said. "I think he was right."

"Oh, go on now! I'm not. But this just makes my day to get to talking about him again. We were so very close. Oh, my yes, it just makes my day."

Zana knight henderson is a wonderfully clever, spunky woman of ninety-one, going on thirty, who lives alone, thinks and reads a great deal, philosophizes, and writes poetry about any and everything.

I got to know her because we've corresponded for about a year, and she sent me a book of poems she published. After reading her letters and poems, I contemplated trying to get her to run away with me. But during a recent visit to her home in Vernon she was in a wheelchair due to an acute attack of arthritis and we decided our get-away would be too slow.

I had telephoned her when I first got to Vernon but there was confusion as to how I should get to her house. "Well, I'm not driving now," she said. "But I suppose I could come and get you in my wheelchair, although it might be a little bumpy, and it doesn't have headlights. I must make a note to get headlights."

Zana is a small, white-haired woman with a clear, strong voice. One of the reasons I like her so much is that she's one of those women who can laugh at themselves, not taking herself too seriously, and also because she loves books. In her home she has books filling shelves, tables, boxes, nooks and crannies.

She probably would have a lot more books, except she also likes to give things away, to friends, the local library, and, I'm sure, to strangers who look as if they ought to be reading a book.

The other evening she led me into her study. She had a "Ronnie's Angels" button pinned to her dress. I told her I had voted for Carter last time but wouldn't do so again. I said I also didn't particularly care for Reagan.

"Then for whom will you vote?"

"No. I think I'll just vote, no."

She smiled, which she does spontaneously and easily.

Zana became a poetess in her later years, although she had been interested and dabbled in writing much of her life. Some of my other feminine friends just think they were suppressed and hampered in creative endeavors by the mores of their times. During Zana's day, if a woman even so much as hinted she might be interested in doing something other than taking care of her husband and rearing a family, it was felt she sure was possessed by the devil.

But Zana persevered, keeping the desire to write poetry burning in a corner of her mind. She grew up and went to school in Tennessee and Mississippi, but was able to go only about half way through the ninth grade. Later she attended business school and learned shorthand and typing.

Her father was in the lumber business but kept copies of the Bible, Shakespeare's works and *Treasure Island* around the house. Zana read them over and over, and even began writing poetry. Her father read one of her poems, scratched his head, and suggested she write something more like Jack London might do.

She helped send a brother through college while doing secretarial work, then married a successful businessman and moved to Kansas. She reared four children, helped her husband take care of a house in town and a farm, and began to write poetry again. She received a great deal of encouragement from teachers at Kansas State and Drake Universities. Gradually she began publishing her poems in newspapers such as the *Christian Science Monitor, Kansas City Star* and the *Los Angeles Times.* She also contributed to the *Kansas* magazine, now the *Kansas Quarterly,* and her poem "Last Harvest," about the death of a farmer, appeared in an anthology. "Last Harvest," reprinted below, also appears in the book of her poems, *Sez I to Myself, Sez I.*

Queer silence runs from house and barn and sheds
To halt the sound of sickles in the mowing;
Somewhere a leghorn cockeral's thin crowing
Breaks on a new deep note; the quiet spreads
Where bees hang listening before the hive.
The new-weaned lambs that yesterday were crying
Drowse in the water-trough's cool shade,
   close lying;
There is no movement of a thing alive.

One instant more . . . no movement and no sound
Through all the house, nor yet quick footsteps
   falling
On stairs and porch, nor frightened voices
   calling . . .
Only the silence holds, peaceful, profound . . .
Even the breeze that stirs the orchard stops
In sudden hush before the ripe fruit drops.

Zana is self-taught, much as a musician plays by ear. And yet, "Last Harvest" is a perfect sonnet.

After her husband died in 1947, she moved to Vernon to be near her daughter. Most felt a woman of her years should settle down to playing bridge. She said she didn't like bridge, didn't want to play bridge, and so she writes poetry and holds court in her house.

"No," she said, "I never remarried. To tell you the truth, nobody ever asked me. I used to wonder why. I wasn't that bad. Then this cousin of mine called me aside and said that I just read too much, acted too smart and this scared off any gentleman. But I love to visit and talk with men. I like men better than women, who are so bitchy. Don't you agree?"

I told her I wasn't about to touch that one, long ago learning the better part of valor when women are concerned. We talked about books, poetry, marriage, the general pursuit of happiness, or at least what is accepted as happiness, and she began to talk about her age.

"You know sometimes the bones of old women break, even if they don't do anything," she said. "It's just age. I'd certainly hate to break a hip. I am a woman, however, and I am old."

"You're not old at all. Not at all."

"And did you hear about that elderly woman in Oklahoma City being kidnapped? I can't imagine why someone would want to kidnap an old woman. A friend of mine asked me what I'd do if somebody kidnapped me. I told her it would be a terrible mistake on their part because I'd just act like I was crazy, which is extremely easy for me to do, as you might imagine, or I'd just talk them to death. I do love to talk. Oh, talking too much is a bad habit I have. But so often I've found the listener doesn't have as many interesting things to say as I have.''

We talked for two hours and it was after 11 P.M. and I worried about her tiring. But she got up out of her wheelchair and walked me to the door. ''I just wanted to show you I could walk if I had to do so,'' she said. ''Besides I reserve the right to talk to people until they actually get into their cars and close the door. But that's what happens when you get old.''

I told her again that she wasn't old. But I didn't really need to tell her that. She already knew it.

Fifty-one years ago Poly and Clitus Kitts adopted a baby. They later found out the baby, which they named Jack, was blind. Doctors could not correct this, saying he had come into the world blind and would go out blind. In his life sometimes Jack Kitts has been very lonely.

Jo Zepeda had high blood pressure, which contributed to a stroke. Doctors performed surgery on her brain. She lost her sense of smell, some use of one leg. One night she was moving along on her crutches when she was confronted by a strange man. He beat her up, threw her to the ground. Then he took one of her crutches and started beating her legs. Both legs were badly broken by the blows. Sometimes Jo Zepeda has been very lonely.

LATE AFTERNOON was full of pictures, sounds of nine to five. The sun's light cast a kind of pinkish whirl against the blue sky. People were coming down elevators, going through the doors in the lobby of the First National Bank in Abilene and scattering, in timeless fashion, toward home. Taken as a whole, the many conversations sounded like a constant buzz.

Jack Kitts, standing behind the counter of the news-tobacco shop in the bank's lobby, heard the elevator going up and down, the people and the buzzing, but he did not see the wide, open western sky nor had he ever seen it. But he stood there, smiling, greeting his friends, the familiar voices who stopped by to buy cigarettes, a soda pop, a candy bar, a newspaper.

Jack has been there for twenty-six years. He always seemed to have been there and so was a part of the people who worked in and around the bank building five days a week. For most of that time he has operated the stand alone but the last year he has had help from Jo Zepeda, a small, thin woman who has sad eyes but a nice smile.

Life, mostly, has ignored her, but Jack heard about a stroke she had had, about how a Crazy had attacked her, beat her up, about the many problems she was having. So he began going to visit her in the hospital. They got to know each other, began to laugh again, play a lot of 42.

"I tell you one thang, he'll play the heck out of you in 42," said Jo.

Earlier this year Jack had to undergo glandular surgery. Shortly afterward the doctors said he couldn't go home unless somebody was there to help him. Jo heard what the doctors had said and she went home with him. And she stayed.

Before Jo began helping him Jack's customers always told him whether the bill they handed him was a $1, $5, $10, and he would make change. Now Jo tells him. "But people always have been so nice to me," he said. "My customers are my friends. The people who run this bank let me have this place for $1 a month. That gives us a legal contract. I know of no other bank which lets a handicapped person work like that. And, really, only a few times has anybody tried to cheat me."

During the "Diamond Jubileee" in Abilene, Jack also sold little hats. A girl came and bought a hat, saying she had given him a $5 bill. It was a $1. Another time a woman came by, got change for a $5. It, too, was a $1. Jack remembered her voice. A few days later she came back and tried to do the same thing. Jack calmly reminded her that she had cheated him before.

"Oh," said the woman, "I must have made a mistake. I'll bring your money back."

"That's between you and the Lord," said Jack. The woman never came back.

A customer who was not familiar with Jack, did not know he was blind, came by the stand and said, "Could you tell me where the mail box is?" Jack, grinning, said, "Over there. You just passed it." When the customer had gone Jack and Jo laughed at the way he pretended he could see.

"Jack," said Jo, "can really surprise you. Sometimes he can tell what a person looks like even though he can't see him. I guess he's just developed a different sense or something."

After we had talked for a while, I asked him if he had any idea what I looked like. He spoke slowly, concentrating, and said, "I sometimes sense things by the voices of people. You are . . . 5–10, 5–11, perhaps 175–170 pounds. And you are . . . light complexioned, perhaps with blue eyes."

I'm 5–10, 174, light complexioned and have blue eyes. Jack was happy when I told him this. So was Jo.

Jack is a member of the Kiwanis, goes with Jo to the Temple Baptist Church, often reads the Bible in Braille, loves to listen to semi-classical music and likes to tape-record things. He often listens to the voices of his parents, now both dead, on tape. He said they were such tremendous people and, after adoption when they found out he was blind, refused to let him go back to the adoption center. Their friends kept suggesting that they do so.

"They were loving, just tremendous to me," said Jack. "Had it not been for them, I might have been full of self-pity. But they encouraged me to live as normal a life as I could."

Recently, Jack had to get an unlisted phone. Since Jo moved in with him they've gotten crank calls. The phone will ring. Jo will answer. The caller might tell her they are living in sin, mutter some obscenity, then hang up. People. Some people.

Jack had worked at small stands in both Dallas and Fort Worth before settling in Abilene. It took him a good fifteen years to build up his business. There were times when his take-home pay would be around $100 a month. Now it climbs as high as $500 a week.

"We're very happy people," said Jack. "I feel no bitterness, anything like that, because I can't see. Any handicap is what you make it. Sometimes (he grins) I tell Jo to turn down the radio because I can't hear what I'm doing."

She laughed. They laugh and talk a lot because sometimes each of them has been lonely but they are not lonely anymore.

My Heroes
Are Cowboys

> The ghosts of long-cooled campfires remain in the eyes of old cowboys. Some of them gray, with saddle-shaped legs and tottery, must continue to look for stars overhead when they awake before dawn. They stir uneasily on the streets of early mornings, as if trying to locate the remunda of an unfamiliar roundup ground. Subjects of a conquered empire, they seek some vestige of lost glory and find it only on the tattered parchment of memory. —*Doug Meador,* Sage of Matador.

I LOVE OLD cowboys the most. You can find them, some rail thin and others with the paunch of age and inactivity, sitting on benches around squares of small towns that touch the ranch country, as it was more than it is. They'll sit there, whittling, chewing, spitting tobacco, and watching people pass, going around in modern-day circles.

And you'll find them in small cafes, just off the square, that serve the Blue Plate Special. They'll drink coffee, always black, and sometimes start to rush, to hurry, before they remember they don't really have any place to go, except maybe to play dominoes, a punctuation mark of growing old.

I can't count the hours I've spent watching and listening to old cowboys talk and tell their stories in twangs and styles from a long time ago, which yet are timeless. Their stories, funny and sad, are excellent not only because of what they say but how they're told. I suppose in the old days cowboys had to be good story-tellers because swapping yarns was the only form of enter-tainment around a night campfire after long days on a desolate range.

Their life was tough. In the end, when they no longer could ride range, the old cowboy would inevitably be as he was in the beginning—broke. His bed was the ground under a tent or a wild and endless sky or occasionally the corner of a plank bunkhouse, and his food was beans, sourdough biscuits, gravy, dried goods, and steak served by a grouchy cook from a chuck wagon. He'd be on the range for a month at a time, spending days that stretched from dawn to darkness on a horse, and his pay was $25 to $35 a month. He loved roundups, the open space and sky, horses and cattle and hated mending fence. The only things he was likely to own were his saddle, the clothes on his back, and an extra shirt, tucked away in a saddle role.

When you find the old cowboys today they will sit with you for a spell and talk about the hottest summer, the coldest winter, the rankest horses, the "baddest" or "toughest" ol' boy they ever met, and Saturday nights on the town, with the number of women and drinks increas-ing with each telling. And some will bull a little but it's all right. Whatever they say is all right.

The old cowboys are bent now, their legs slightly bowed. They still wear their sideburns short and thin, sticking out from under soiled, naturally creased hats. They have hands and faces of leather, lined by the sun and wind long before time began doing it. They squint, searching for focus, and their teeth are yellowed by tobacco. But their faces inevitably brighten when you get them to talking about the old days and old friends, now mostly gone, because you've unlocked the past, what they were, not just put the key in the door of the domino parlor.

Of course, times changed; the sky and space narrowed and the cowboy, the real cowboy, one of society's last truly romantic figures, was just about squeezed out, his life becoming memories and plastic portrayals.

So the old cowboys are fading away now. They will never pass this way again, but I'm glad they did.

AT MID-EVENING, the legendary Bill Cole sat in an easy chair, just half watching a program on the big color television set across the living room of the small frame house in which he lives in Vernon, Texas. The house, across the street from a school in a quiet, tame neighborhood, is nondescript and far from where the action is.

Bill Cole was bored. He's seventy-five now, sporting a slight paunch over what was once a tight, lean stomach. His face and neck are deeply creased. He's quick to grin, but his eyes are steel-like, his jaw is set, and his bent, twisted nose makes him look like an old boxer. And his hands are scarred and huge, oversized like mitts. His wife died about a year or so ago, and now he lives alone, with occasional visits from his sister who helps around the house.

"I tell you what I am," he said. "Bored. Bored as hell. When you've been a-goin' all your life, it's hard to come and sit down."

He moved nervously in his chair. "All I do now is watch that danged television, go down the hall and play dominoes, and take walks. But mostly I'm just bored as hell."

His current existence, dictated by the inevitable passage of time, belies everything he was, and still is just below the surface. He was a working cowboy on the nearby Waggoner Ranch from 1936 until 1975. You talk to the old cowboys around Vernon, most anybody who's been connected with the ranch for any length of time, and they'll tell you stories about Cole.

"If half the stories are true," said H.A. McCarthy, longtime employee of the Waggoner Estate and currently publicity director, "then Bill must have been the toughest man in Texas."

A few years ago Bill came home to find his wife all in a dither. "Bill, there's a rattlesnake here," she said. Bill didn't have time to find a stick to kill the snake because it began crawling under the house. He ran over and caught the snake by the tail just before it disappeared. He held it up by his left hand, clamped it around the neck with his right, and jerked its head off. He told his wife, no, the derned snake didn't bite him.

"But then," he recalled, "I commenced to get a little dizzy, and sure enough, the thing had bitten me. I had to go to the doctor and get treated." (Some of the old cowboys said what actually happened was that Bill had bitten the snake and it had died.)

Bill used to have some run-ins with a couple of brothers, also cowboys at the Waggoner. One day they met at an old rock house to settle an argument. An eyewitness said that when Bill got to the house and opened the door, one of the brothers slugged him, shattering his nose. Blood was running down Bill's face, but he had a kind of grin on it and drew back and smacked the guy, just to the side of his chin.

"I swear," the old cowboy said, "that ol' boy's feet touched the rafters when Billy hit him."

Bill turned to the other brother and told him they'd best settle up, too. But the brother said, "You ain't a-goin' to fight me, Bill. I seen you get hit smack in the face and you didn't even blink. I ain't fightin' nobody who don't blink when he gets hit smack in the face."

"Everybody used to say," another oldtime cowboy, Frank Handley, remarked, "that the only way to whip ol' Bill was to kill him. And I reckon even the Germans couldn't do that during the war."

Bill was in Europe during World War II. He got shot through the shoulder with a machine gun and almost blown up. He was standing around with two German prisoners when a shell hit right by them. It killed the Germans but only knocked Bill down for a spell. However, he says he hasn't been able to hear very well out of his left ear since then.

"He come back from the war all trim," Handley recalled. "He asked me if I had any idea where he lost his belly. I said, no, I surely didn't and he said, 'Handley, I got it off a-crawlin' on the ground all over Europe.'"

There used to be a little drinking establishment just south of the old Vernon drugstore. One day a peddler came to town, all dressed up and talking a mile a minute. He spotted Bill and told him to come on in so that he could buy him a beer. Bill obliged. When it was time to pay, the peddler disappeared. Bill paid and the guy came back in.

"By gawd," said Bill, "when I ask a feller in for a beer I figure on paying for it." When the peddler said he HAD paid for the beer, Bill turned to the bartender, Charley, and asked him. "You paid for it, Bill," Charley confirmed.

"Charley," said the peddler, "you're a li . . ." Before he got out the final word Bill busted him upside the head, sending him through the door and out into the street. The peddler got upon all fours, and Bill, right behind him, began kicking him in the tail. Finally, some cowboys came out and stopped him.

Another story has it that one time when Bill got drunk, two officers were sent to get him. "I knowed that wasn't true," an oldtimer said. "No way they'd send ONLY two officers to get ol' Bill."

In 1975, Bill, then sixty-seven and still going strong, was out on the range getting numbers off some mares. A stud was with the mares and didn't take too well to the intrusion. Bill shoved the stud away, but as he got onto his horse, the stud came over, bit down on his leg, and jerked him completely out of the saddle. The stud scraped most of the flesh off his lower leg and bit completely through both bones. This happened at 8 A.M., and they didn't find Bill until 5 P.M. He had pulled up grass to stop the bleeding. If this accident hadn't happened, everybody says Bill probably would still be cowboying on the Waggoner.

"I wished I was," he said, getting up to turn off the television set. "This life sure is boring. No, I don't drink at all now. You get so old and have to sit down, and if you start a-drinkin' you can't stop. Pretty soon, every time you get bored or something you take a drink. I don't want to end up like that so I don't drink at all."

I asked him if all the stories I'd heard about him were true. "Aw, you can't believe all those stories," he said. It was a little dark in the house but I could see he was grinning and thought he winked at me.

Now FRANK HANDLEY is one of those oldtime cowboys who moves and talks in a slow, easy manner and can keep you entertained for hours, spinning yarns about the old days when he was a bronc rider in the rodeo or a cowboy, first on the Matador and later on the Waggoner Ranch, a spread of about a half million acres near Vernon. Oh, he'll tell you how much easier it is to break horses nowadays than it used to be because they're treated more gently from birth and don't grow up so ornery. He'll tell you how in the 1930s he used to cowboy sixteen hours a day for $35 a month. But the most amazing story he tells concerns the time he had his head on crooked.

We were sitting in the office of the Waggoner Estates in the Waggoner Building in downtown Vernon. He leaned forward in his chair, smacked his lips ever so slightly, and said, "Well, when I was a-workin' on the Waggoner we used to have wild cattle, and I mean wild. I cowboyed, broke horses, did a little bit of everything, and sometimes also drove stock in a truck to Fort Worth.

"Well, sir, one day back then we loaded up, and I was a-driving down yonder to Fort Worth when the cattle commenced to get tangled up. I stopped and went back and took a look. This one bull and some cows were tangled. So I grabbed the ol' bull's leg and set it over one of the cows so she could get loose. It touched another bull standing back there, and the danged animal just up and kicked me upside the head.

"I got up and my nose was busted and bleeding, and there was a cut over my eye. But something else felt pretty funny, I can tell. My head was turned plumb around. My chin was over my shoulder, and when I tried to turn it, I couldn't."

Frank stopped a truck. The driver got out and Frank told him what had happened. "And say, buddy, you rec'on you might help me turn my head around?"

"I rec'on it might kill you if I did," said the truck driver.

"Well, I rec'on it might kill me if you don't help me turn it around straight."

Frank grabbed hold of the back of the truck and braced himself, while the man helped him turn his head straight.

"But it was bothering me and I got to a-worryin' so I stopped in Olney and phoned the doctor," said Frank. "But he wasn't in. So I went and washed up and decided to go on to Fort Worth."

He unloaded in Fort Worth, turned around, and drove back to Waggoner, arriving about 2 A.M. In those days the cowboys got up at 4:30 A.M. "My wife told me it was time to get up," he continued. "I told her I believed I'd just lie for a spell. Then she turned on the lights and almost fainted. I looked pretty bad. Anyway, I got up, went to get some bulls, and carried them out to the field. But everybody kept on a-sayin' I ought to see the doctor, so I did."

The doctor took x-rays. "Well, he looks at me, then at them x-rays," said Frank. "Then he looks at me again and back at them x-rays. Then he takes some more. He says, well, these x-rays show you have a broken neck. But they're wet x-rays and might be wrong. So come back in the morning. So I did and he said, sure enough, the x-rays showed a broken neck. So he told me to go on to see this other doctor in Wichita (Falls) and see what he said.

"So I went to him, and he took some more x-rays. He called me into his other office, where he had the desk you know, and said feller you've got a broken neck. And then he told me I better go see this doctor in Dallas. He said he'd call this doctor and that I'd be put in traction. He explained traction to me, but I got to a-thinkin' that if they did that to me, tying up my neck and mouth and all, I wouldn't be able to chew tobacco with that harness on."

But Frank packed his jeans, pajamas, and a clean shirt and went to see the doctor in Dallas. The doctor told him that he had a broken neck and, sure enough, he'd have to put him in traction. Frank thought for a second and told the doctor, "Well, it'll be a mite hard to chew tobacco in traction. And doctor, there's something I haven't told you. I been a-using this horse medicine on my neck and it's a-doin' pretty good. Besides, I just don't know how I am a-goin' to get by without chewing tobacco."

The doctor shrugged and told him he wasn't his patient anyway. "Go back to your doctor in Wichita Falls and talk to him." Frank went back to Wichita Falls. When he went to the office, the doctor said he'd talked to the one in Dallas. Then he started laughing.

"He was laughing so hard I thought he'd die," said Frank. "And he told me to go on home and use that horse medicine. He said if I got to a-hurtin' to come back in. Well, in those days if you could walk a-tall, you went to work. So I went on back out there to work and kept a-using that horse medicine and never did have any trouble with my neck."

He paused, smacked his lips, and said, "I guess you might say the horse medicine cure it."

ROBERT KALKA, the bartender at Arkey Blue's Silver Dollar in Bandera, Texas, and a cowboy of piddlin' nature, had eyed the old saddle for a long time. It was a real collector's item with its old iron-ring stirrups and worn, partly cracked leather.

"Hondo," said Robert to the saddle's owner, "how 'bout sellin' me that saddle. How much you asking for it?"

Hondo eyed Robert and then said, "Son, I wouldn't sell that there saddle. I been th'owed off that saddle everywhere from Calgary to Mexico during my time. Now that I'm old and retired, I plan to put that thar saddle by my bed. Every mornin' when I wake up I'm a-goin to look at that saddle and say, 'Well, you sonuvagun, you ain't a-goin to th'ow me today.' "

Hondo recalled that he won the saddle in bronc riding at Pendleton in 1925, rode on it, and fell off it for fifty years. The saddle and a pair of spurs and chaps are about all he has from his days as a cowboy, both the working and rodeo kind.

There are drugstore and rhinestone cowboys in Bandera—instant cowboys who ride in a pickup and carry a can of Skoal in their hip pocket—and modern-day working cowboys who ride the range in a jeep. But there is also Hondo. His last name actually is Marchand, but most people around here don't know that. He's just Hondo, the oldtimer who figures he was born about 1900 and just sits around and takes in the changing scene. He's a small, thin man, five feet six, 130 pounds, and is bowed and bent. He squints a little from the wind and dust that used to blow into his eyes, and sometimes feels like it still does. His sideburns remain short, sticking out just below his hat, as they always have done. He might have been the Marlboro man. Before he retired five years ago to his place, a half acre with a house and a cabin about nine miles from Bandera on Medina Lake, he worked at various dude ranches in the area.

"Working the dude ranches is being part cowboy, part entertainer, part gigolo, part about anything else you can think of," he said. "You know, a feller goes on a bender once in a while, maybe a day or two. You work one of them dude ranches and you're on a bender every day of the year. It plum tuckers you out.

"So I just up and retired and got me this little place here. It's paid for, and I got me a real good wife and a little critter of twelve (a son). I was out workin' on the cabin. I washed it, scraped it, sanded it, and painted it. That ain't bad for an old man, but right now you might say I been rode hard and put up wet."

Hondo was raised on his father's spread about twenty miles from Calgary in Alberta, Canada. He said his neighbor was the Prince of Wales. When it was time to move on, he worked ranches around the Northwest, Southwest and in Mexico before settling in the Hill Country.

"I 'spect the last time I saw a chuck wagon, the real McCoy, was back in 1934–35. I mean where the cowboys actually follow a chuck wagon. Oh, you could make yourself twenty to fifty bucks a month, but it was a good, tough life. Many was the day I'd ride ten, fifteen miles out at daybreak, swap horses, ride for a while, and then swap again. Finally, I'd get me another one and ride on in after dark.

"Oh, in my day there was a lot of pranks a-goin' on. You know, puttin' a scorpion in a feller's boot or maybe a rattlesnake in his bedroll. I'm awful little, so everybody figured they could pull a lot of stuff on me. They figured I couldn't whup anybody anyway. But some of them fellers found out differently."

Hondo still gets up early and goes to bed early, like he always used to do. Sometimes he'll go into Bandera and chat with some of his friends. "Oh," he said, "you might say I do a lot of reminiscing about the old days." He paused, looked at his saddle and said again, "No, you sonuvagun, you ain't a-goin to th'ow me today."

EVANS MEANS WAS a loner who lived in a two-room rock-and-mud hut at the base of the towering rimrock of the Sierra Viega Mountains in extreme Southwest Texas. The rimrock, or the Rim as they call it, forms a kind of natural wall some ten to twelve miles this side of the Rio Grande. If you travel south from Evans' house you'll eventually pass the rim and be able to look into the unfocused distance and see Mexico.

Now on his spread of some three sections, Evans had a few horses, a small bunch of cattle, fruit trees, a mine he'd dug in hopes of finding gold, a stream and, of course, his house. Made mostly of rock, which protrudes over the cementing mud and keeps it from washing away in the rain, the house is very primitive, without plumbing or any modern conveniences, but that's the way Evans liked it. Oh, in recent years he did buy a bathtub and put it in the back of the house. Other than that, though, the house is as it had been for Lee Means, Evans' father. Lee, his brother John, and a man named George Evans, they say, originally bought and settled a much larger spread in the area. Lee thought enough of George to name his son, Evans, after him.

Evans grew up in the late 1800s and early 1900s, first learning about being a cowboy, then becoming and being one in the area, which is made up of mountainous, rocky terrain. Horses raised there form strong legs and ankles. It's been said that if you could get a wild horse and stay on it for fifteen or twenty miles, it would be broken. Evans broke a lot of horses, and many people brought their horses to him to be broken. It's something he liked to do.

Evans stayed where he was after his father died. Mostly, he stayed alone. He did serve in France in World War I and, when once asked how he communicated with the natives in French, said, "Aw, I'd just talk Spanish to them and put a little curlicue on my words. They understood me good enough."

Once a girl from the East came to the area. She was taken with the tales, both real and imagined, of the romantic cowboy. She met Evans, fell in love, and they were married. They had two children, a boy and a girl, but soon the rugged existence got to her and she left. Some say he ran her off. She took the girl with her. The boy spent sometime with his father and then left, too. Again, Evans Means was alone.

It was almost impossible to get to Evans' place in a car or truck, unless it was specially equipped. But that suited Evans fine because he was more at home on a horse. Some of the people around Marfa, Ft. Davis, and Valentine, which is about forty miles away and the closest community to his place, would tell you that Evans was just a hermit, a little odd, maybe a little touched in the head. But when someone remains alone, preferring to keep his own counsel, he often is classified as being odd because people consider such behavior different and abnormal.

Certainly, Evans was a man with both feet firmly planted in the past. He was a thin, dark-complexioned man of about five feet eight. He wore a wild-looking mustache, which would have been more appropriate in the Old West, and usually was unshaven, whiskers growing wild on his leathery and deeply creased face. He wore an old cowboy hat and usually had a six-gun strapped around his hip. He looked very rugged, exactly like a cowboy you see in one of those old, yellowing hardback photographs, not the kind invented in Hollywood. Some felt he looked more Mexican than American, and at times this became confusing. He spoke perfect border Spanish, not the textbook kind.

One story has it that the Border Patrol, thinking he was an alien, picked him up on the highway. They questioned him, but Evans refused to speak. They took him into town, and only then did he tell them who he was. "Shoot," he said, "I wasn't a-goin' to tell them who I was because I wanted a free lift into town."

J.K. Miller, whose spread borders the one belonging to Evans, said Means didn't always take very good care of himself. Often aliens would cross the Rio Grande and stop at Evans' place. He didn't leave the door closed to them. A few years ago an alien who had been staying at Evans' place came riding to Miller's and said the old man was dying.

"Señor Evans, he's in bad shape," the man said, breathlessly. "All he takes into his stomach is coffee, no food. He takes coffee and smokes cigarettes. Nothing more. I think he is dying."

Mrs. Miller fixed some aspirin and soup for the man to take back. Miller then went to check on Evans and, indeed, found him very sick. He took Evans to the hospital in town. "If you hadn't of come," said Evans, "I'd have died for sure." Evans didn't want to die. He'd just get on his coffee-and-cigarette jags for days at a time.

When the big land boom started and ranchers began cutting up their land and selling small tracks to people who wanted to use it for retirement or vacation and recreation, Miller asked Evans why he didn't do the same thing. He told Evans he could make a lot of money.

"Nope," said Evans. "If I sold it, moved into town, and started sitting on my butt, I'd be dead in two years." Evans knew it would kill him to change a lifetime of habits.

Nobody saw Evans much in recent years, although one story had it that he had gotten religious and began spending some time going up and down the Rio Grande preaching the word of God to anybody who would listen. But whatever he did he'd still return to his place, living alone and not seeing another human being for weeks at a time.

On January 23, 1980, Presidio County Sheriff Rick Thompson got a call at his office in Marfa. A man said that he'd been out around Evans Means' place and he thought the old man was dead. Sheriff Thompson made a trip to Evans' place, below the Rim. He found him outside the house, by his mine. He was dead. At first, foul play was suspected because Evans had a number of bruises around his head. I heard a lot of talk about that in Ft. Davis. But after an autopsy, Sheriff Thompson decided that Evans probably had fallen some fifteen feet off a nearby bluff, fracturing his skull. This likely knocked him out cold, and while he was unconscious, he died from exposure. They said he was eighty-eight years old.

Perhaps had someone been there Evans could have been saved. It was a shame, really, that he died alone. "If you're going to live like he did," said Sheriff Thompson, "I'd say your destiny is kinda set for you. You're going to die alone. You know what I mean."

Sure. And I guess Evans Means knew, too.

THERE WERE SO many tears at the funeral of Randy Spears I thought it might be best if I could hold on, not crack in spite of the feeling I had inside for the man, as did others who knew him. Then at the graveside Larry Mahan, tears in his eyes and his voice cracking with emotion, began singing the first verse of "Red River Valley."

From this valley they say you are going,
We will miss your bright eyes and sweet smile,
For they say you are taking the sunshine
That brightened our pathway the while.

When he led in the singing of that there were no dry eyes.

Randy was such an upbeat boy, always smiling, encouraging, trying to be helpful. I honestly can't remember him ever being selfish. He was always complimenting, helping, promoting, somebody else and seemed most happy when standing in the wings, watching his friends in the flood-lights of success.

As I sit here now, I keep thinking the phone will ring, and it will be him saying, "Bob! How's it goin'? I'm here in Phoenix and just got to wondering how you were doin'." But if it rings, it will not be him because on what now seems a crazy, senseless Tuesday, he died at thirty-one for reasons none of us can understand, although we keep trying. I guess we're not supposed to understand.

Randy would do things like that, just call you from here or there, because he sincerely wanted to know how you were doing. After he died, Mahan and Billy Bob Harris were telling me how Randy always was saying nice things about me. But when I was around him, he always seemed to be saying nice things about somebody or other. I've been thinking a lot about that, about how much he gave to so many of us and regret that we didn't give more to him.

I know. It's human nature, natural to feel this way after someone has died, but I just hope it becomes more natural to feel that way when they're alive.

Randy was a tall, very thin man who always wore glasses and dressed Western because he was a cowboy. The first time I met him was while he was working for Neal Gay at the Mesquite Rodeo. I'd talked to him, on and off, for years, and he'd always been extremely helpful. But after I began working on a book about the rodeo cowboy culture, I spent a lot time with Randy, and we became friends. If it hadn't been for Randy, the book wouldn't have been possible. He worked tirelessly and unselfishly, making suggestions, putting me in touch with the proper people, and opening doors that might have been closed to me but for him.

So many memories came to mind during the funeral. Once we had an all night session of pickin' and singin' in a motel room. Randy, Monty Henson, Steve Davis, Ed Knocke, and I were there. Randy encouraged anybody who performed but refrained from joining in. Then, suddenly, he stood up and began doing a very fine imitation of Elvis Presley. I don't think any of us were aware he could do that.

Once in Oklahoma City during the National Finals Rodeo, a bunch of us were in a club. Suddenly, Bob Wills became the king again, and somebody suggested that Randy get up and join the fiddlers in "Faded Love." After they finally got him on stage, he borrowed a fiddle and played tremendously. I later found out he had been a violinist.

A few years ago, after Randy left the rodeo, he went to work for Mahan, eventually becoming the president of Larry Mahan Productions. Mahan was then embarking on an entertainment career after gaining six All-Around Championships in professional rodeo. When Mahan opened the Waylon Jennings show in Fort Worth a few weeks before Randy's death, I went back stage and talked to Randy and his wife, Karen. I asked him how he liked working in what can become the madness of the entertainment world.

He said he loved it, the pressure, everything. He was extremely proud of Mahan, who had started his second career with little natural talent and, through hard work and a lot of desire, had become a good entertainer.

Outside of Karen's and Randy's immediate family, nobody took Randy's death harder than Mahan. Larry is such a positive, turned-on guy that he really didn't know how to cope with the hollow, gnawing, heavy feeling inside.

At the funeral he'd tried to handle it, put on his old face, but then crumbled like the rest. After the service at the graveside Larry tried to do everything: talk to Karen, Randy's parents, everybody. But he almost cracked again because of that awful feeling. He didn't know what to do with it, where to put it.

He couldn't ride it, think it away, fist-fight it. Nothing. When I walked over and put my arm around him, he said, "This is just the toughest bull I ever rode. I've already been on the full eight seconds but there ain't no way to get off and it's still bucking and it don't look like it'll ever stop."

The only thing I know is that if you hang on you can handle it just a little better the next day, a little better the one after . . .

At the funeral were lawyers, entertainers, and many of the cowboys that Randy loved so much. They were there in their big hats, wearing unfamiliar dress shirts with too much starch, ties, sports coats, boots, and jeans. There were so many people there. I think Randy might have been embarrassed by all that attention he got, but we needed to give it. Finally.

nick's
secret

nick's secret

Claire H. Blatchford

Lerner Publications Company ■ Minneapolis

Text copyright ©2000 by Claire H. Blatchford

All rights reserved. International copyright secured. No part
of this book may be reproduced, stored in a retrieval
system, or transmitted by any means—electronic, mechanical,
photocopying or otherwise—without the prior written permission
of Lerner Publications Company, except for the inclusion of
brief quotations in an acknowledged review.

Lerner Publications Company
A division of Lerner Publishing Group
241 First Avenue North
Minneapolis, MN 55401 U.S.A.

Website address: www.lernerbooks.com

Library of Congress Cataloging-in-Publication Data

Blatchford, Claire H.
    Nick's secret / Claire H. Blatchford.
        p.   cm.
    Summary: Nick, a deaf seventh grader, befriends a mysterious girl
who is training and protecting a pack of valuable sheepdogs on her
own.
    ISBN 0-8225-0743-9 (lib.bdg.: alk. paper)
    [1. Sheep dogs—Fiction. 2. Dogs—Fiction. 3. Deaf—Fiction.
4. Physically handicapped—Fiction.] I. Title.
PZ7.B6139 Ni 2000
[Fic]—dc21   00-008274

Manufactured in the United States of America
1   2   3   4   5   6   –   BP   –   05   04   03   02   01   00

For Laurel and Christa,
our adventure-loving,
dog-loving loves!

chapter 1

Nick hadn't seen her come into the pet shop, and that bugged him. Being deaf, he considered himself pretty quick at seeing things and keeping track of them. He thought he was aware of *every* customer who had walked into the store since he'd started work that morning—and the store was swarming with December twenty-first Christmas shoppers—but suddenly there she was.

She was a couple of inches taller than he, and wore jeans, a red turtleneck, and an oversized tweed jacket. No kid at school would be caught alive wearing a jacket like that. It looked like something an old woman would wear. What really struck Nick, though, were her hair and the expression on her face. Her wiry brown thicket of hair resembled steel wool. It looked ready to burst out of the confines of the elastic band at the nape of her neck. Her expression seemed distant, almost secretive. Since he had started working for Mrs. Firth five months earlier, Nick had noticed that most people who came in wore an open, blank look, even if they knew what they wanted to buy. This girl was different. She looked closed, aloof—almost unfriendly.

Who is she? Where'd she come from? Nick wondered as he ran a hand through his own curly red-blond hair. He decided she was fifteen or sixteen. Ninth or tenth grade. Nick himself had turned thirteen in September, shortly after starting seventh grade.

The girl was looking over the shelves with the various kinds of dog foods, leashes, collars, and other dog stuff. She picked up several items, fingered them thoughtfully, and put them back.

Nick started toward her to ask if she wanted help, but Mrs. Firth grabbed him by the arm. Her blue eyes were blazing. The bun of gray-white hair on top of her head was close to unraveling.

"There's a ton of rabbit pellets in the fifty gallon goldfish tank!"

"How—" Nick started to say.

"Clean it up!" Mrs. Firth snapped. "The fish will die if they eat it! I've got to be at the cash register."

Nick knew his boss had a temper, but he

8

respected it. She really cared for her animals, every one of them, and she expected others to also. When they didn't, she spoke up, even if it meant turning customers off or scaring them away.

Nick raced to the back of the store. The normally clear water in the largest tank was as thick as pea soup with disintegrating pellets. The twelve fish could barely move. They were large goldfish, from four to six inches long, raised specially for indoor and outdoor garden pools. They had sunk to the bottom of the tank, their fins flapping feebly, their mouths opening and shutting slowly in silent desperation.

A bunch of little kids gathered around the cloudy tank to watch. Some were pointing, others were imitating the fish and laughing.

What kind of a crazy joke was this?

"Get back!" Nick barked.

The kids shrank back as Nick grabbed a bowl and rushed to the sink.

Lugging the bowl to the tank, Nick put it on the floor and swung around in search of a fish net. He knew he could fit only one or two of the big fish in this bowl. He would have to get more bowls for the others. Later, if the fish survived, he would return them to the tank.

There were no nets in sight. Where were they? There were usually half a dozen on hand for use in the different tanks.

Nick reached for a brand new net, tore the plastic wrap off, and turned back to the tank. To his surprise, the girl in the tweed jacket was there.

She put a hand out for the net, and Nick noticed she wore two silver bands with snakelike patterns on her forefinger.

"I'll help." Her lips were easy to read.

Nick paused. *Who* was she? He found her steady gaze oddly unsettling.

"This isn't big enough for all of the fish," she said with a glance at the bowl Nick had brought. "You'd better get some more."

Nick flushed. Of course it wasn't big enough! He wasn't *that* stupid! Who did she think she was anyway, bossing him around?

She took the net from him. "Come on! HURRY!"

The last word jolted him into action. There wasn't time to argue or ask her who she was. The fish were suffocating. Every second was important.

The girl had transferred two fish to fresh water by the time Nick returned with another bowl. She clearly knew what she was doing.

When Nick finally lowered the sixth bowl onto the floor beside the others and straightened up, the girl wasn't in sight. Nick turned around and around. Where was she? The net rested over the top of the tank, ready for him to finish the job.

Nick netted the last two fish, got a hose, and began suctioning the dirty water out of the huge tank. He was about to go up front to look for the girl and tell Mrs. Firth things were under control, when his heart almost skipped a beat. Was that a gray baseball cap bobbing around in the crowd near the cash register?

He squinted. Yes, it was gray with black lettering. He knew that cap a mile away. It belonged to a tall eighth grader from his school, Daryl Smythe. Nick had been avoiding the older boy for weeks.

Nick started to back into the hall that led to the rear entrance and the downstairs office where Wags, his mutt, stayed while Nick worked, but he wasn't quick enough. Daryl had caught sight of him. A slick grin spread over the tall boy's lips. Two girls and another guy stood behind him. Nick recognized the girls but not the guy. One of the girls was in his English class, the other rode on his bus. Neither of them had ever bothered to look at Nick in school, and here they were staring as if he was the only other human on the planet!

What now? Nick wondered, his hands clenched in fists.

Daryl's grin broadened as Nick returned his stare. He motioned for Nick to come over to him.

What's he want? I have to work!

Daryl motioned again.

Quickly and firmly, Nick shook his head once

He wasn't going to be intimidated. He wasn't going to be ordered about like a dog.

Daryl motioned yet again.

Nick pointed at the front door to say he'd meet him outside. If they were going to scuffle, he didn't want the store getting messed up or the animals getting hurt. Daryl's grin faded away. He whispered something to the other kids, and they fanned out behind him, all facing Nick.

Whoa! Nick stepped back against one of the tanks. Daryl clearly thought Nick was telling him to get out of the store. He looked ready to fight.

None of the customers seemed aware of what was going on. Mrs. Firth was at the other end of the store, out of sight. Nick pointed at himself and pointed at the front door to tell Daryl he would go outside, but Daryl didn't get it. He was too angry to listen to Nick's signs. His customary grin had been replaced by a sneer.

Nick's knees felt weak. What would they do?

Nick didn't wait to find out. He dropped down low to confuse Daryl, slid around the edge of the reptile tank, vaulted over a cage full of puppies, nearly collided with an elderly gentleman, and dashed down the back hall. Should he go out the rear entrance or lock himself in the downstairs office? The fact that Wags and his jacket were downstairs settled the matter.

Wags leaped up, her stringy brown tail bouncing back and forth in happy surprise, as Nick tumbled into the room. It reeked of sweet soapy scents. Esmeralda, a distant cousin of Mrs. Firth, ran a dog- and cat-grooming salon there from the end of April to the end of October. The rest of the time she took it easy in Florida.

Breathing hard, Nick slammed the door shut, turned the lock, and sank onto the plush swivel chair. Minutes passed. Wags licked his hand and leaned against him as if to protect him.

Someone banged on the door. Nick could hear it through his hearing aid and his feet, even though there was a thick carpet on the floor. He didn't dare move. He was certain Daryl was right outside. His throat tightened. *He's really after me!*

There was more banging.

Wags barked.

"Shhh!" Nick hissed.

Wags was immediately quiet. Her tail went down. Her eyes never left his face.

Nick stared at the telephone on the desk. The health food store where his mother worked was seven stores away. He wished he could call her, even though he couldn't use a regular phone. Then he remembered she wasn't there. She wasn't at home either. She'd told him the night before that she and Peter were doing an errand that afternoon. When Nick had asked what kind of an errand, she had shrugged and given a mysterious smile.

What am I going to do if Daryl breaks in here?

13

WHERE is Mum? This is the second Saturday she's taken time off with Peter.

His rambling thoughts were interrupted by the sight of Wags's perked ears. She was listening to something—something very close.

Seconds later a scrap of paper appeared under the door.

Wags sprang forward to sniff at it.

Nick picked it up. On it, in an unpleasantly familiar hand, he saw the words:

**Be at the Tower Motel
tomorrow morning at 10.**

Nick shivered. He didn't like the idea at all. Until that fall, he had only known Daryl from a distance. The older boy was one of the obvious kids in junior high. You couldn't miss seeing him even if you tried. Daryl's swagger said, "I'm cool," and he was a daring skateboarder who knew every slab of concrete in town. Nick hadn't done much skateboarding but had sometimes admired Daryl's twists, jumps, and turns. He had also noticed the four or five loud-looking kids who trailed Daryl. Nick, who had difficulty following group talk, kept to himself, and Daryl had paid no attention to him until recently. It had all started the night Nick was riding his bike home from the pet shop with Wags and decided to take a shortcut.

Nick's shortcut was a back road that went up a hill and under a thruway bridge. As he neared the bridge that night, Nick saw moving lights, then a spray of something that looked like milk. Next, he narrowly missed hitting someone. Alarmed, Nick slid off his bike and put up an arm to shield his eyes from the glare of flashlights on his face.

"Gimme a break," he said.

When the flashlights were lowered, Nick saw two guys. He didn't know the short, stocky one. The tall one was Daryl.

The lights were bright enough for Nick to catch two words on Daryl's lips, "deaf jerk."

"DEAF JERK?" Nick growled.

Daryl's mouth fell open. "You heard me?"

"I hear with my eyes."

Daryl grinned.

The other boy grinned too and pointed the flashlight on the wall to illuminate the white outline of a monster with horns, fangs, and a single bulging cyclops-like eye!

"*You* guys did that?" Nick gasped. A similar monster had appeared on the back of the supermarket in the spring. It was big and bold, but unfinished. The vandal had departed in haste, leaving the aerosol cans behind.

Daryl stepped close to Nick—he was at least six inches taller—the nozzle of a spray paint can pointed straight at Nick's eyes. Nick tried to back away, but the other guy moved behind him. For one minute Nick was scared, truly scared. He shut his eyes tight, knowing he could be blinded if they sprayed paint into them.

Nick waited, not breathing, till he sensed a commotion. He opened his eyes and saw flickering flashlights and retreating figures followed by Wags. Wags was after them! Farther down the road, he saw the headlights of an approaching car.

Nick yelled to Wags as he ran with the bike in the opposite direction, out the other end of the bridge and up the side embankment to get out of the way of the car. It passed through the tunnel and gone on. Then there was darkness. Daryl and his friend had left.

Nick hugged Wags long and hard after that. He could still see the can of paint up close to his face. He hadn't been sure what to do. He knew his mother would be furious if he told her what had happened. She would tell the cops, and then what? They might have wanted him to prove Daryl had done it, and he didn't even know who the second guy was.

Nick's mother wasn't home that evening. Exhausted, he lay down on his bed and fell asleep fully clothed. The next morning, he decided he'd keep quiet until he knew how things stood with Daryl. He didn't have to wait long. Two days later, he found a sketch of the one-eyed monster stuck to the inside of his locker.

Beneath it were the words:

**Any ratting
and we'll get you—
or your dog.**

There had been no more notes since then, not until this one.

Why do they want to meet me at the Tower Motel? Nick wondered. *I haven't said anything to anybody.*

He sat with his head in his hands.

When Wags curled up and rested her head between her paws, Nick knew that the kids must have left. Mrs. Firth was probably mad as a hornet, wondering where he was.

He turned the lock, opened the door, and peeked out. Nobody there. He motioned for Wags to stay in the office, stuffed the note into his pocket, took the back stairs two at a time, and made his way cautiously down the hall.

The store was still thick with customers. Nick squinted as he surveyed the crowd. As far as he could see, there was no gray baseball cap in sight. Mrs. Firth was still at the cash register, apparently unaware that Nick had been elsewhere. The tension ebbed out of his arms a bit, but not entirely.

By closing time, Nick had cleaned and refilled the huge tank, and the goldfish were back in it.

They seemed to be all right. While cleaning up, Nick found the missing fish nets shoved behind the tank. It looked as though someone, probably the same person who had dumped the rabbit pellets in the water, had wanted to slow down the rescue operation. Was Daryl Smythe responsible? Nick had a feeling he probably was.

"Good work," Mrs. Firth told Nick as she pinned loose strands of hair back into her bun. "What's the matter with people? Don't they have brains in their heads? I sure would like to get my hands on the nut who thought fish eat rabbit food!"

"I don't think he was trying to feed the fish," Nick replied.

"Uh?" Mrs. Firth peered at Nick. "Did you see him?"

"No."

"Why do you say it's a him? And what do you think he was doing?"

Nick gave a little shrug.

Mrs. Firth tapped at his arm. Her big, curved nose was almost pointing at him. "Is there something you know that you aren't telling me?"

Nick put both hands up. "I don't know who put the pellets in the tank. Honest, I don't."

She regarded him for a minute. Then, satisfied, she went on. "Well, I wondered if a girl did it."

"A girl?"

"Because there was a girl in here today I've

never seen before—"

"Hey!" Nick interrupted. "She had lots of hair—stiff wiry hair—didn't she?"

Mrs. Firth nodded. "And a ratty old coat, and a poker face."

A ratty old coat? Nick almost laughed. He had never thought of Mrs. Firth as being fashion conscious. Most of her clothes looked as though they came from the thrift shop.

"You saw her too?" Mrs. Firth asked.

"She helped me! She took most of the goldfish out of the tank while I got the bowls. She knew how to net them without dropping them."

"Well now." Mrs. Firth actually smiled. "SOMEONE in this crazy world has SOME sense in their head."

"Then she disappeared," Nick added. "I wanted to thank her, but..." He shrugged again. He wasn't about to tell her why he hadn't been able to look for the girl.

"Maybe, if she comes in again, we can get her to help us during the next few days." Mrs. Firth spoke more to herself than to Nick. "Because I'm getting too old for this. Today was horrid. HORRID. Worse than the flea season. If it's not fun anymore, maybe I shouldn't bother."

"Don't say that!" Nick put a hand on her arm. He loved the pet shop almost as much as his own home. He even liked the smells of molting birds, kitty litter, puppy drool, and slimy tanks. "I'll help you, I will!"

"I know you will." Mrs. Firth put her hand on top of his. "But two of us isn't enough. And if something happened to me, and you were alone here, your mother would never forgive me."

Nick frowned. What was Mrs. Firth saying? He was going to ask if she felt OK, but she had gone on to the aviary to talk with her favorite cockatiel before closing up. Nick got his jacket and mittens from the back office. Wags ran on ahead to the front door.

"Good night." Nick tapped on the aviary window.

She turned, the big white bird on her arm, and mouthed the words, "Be here tomorrow at 10:00. There's a lot to do before the store opens."

Nick hesitated. He could feel the tension building up in his arms again. That's when Daryl had ordered him to the Tower Motel. How could he be in two different places at the same time?

Mrs. Firth didn't wait for his response. She assumed the matter was settled.

What am I going to do? Nick wondered as he stepped outside. It was cold—cold enough for snow. For a second he was excited. He'd asked for a snowboard for Christmas, even though he'd never gone snowboarding. Both his mother and his father had dropped hints that he might be getting one. Then his thoughts returned to Daryl Smythe. *The Tower Motel is at least five miles from here, way out on the other side of town. How long would it take me to get from there to here?*

Wags dashed off toward the grassy area near the parking lot.

"Hey!" Nick gave a quick, sharp clap of his hands. If Daryl happened to be waiting for him near the bike rack, he wanted his dog close by.

Wags circled back, a questioning look on her face, then fell into step beside him.

Only the bike was at the rack.

The Tower Motel? Nick shivered again. *It's a creepy place.*

chapter 2

There had been a fire at the Tower Motel six years earlier, when Nick was in first grade. A man had fallen asleep while smoking his pipe in bed and, because his cabin was the last one in a row of eight set back in the woods, the motel owners hadn't realized right away that a fire had started. To complicate matters, the firefighters had a terrible time getting to the cabin because a blizzard had dumped more than a foot of snow on the town hours before. The road leading up the bluff to the motel was packed with snow. Rescue workers couldn't save the man.

Wild stories about the man had circulated at school among the older kids. The newspaper had printed little information about him. All it said was that he was in his seventies, was a friend of the motel owners, often stayed there on his way to or from Florida, and always wanted that particular cabin. Some of the fourth and fifth graders, however, said the man hadn't been smoking a pipe—he'd been building bombs, and one had exploded by mistake. Others claimed the motel owners had started the fire knowing the man was snowed in and wouldn't be able to get out.

Nick's mother had become very angry when she heard about the stories. She had told Nick they weren't true—that the fire had been a terrible accident. Besides, she had pointed out, why would the motel owners set fire to one of their own cabins? But Nick hadn't been able to stop thinking about it. He could just see the snow drifts blocking the door, the huge, orange flames flickering up out of the cabin windows, and the fire engines slipping and sliding off the road.

"Nicholas Wilder," Nick's mother had said when she realized how scared he was. "Don't think about it. OK? Let's think about something else."

"But Mum!" Nick had been close to tears. "Suppose the water from the fire engines froze in the air, they couldn't put the fire out, and that's why the man died?"

"What a imagination you've got!" She said, putting her arms around him. Seconds later she exclaimed, *"You're* on fire!" Nick had a fever. He was admitted to the hospital with meningitis the next day. The disease damaged nerves in his ears. When he came home a week later, he couldn't hear. It was as though his ears had been switched off overnight.

Now, as he bicycled home, Nick thought of the Tower Motel. He knew the motel was still in operation during the summer—he'd passed the green and yellow sign for it on Route 77 lots of times—but he never went anywhere near it and didn't even know if the same owners still lived there. As far as he was concerned, the place was spooked.

Nick rode alongside Peter's old Honda in their driveway. *So he's here for dinner again,* Nick thought as he put his bike in the garage. He gritted his teeth and realized he wasn't looking forward to seeing his mother's boyfriend, even though he had introduced Peter to his mother.

Nick had met Peter, a newspaper reporter, the summer before. Peter had asked Nick to row his rubber raft across the town's lake and take some photographs for a story. The assignment hadn't turned out the way they expected. Nick's raft had sprung a leak, forcing him ashore on the far side of the lake. There, Nick walked into a boathouse that bird smugglers were using for a hideout! The pictures he took of the illegal birds led police to the smugglers.

Nick started for the house. Peter was a cool

guy, but Nick just didn't want to see him right then. Why couldn't Peter give his mother a break from cooking? Why couldn't they just have plain old spaghetti and then go to the drive-in for yogurt cones afterward? Almost every meal now that Peter had come into the picture had to be what his mother called "an eating adventure."

Peter was seated in Nick's chair, tilted back against the kitchen counter, laughing. As usual, his longish brown hair was tousled. He nodded when Nick and Wags came in and made the sign for "hi," a quick, friendly salute.

Nick didn't respond. He was hanging up his jacket when his mother put an arm around his neck from behind and hugged him. Nick wiggled out of her embrace. He didn't like being cozy with her in front of other people.

She caught his arm before he could move away. "What's the matter, sweetheart?"

"Don't sweetheart me!"

Nick saw the hurt look in her blue eyes and was sorry. But not sorry enough to say anything more.

"Well..." She put a hand on the barrette that held back her long golden-blond hair. "I didn't realize you don't like being sweethearted."

Nick groaned. Why did she have to make a big deal of it? He'd *never* liked being called sweetheart, and suddenly it had become a huge problem. He nodded at the dog. "I'd better feed Wags."

His mother caught his arm. "You know what day it is today?"

"Saturday."

"It's December twenty-first. We're going to the Floyds' farm to cut the tree after supper."

Nick shrugged. They always cut their Christmas tree on the winter solstice. Mr. Floyd let Nick ride on the tractor to the upper field, where the best trees grew. Last year he let Nick drive the tractor. When they got back to the farmhouse, Mrs. Floyd always invited them in for popcorn and mulled cider, while Mr. Floyd tied the tree to the top of their car. Nick wondered if Peter was going to come along this year.

Nick's mother squeezed his arm again. "Really! What's the matter? You're behaving like you've had a rotten day."

A rotten day? Nick rolled his eyes. He could have been beaten up by Daryl Symthe *and* lost his job while she took the afternoon off with Peter. She had no idea what he'd been going through. If she knew what had happened at the bridge, if Peter knew what he knew about the graffiti....

Peter got up, knocking the lampshade off the wall lamp as he stood. He was so tall he was always bumping around. The lampshade bounced off Peter's arm, rolled across the kitchen table, and onto the floor. Nick giggled as Peter and his mother both scrambled for it.

"Nicholas Wilder!" his mother said as she straightened up. "You're being rude!"

Peter waved the lampshade to get Nick's attention. His green-brown eyes were concerned. "Look, Nick, I can leave if you want to be alone with your mom."

"No, Peter." Nick's mother's eyes flashed. "That's not the answer. Not if you're going to be living with us."

Living with us? Nick looked from one to the other and back again. His mother nodded. Her face was very pink. Peter gave an awkward shrug and clownishly put the lampshade on top of his head.

"We want to talk with you about it," Nick's mother said.

Peter nodded.

Nick didn't know what to say. How could he talk about it with them if they had already decided? What about him? Where was he in this? They were both watching him, waiting.

Suddenly the air seemed close and thick, almost unbreathable. Nick grabbed his jacket off the hook again and headed back out the front door.

* * *

Nick climbed and climbed until he could go no farther. He sat leaning against the trunk of the

27

pine—*his* pine—one arm around it, the other hand on the last thick limb that could hold him. When he was younger he'd been able to go higher, closer to the sky, but a hurricane two years earlier had snapped the uppermost branches off like they were pretzel sticks.

Pine scents filled his nose, pine needles brushed his forehead, and pine creaks sounded through his body. Nick shut his eyes. Gradually the stillness of the tree, the winter air, and the stars seeped into him.

When he opened his eyes, he looked down. He saw two dark figures in the driveway, one short and one tall—his mother and Peter. He knew they were talking. Then they merged into one form. He squinted. What were they doing? Hugging? Kissing? Nick swallowed. Then they were two forms again.

Seconds later the headlights on Peter's Honda switched on, and the car backed out of the drive and disappeared down the road. Nick's mother didn't go in. Instead, she looked up at the pine. Nick leaned back even farther against the tree, holding his breath, hoping she couldn't see him. He could sense her calling to him. He knew she was telling him to be reasonable, to come down, get warm, have supper, and talk things over. But he didn't move or say anything. Finally she went back in the house.

So Peter wanted to move in with them. How

could he do that? There wasn't enough room in their apartment. Peter took up miles of space whenever he came over. He always had a ton of camera equipment and other stuff with him.

Were Peter and his mother going to get married? Was that what they wanted to tell him? Nick's parents had divorced when Nick was in second grade, but, oddly, Nick couldn't really remember a time when it hadn't been just him, his mother, and Wags. Sure, he and Wags went to see his father in Maine for a couple of weeks in the summer and a few days after Christmas— that visit was coming up soon—but home for him meant being with his mother.

The wind picked up. There was a cold, shrill edge to it. Nick's hands began to feel raw, almost numb. And it was dark, so dark. It really was the darkest day of the year.

He huddled closer to the tree. What was he going to do? Everything was a mess. *Everything!* If only people—his mother and Daryl Symthe— would leave him alone, things would be OK.

The wheels in his head began to churn. Darn it! He was *not* going to the Tower Motel! What did Daryl plan to do there anyway? Throw him off the bluff for catching him spray painting a wall? Maybe he ought to try calling Daryl on the TTY. The guy had surely never gotten a call on a TTY in his life.

That thought and the cold wind brought him

back to the ground, where Wags was waiting. She jumped on him and licked his cold hands. Nick hugged her while she wiggled and wagged. At least he had one real friend.

"Well?" said Nick's mother when he appeared in the kitchen. She was seated at the table, the newspaper in front of her. From the expression on her face, Nick knew she probably hadn't been reading but had been sitting there waiting for him.

"Hungry?" she asked as he peeled off his jacket. He nodded.

"Spaghetti?"

Nick frowned. Was she trying to be nice? "Was that what we were going to have?"

"Yup. It was Peter's idea. He was going to cook it."

"Oh." Nick turned to hang his jacket and then get Wags's bowl. Maybe Peter felt the way Nick did about spaghetti, but he wasn't ready yet to talk about Peter.

Nick avoided his mother's eyes as he ate.

Finally she banged on the table to get his attention. "Can we talk now, Mr. Wilder, or are you going to be stubborn and refuse to say a word?"

Nick's eyebrows went up. Mr. Wilder? This was new. His mother usually called him by his full name when she had something important to say.

"Well?" she challenged him.

"Well." Nick paused. "I guess I have to, Ms. Pierce."

She grinned and slapped the table again. "OK, Mr. Wilder, since I have learned that you don't like being called sweetheart, we can proceed."

"Mum," Nick got right to the point, "are you and Peter getting married?"

She sighed. "I don't know, Nick. I really care about Peter and I think he cares about me...about us."

Nick swallowed again. "If...if you don't know, Mum, why would he live with us?"

"So Peter and I can find out if it would be right to get married."

"Oh." And then again in an even smaller voice, "Oh."

Tears welled up in her eyes. "It didn't work out with your father, Nick. That hurt a lot. I want to be sure, really sure, before I get married again."

Nick felt helpless. He hated when she cried. But then, really, it was her own fault. Why did she have to bring it up now, right at Christmas, right when Daryl Smythe was being so mean?

The thought of calling Daryl on the TTY suddenly seemed far, far away and pretty stupid. What was Nick going to do? What would his mother say if she knew about Daryl? She was probably so busy thinking about Peter, it wouldn't matter.

"Nick, I thought you liked Peter. I thought you

liked swimming, snorkeling, hiking...doing all your favorite things with him."

"I do...."

"We met because of *you.*"

"I know...."

"Peter thinks you're great. I've had the impression you two get along really well."

"Yeah, but...."

When Nick's voice trailed off yet again, his mother threw up her hands. "This conversation isn't going anywhere! What am I supposed to do? Put my life on hold until you're more agreeable?"

Nick took his empty plate to the sink. His mind was going in circles. *Mum, I do like Peter. He doesn't talk down because I'm deaf. He doesn't treat me like I'm two years old. I like it when we go snorkeling and hiking. I like talking to him about wilderness survival and stuff like that. But does he have to be around* all *the time?*

He turned the water on so hard it splashed right off his plate onto his shirt.

"Aargh!" Nick jumped back, but he didn't look at his mother. *Mum, I know you think I need a father figure. I know! You've talked about it a hundred thousand times. Male bonding and all that crap. You don't get it. You don't understand that even if Peter was my father, I'm not sure I could tell him about Daryl. I don't know what to do....*

Nick swung around, suddenly determined. If

he couldn't do anything about his mother and Peter, at least he could deal with Daryl. "Mum, I've got to make a call."

Her face looked ready to collapse. Without saying a word, she got up and left the kitchen. She usually did that when Nick talked with his father on the TTY, to give him more space.

Nick sighed again. He knew she'd gone to her room and was probably crying. Nick felt terrible. He hadn't meant to upset her. He just didn't want to talk then, that was all. She was overreacting. He hadn't really said no to Peter living with them. It had come up all at once, so fast—*too* fast.

Nick got the phone book and took the lid off the TTY. Only one Smythe was listed. He put the phone receiver face down on the machine, on the suction cups designed to hold it. Beneath the suction cups was the small screen where all typewritten words—Nick's and then those of the person he was talking with—would appear. Below the screen was Nick's keyboard. Nick dialed the relay operator and typed out Daryl's name and number.

Seconds later the operator typed back that she had dialed the Smythe's number, and the phone was ringing.

Nick panicked, plucked the receiver off the TTY, and slammed it back down on the hook. *What* was he going to say? He hadn't figured that out yet.

33

He decided he would tell Daryl he couldn't make it to the Tower Motel because he had to work. It was that simple. He was glad the operator would be saying the words, not him, because he knew his own voice would probably sound squeaky.

Minutes later the operator's typed words appeared on the screen, telling Nick that a woman had answered the phone at the Smythe house.

"Is Daryl there?" Nick typed back.

"Just a sec," said the person at Daryl's house.

Daryl came on with, "Who's this?"

"This is Nick Wilder. I'm using my TTY to say I can't meet you at the Tower Motel tomorrow," Nick replied.

"Uhhh…" the operator typed out Daryl's slow response. It was followed by another long "Uhhh…" and then, "Tell him I'll be there and…uhhh…only a wimp would make up an excuse for not coming."

Nick gritted his teeth as he typed, "I can't be there. I have to work."

"Sorry," the relay operator typed to Nick, "he hung up without waiting to hear what you had to say. Do you want me to redial?"

He'll come looking for me at the pet shop again, Nick knew. *If he's the one who put the rabbit pellets in the tank, what else would he do?*

Nick needed time to think. "No, I don't want to

redial," he typed. "Thanks. Bye for now."

He sat staring at the TTY after he had hung up. What if he didn't go to the motel or to the pet shop? What if he just disappeared and spent the day in the pine tree?

Tempting as the thought was, he knew it wouldn't solve anything. *I guess there's only one thing to do. If Daryl's sharp, I've got to be even sharper. I've got to play his game and beat him at it. I'm not going to be scared, I'm gonna show him.*

Nick drew his breath in quickly as he realized what that meant: He was going to have to meet Daryl Smythe at the Tower Motel. There was no backing out of it. He would have to meet Daryl and his gang face-to-face.

chapter 3

The sky was dark when Nick woke the next morning. Pitch dark. The red digits on his bedside clock read 6:11. He blinked and peered at the clock again, convinced he had never fallen asleep and it was still Saturday evening.

The clock blinked from 6:11 to 6:12. He had made it through the night.

Thump, thump, thump. Wags's tail beat a greeting on the wooden floor.

She can hear my eyes open. Nick grinned as he put an arm over the side of the bed and felt for the dog. Wags met his hand with a cool, wet kiss.

"Stay with me," Nick whispered. "I need you."

Thump, thump, THUMP! replied her tail.

"SHHH."

Nick didn't want Wags to wake his mother.

They hadn't gone to the Floyds' farm and had barely exchanged words the night before. He had switched aimlessly from one TV station to another while she stayed in the kitchen. He didn't know what show he was looking for. He only knew he had to keep away every thought of Daryl Smythe or the Tower Motel. He didn't want to get his imagination going by thinking about them. He'd be a nervous wreck.

When Nick had finally headed for bed, he peered in the kitchen. His mother was perched on the countertop, talking on the phone, fiddling with one of her turquoise earrings, and looking pretty upset.

"Night," he said with a wave from the door.

She mumbled something into the receiver, put a hand over it, and said, "Night, Mr. Wilder."

She looked far away. Calling him Mr. Wilder made the distance even greater. Nick was sure she had been talking about him with Peter.

Now, as he lay looking at the red digits on his clock, he found himself wondering about names. His mother had used his father's last name—Wilder—until their divorce. Then she had changed it back to Pierce.

If Mum married Peter, would she become Suzanne Harkins? Suzanne Pierce Harkins? Mrs. Peter J. Harkins? How many kids at school have mothers who keep changing their names? Is Daryl Smythe's mom called Mrs. Smythe, or does she have some other name?

Then Nick remembered Mrs. Firth was expecting his help at the same time he was supposed to be at the Tower Motel. Should he call and tell her he couldn't be there, or that he'd be late?

He wanted to be there, that was his life. His day didn't really begin on weekdays till 3:00, when school got out. And on the weekends, he often came in early—before Mrs. Firth. He'd even spent two nights there when the puppies arrived. Mrs. Firth had been concerned about one of the pups, so Nick had brought his sleeping bag and slept in Esmeralda's office, with Wags beside him. Wags hadn't been too happy about the puppies at first, but by the end of that weekend she was acting like they were her own. Nick had had such a good time he'd left his sleeping bag there, hoping they could do it again.

Nick decided he would tell Mrs. Firth he was coming in late. If Daryl beat him up, well, he'd still try to get to work. Whatever happened he wasn't going to be a wimp.

But what excuse could he give Mrs. Firth for coming in late? Maybe he could tell her he'd eaten something bad the night before, had thrown up, and needed a couple more hours to recover. But she might talk with his mother, so that was out. Besides, Nick didn't like telling lies. It was extremely hard for him to tell a lie because it was so easy for him to see one. He'd discovered that six months after he'd gone deaf. He had asked his mother why his father had gone to Maine, and she had talked about the great fishing trip his father was on and how badly he needed a break from work. The edges of her mouth were pulling down, though, no matter how cheerful the words that came out seemed.

"Your mouth isn't right," he told her.

She was startled. "What do you mean?"

"Dad didn't really go fishing, did he?"

Her mouth fell open when he said that. She'd cried and cried. Afterward she always made a big point of being honest and direct with him. Sometimes too honest and direct! She never failed to tell him when she thought he was being a pain. And she wouldn't ever let him wiggle out of speech therapy.

Nick decided he would tell Mrs. Firth there was something important he had to do that would make him late. That was the truth. If he didn't go to the Tower Motel, Daryl Smythe might do something worse at the pet shop.

He tiptoed into the kitchen, put the phone on the TTY, dialed the relay operator, and gave Mrs. Firth's number, which he knew by heart.

The operator let Nick know that the phone rang eight times before it was answered.

"Err... Hello?"

"Mrs. F.," Nick typed fast, "this is Nick. I can't come in at 10:00 today. I'll come in later."

"Good grief, Nick! Do you know what time it is?"

"Yes, Mrs. F. I'm sorry to be calling so early, but I had to let you know that I'll be coming in later."

"How much later?"

Nick frowned and did some quick calculations in his head. "Maybe 11:30 or 12:00."

"That is late! I need you before the mob arrives. The cages have to be cleaned out."

"I'm really sorry, Mrs. F. I'll do everything I can to get there as soon as I can."

"You'd better!" There was a pause. "I'm not used to being called at this hour, Nick. I haven't had my cup of tea. In fact, I haven't brushed my teeth, and my hair is a mess. Since you have gotten me out of bed at this ridiculous hour, why, may I ask, can't you come at 10:00?"

"I'm sorry, Mrs. F...." Nick glanced around the kitchen frantically. "I can't. I have something else I have to do."

"Look, young man, I plan to hire you full time some day. You might as well learn now that you have to be accountable. Especially with animals. You can't just come later because you have something else to do. It doesn't work that way. Animals have to be taken care of."

Nick squirmed. She sounded desperate for help. But he couldn't see any way out. "I know, Mrs. F. This won't happen again, I promise."

"I could tell you right now not to come in at all."

She's angry! Nick squirmed even more. "Please don't say that, Mrs. F. I like working for you. I want to work for you." Then, before he could stop them, his fingers had added some other words. "My mom's getting married."

Nick stared at the TTY screen, horrified. Why had he said *that?* He wanted to take the words out, but the operator had already passed them on.

"FANTASTIC!" Mrs. Firth's response flowed back in big letters. "Now that I'm awake, I must say that's the best news I've heard in ages! That's wonderful, Nick! Who's the lucky fellow?"

Nick's face got hot. His mother would shoot him if she knew he was talking like this. He'd better get out of this fast!

"Wait a sec!" Nick replied. "Mrs. F., I made a mistake. I'm not supposed to talk about it. Please don't say anything to my mum. I'll come in as soon as I can."

Mrs. Firth, however, wouldn't be deterred. "Is it that newspaper reporter, Nick? Is your mother going to marry him?"

"I'm sorry, Mrs. F. I forgot I'm not supposed to talk about it. I'll see you later."

"It had better be him!" Mrs. Firth wouldn't hang up. "Because they're MADE for each other! We could throw a surprise shower for them in the pet store, and Ralph could provide the food. Wouldn't that be fun?"

Nick groaned. Ralph was his mother's boss at

the health food store.

"Do you think," Mrs. Firth went on, "they'd like a white cockatiel or a pair of love birds as a gift?"

Nick didn't wait to hear any more, or even to thank the operator for making the call. "I have to go, Mrs. F. Bye." Then he pulled the phone off the TTY, clamped it back on the hook, and put both hands over his face. Why in the world had he said that about his mother?

A hand ran across his shoulder.

Startled, Nick looked up.

His mother was standing beside him in her nightgown, her long, golden-blond hair falling free, framing her face. There were circles under her eyes.

"I'm sorry," she said.

What was she talking about? Nick gave a puzzled shrug.

"I'm sorry I didn't talk earlier with you about Peter." She pulled a stool over and sat down beside him. "I was only thinking about myself, what *I* wanted. I didn't stop to think of how long it's been just the two of us living here together, doing things together."

What could he say to that? Nick gave another shrug.

"Peter and I have agreed to wait till after the holidays. Then we'll *all* see about sharing space," Nick's mother continued, as she tugged a bit at her earring.

42

"You mean you aren't going to get married?"

"I never said we were getting married. You seem hung up on the question of whether we're going to get married or not."

His face got hot. What if Mrs. Firth didn't keep quiet and told Ralph his mother was getting married? She could be quite a squawker! She would probably want to tell all the other store owners on the block. What had ever gotten into his fingers to type a message like that?

Nick's mother squeezed his arm. The squeeze told him how much she wanted to talk. His chest and arms began to feel hot too. But he couldn't say anything.

She sighed and threw up her hands. "I'm sorry if you don't want Peter around."

"I didn't say that."

"Maybe you didn't say it with words, but you sure said it. Not even saying hello when you came in last night, then running out and hiding in the tree. What's all that supposed to mean?"

Nick rolled his eyes. How much more complicated could things get? Why'd she have to make it sound like everything was *his* fault? Couldn't she see he had other things on his mind? Before Peter came along, she had always been so aware of what was going on with him. Sometimes it had seemed as though she could hear his thoughts.

He shut his eyes. He wanted to tell her about Daryl Smythe. If only he hadn't taken that shortcut! If only she'd been home that evening! She would have known something wasn't right. She would have seen, and he would have told her. And then it wouldn't be his problem anymore.

He caught himself. If he told his mother, she would tell his teachers, the principal, the social worker, the cops. Everybody would know he'd snitched on Daryl. That would really make him a wimp. What was so bad, really, about painting a monster on a wall? It wasn't a bad painting. It looked like something out of science fiction. It wasn't like Daryl was writing dirty words all over.

Nick's mother punched his arm.

He opened his eyes.

She looked so tired. "Please don't cut me off like this, Nick. I want to find out what's best for us. And I want you to know that whatever happens, Peter and I love you. That's right at the top of our list."

She didn't wait for Nick to reply. She got up and went to the refrigerator as though the conversation was over.

Nick went back to his room, flopped down on the bed, and stared at the ceiling. He didn't know what he felt about his mother and Peter. All Nick could think about was going to the motel. Should he take a weapon? What about his knife or the red pepper spray his mother had given him?

He got up, went to his desk and rummaged through the top drawer. He found a jumble of feathers, fossils, arrowheads, stones, shells, his compass, goggles, pocket microscope, and Swiss Army knife. He opened the knife and felt the blade with his finger. It was fairly sharp. He'd used it to whittle, cut twigs, and clean trout when visiting his father. He had hated using it on the trout, because he loved fish—all fish—and he loved them alive and quivering in the water, not limp and heavy in his hands. His father had called him a marshmallow.

Nick snapped the blade shut and dropped the knife back in the drawer. He could not fight Daryl with a knife, even if the guy *was* so much bigger than he was. If his father knew, would he call him a marshmallow again?

He started tossing things out this way and that. Where was the red pepper spray? Where was the slingshot that had belonged to his grandfather?

Neither were to be seen.

What a mess! Nick sank back onto the bed. It looked like his own two hands, his wits, and Wags were all he had.

Then he wondered if he should wear his hearing aid. If they got into a fight, it might be damaged. But he wanted to be able to hear Daryl too. He realized then that he was actually more worried about being able to lip-read Daryl and his friends than having to fight them. There was something clean about fighting, even if things got a bit bloody. When you fought, you won or you lost. You knew what you had to do and you knew pretty quickly whether to depend on strength or on speed. It was different when you had to look at lips and figure out words. Nick knew he was a good lip-reader, but he also knew there were times when he couldn't make sense of *anything* that was being said. That's how it was when he was tired, angry, or stressed out. It could be scary.

The thought of having to read Daryl's lips made him nervous. He could just see the smug, knowing grin. It could be as sharp as any knife. In the last few weeks, he had felt it poking at him, cutting him down to nothing.

Nick dressed quickly in his favorite jeans, T-shirt, and fleece pullover. He was pulling on his socks when an idea popped into his head. He could try throwing Daryl off balance by talking.

He wouldn't even wait to see if he could read Daryl's lips—he wouldn't give Daryl a chance to speak. He, himself, would talk and talk and talk. He would tell them how he'd dodged the bird smugglers the summer before and had outwitted them. He would show them he knew something about the world, maybe more than they did. He would talk so much that Daryl and his gang would either let him alone or would tell him to shut up and leave.

Nick grinned, because he was no talker. Since he couldn't hear his own voice, his words didn't always come out right. He had therapy to help him with that. No, he didn't like talking. In fact, he had once refused to talk at all in order to get out of speech therapy. In class he hardly said anything. He would pretend to be reading or taking notes when the teacher looked as though she was about to call on him.

He was so absorbed in the idea he didn't realize his mother had opened the door and was watching him. She waved to get his attention. She was still in her nightgown, still weary-eyed. "Why are you smiling?"

Nick's face went flat. He gave a careless shrug.

"Ha!" She wagged a finger at him. "I know you. You're up to something."

Nick shrugged again and reached for a sneaker. She still knew him through and through. He didn't know if he was glad or not.

"You'd better wear boots. It's supposed to snow."

"Snow?" Nick dropped the sneaker.

"The radio says we may get several inches. Looks like we're going to have a white Christmas, and we haven't even gotten our tree yet!"

Nick twisted around and looked out the window. The sky was a heavy, thick gray. Now what? Would Daryl's plans change? Would Mrs. Firth still open the pet store?

Nick's mother punched his arm. "What's the matter with you? You usually jump ten feet in the air and dive off your desk onto your bed when you hear the first snow is coming. And you've always loved finding our Christmas tree. And you're still expecting a snowboard for Christmas, aren't you?"

Nick nodded absentmindedly. He knew she wanted things to be OK between them. But what about the snow? What should he do?

"Do you want me call Mrs. Firth for you to find out if she'll be opening the store today?"

"No!" Nick put both hands up.

"Oh, all right."

"The animals have to be fed anyway, Mum. And the cages have to be cleaned out."

"You sound like a farmer. I can drive you to work."

"No!" His hands went up again. "I'll ride my bike."

"Even if there's a blizzard?"

He wasn't in the mood to joke. "Really, Mum, you don't have to exaggerate. I'll be fine."

He saw the hurt look in her eyes again.

"Oh, OK, Mr. Wilder," she said, and left.

Blizzard? Nick looked out the window again. *Mum's just exaggerating, like usual.*

But the sky really did look dark.

chapter 4

The morning's snow began soft and slow, a tiny feather here, a bit of dandelion fluff there. Then around 9:15 it started coming down faster: like flattened popcorn being tossed out an overhead window.

Nick switched from sneakers to hiking boots, got his backpack, parka, mittens, and ski hat and went to the kitchen for the bag lunch his mother had prepared for him. He checked it to make sure she had included a couple of biscuits for Wags. She had.

"Ralph called," she said. "He told me not to come today because of the weather. So I'll be here."

Nick stuffed the bag into his backpack.

"Promise you'll stay at the store if the weather

is really wild?"

Nick nodded.

"Otherwise I'll see you around 5:00. We'll get the tree before supper. How's that?"

Nick nodded again.

She caught his arm before he could leave, pulled him close, and kissed him on the cheek. She smelled of cinnamon apple tea. "I really do love you, Nick, even though I don't know what the heck is going on with you."

Nick could see tears forming in the corners of her blue eyes. He backed away quickly and awkwardly, and he headed for the door.

The snow was beautiful. It was coming down straight now. *This doesn't look like a big deal*, Nick decided, as he put his head back and opened his mouth to catch a few thick flakes. Wags ran in circles, begging him to make snowballs for her to catch.

"There isn't enough snow yet," Nick told her.

Once on his bike, Nick headed north, rather than south into town, with Wags trotting behind. They went under the thruway, past the police station and the cemetery, and along the lake where Nick swam and snorkeled every chance he could get in the summer.

After they passed the town beach, the wind suddenly rose and the snow fell at a slant, right into Nick's eyes. He bent his head to see where he was going. Wags stayed close to the back tire, her head bent too, her tail down.

They started uphill in the direction of the road that led from Route 77 to the bluff. Only a few cars passed Nick—all had their windshield wipers and headlights on. Every few minutes, the wind would shift and the curtain of snow would flutter open, revealing a bare field or a house. Then it would whip closed again.

Nick's eyes never left the edge of the road. He knew the way to and alongside the lake by heart. He knew every driveway, mailbox, guardrail, stone wall, bridge, brook, and beach. He did not know the roadside beyond the lake in the same way—and this had him worried, because the snow was starting to make him feel a bit disoriented.

About fifteen minutes after passing the beach, Nick and Wags came to a road. Nick thought it was the road that went to the bluff, but he couldn't see where it led. The green and yellow sign for the Tower Motel was nowhere in sight, and there were no other markers of any sort. Was the road he wanted farther on?

He stood there, confused. A tall hemlock grew near the turnoff. Nick stared at it, trying to remember it. His mind drew a blank. He hadn't paid much attention to landmarks when he and his mother were in the car on this part of Route 77. There were lots of tall hemlocks. All he could remember was that the road to the motel went straight up. And this road looked as though it *did* go straight up. He decided to give it a try.

The going was so steep and bumpy Nick had to stop and dismount. Parts of the road looked like they had been washed out, and now the snow was rapidly covering up everything. It would be tricky riding a bike back down without crashing. Nick shivered as he remembered the fire engines that had tried to get up the bluff six years before.

Don't think about that at all! he warned himself.

He wiped the wet snow off his eyebrows—it was starting to freeze—and looked at his watch. It was after 10:00. Should he leave his bike there and get it later, on the way out? Where was Daryl? Was he waiting up on the bluff, or would he be arriving any minute? Nick was determined to keep the appointment. If Daryl didn't come, then he, Nick, would be able to say *he* had been there no matter what.

Nick left his bike under the hemlock, leaning against the trunk of the tree, and started up on foot. Wags lingered behind, a questioning look on her face.

"Come on, Wags!" Nick urged her on.

She followed reluctantly, as though she had doubts about the whole expedition.

The going was steep. The snow blew right into Nick's face. *I'd rather be going downhill on a snowboard,* he thought grimly. He stopped to pull his hat farther down over his ears, then went on, keeping an eye on the rocky ditch that lined one side of the road.

Up and up.

After a while, the ground began to level off a bit. Nick tried to look ahead, but he couldn't see very far. Then he realized there were fewer and fewer trees on the ditch side of the road. He stepped across the ditch, scrambled up the slope on the other side, and nearly stumbled into a stone wall.

It was what Nick's mother called a meadow wall—a wall made of stones of all sizes and shapes, dug up when the land had been cleared to make pasture. As Nick stood there, the wind died down, the snow fell straight, and in that instant he saw, to his amazement, an enormous pack of dogs—there must have been half a dozen—barely ten feet away, gathered around a lone figure.

The dogs were jumping and barking, smoky puffs coming out of their mouths, while the figure whirled and waved its arms as though doing some crazy dance. Wags's ears and tail went straight up. The fur on her neck rose in a defensive arch.

Nick knew she was alarmed. He grabbed her by the collar, put a mittened hand over her muzzle to make sure she wouldn't bark, and dropped down behind the wall.

He wasn't quick enough. One of the dogs had seen Wags and was headed straight for them. Nick's heart nearly leaped out of his throat. Ordinarily he left Wags alone with other dogs, knowing she could settle business and figure things out on her own. But this was different. There were so many of them! If they attacked her, they could kill her.

There was no escape. Nick threw both arms around Wags, leaned over her against the cold stones, covering her body with his, and buried his face in her snowy fur.

He felt them nosing at his arms and legs. He couldn't tell if they were playing, teasing, goading him on, or preparing to attack him. He didn't dare look. He felt the icy hardness of the stones underneath and Wags wiggling in his arms. The loud BOOM, BOOM, BOOM of his beating heart sounded in his chest.

And then, suddenly—nothing.

Nick knew the dogs had either left or were holding back, but still he didn't dare look up. Wags stopped struggling.

After a few more seconds, Nick took a peek out over his arm. The wind had picked up again, blowing the snow sideways. Nick peeked higher, out over the wall.

The dogs were crowded around the figure, watching Nick, and waiting. He could see their tails bouncing back and forth and their pink tongues hanging out of their mouths. A couple of them were barking. But it was clear, from the way their owner stood, that they were under orders to leave Nick and Wags alone.

Nick slowly got to his feet. Wags leaned against him. He could feel her shivering and was aware that his own legs were wobbly.

What a lot of dogs!

Nick knew people who owned two dogs, but never this many. How many bags of meal and cans of dog food a day would it take to feed them all? Suppose you wanted to go somewhere in the car with them, how would they all fit? How would *you* fit?

The owner, who was wearing a long, dark jacket and a knitted hat with a bright red and white pattern, waved and gestured for Nick to come over the wall.

Nick pointed at Wags. He wanted to be sure she would be safe. The owner nodded and gestured again.

The other dogs came to sniff at Wags after Nick pulled her over the wall. Wags stood with her tail down tight between her legs, her ears flat. Despite the snow, Nick saw that the dogs looked as though they were all of one family, with long black and white fur, bushy tails, and pointed ears and muzzles. One in particular, the one that had first spotted them, appeared to be the alpha dog, the leader. It was larger than the others and inspected Wags very carefully. It sniffed Nick as well, its tail held at a cautious angle.

"Are they all yours?" Nick shouted to the owner.

The owner cupped a hand behind one ear.

As Nick came closer to repeat his question, he recognized the long, dark jacket. It was the tweed jacket he'd seen the day before in the pet shop.

Nick let out a small gasp. It was indeed the girl who had helped him save the goldfish from the tank full of rabbit pellets. Her dark wiry hair poked out from under the red and white cap.

She evidently recognized him then, too. She didn't smile, but her expression did not seem hostile. Just reserved.

"Didn't you help me yesterday?" Nick asked.

She nodded. She seemed quite a bit taller than he was. Nick wondered how much of that was because they were standing on a slope.

"Will your dogs leave my dog alone?"

"As long as I'm with them."

"Thanks for helping with the fish," Nick said, not sure what else to say. "They could've died."

She nodded again and said something.

"Sorry." Nick pointed at one of his ears. "I'm... I'm deaf."

She came closer. She spoke slowly, clearly. "How did you know I'd be here?"

"I didn't know."

"What are you doing here?" Her eyes weren't

angry, just curious. They never left his face.

"I'm supposed to meet somebody at the Tower Motel."

She stared at him. "Who?"

It's none of your business, Nick thought. He didn't say it, though—he just shrugged.

"The Tower Motel isn't on this road," she said.

The small, quick sideways movement of her eyes and the set line of her mouth caught Nick's attention. They gave her away. She wasn't telling the truth.

She waved vaguely out to the right. "It's over there."

Why is she lying?

The girl came closer. "Did you walk here?"

"I left my bike at the bottom of the hill."

The wind blew snow into their faces. Nick put an arm up to shield his eyes.

"You don't want to go there," the girl warned when they could see each other again. "Certainly not in this weather. Go home."

Nick stepped back. She was not only bossy, she was, as his mother would say, rude.

As though regretting the harsh way she had spoken, she grabbed his arm and gestured. "Come on. I'll show you a faster way down."

They cut across the field, all the dogs but Wags bounding on ahead, the big dog in the lead. There was something wild and clean about the dogs moving together, shoulder to shoulder, all at the same speed. They were like a single breaking wave.

Nick, Wags, and the girl followed the pack into a woodsy area. The girl stopped and turned to Nick. "See the path?" She pointed on ahead.

Nick could see from the narrow clearing that there was a path. He nodded.

"You'll come to a river. Follow the river. Just be sure you're on the right side of it. It'll take you to Route 77."

"I left my bike near a hemlock at the bottom of the road. Where would that be?"

"Go left on Route 77. You'll come to it."

Nick nodded. "Thanks."

She grabbed his arm again. Nick was startled by the tightness of the squeeze she gave him. "Don't tell anyone about me. OK?"

Nick paused. "What about the dogs? Are they all yours?"

She gave a quick, fierce nod. "They're mine. Nothing about them either. OK?"

"How come?"

"Because I'm asking you." Her eyes were very steady, very direct. "If you're the kind of person who saves fish and other animals," she continued, "then don't say anything to anyone about my dogs or me."

Nick stared at her.

Her eyes didn't flinch, but her mouth tugged down a tiny bit. There was something sad in the downward pull.

"OK?"

"OK," Nick agreed.

"Promise?"

Nick nodded.

"Say it." Her mouth was no longer sad—it was insistent.

"I promise."

She smiled then for the first time. The smile was in her brown eyes too.

She peeled off a mitten and put out a hand to seal the agreement.

Nick took off his right mitten and shook her hand. Hers was warm and strong.

"Bye." The girl said, still smiling.

Then she put two fingers between her teeth. She gave a whistle that even Nick could hear through his hearing aid. The dogs, who had stopped farther down the path, immediately turned and moved back up toward their owner. When they reached her, she said something, and they all sat down at once in the snow.

Amazing! thought Nick. *How does she do it? It's almost like they're a part of her.*

"Bye," she said again and waved.

Nick knew she wanted him to leave. Was she concerned for his safety, or did she just want him to go away? He wasn't sure, but he turned and started down the small, winding path, with Wags close at his heels.

Once he looked back through the falling snow. She was still watching him.

Who is she? Nick wondered. *Why doesn't she want me to tell anyone about her? What's she doing with all those dogs?*

She waved.

Nick waved back. *Why did she lie? Why does she want me to go away?*

The girl stood there watching.

Nick frowned. He was certain the Tower Motel was farther up the road and that Daryl was waiting for him.

chapter 5

When Nick had hiked around a bend and felt sure he was out of sight, he stopped beneath a pine. Wags stayed by his side. The snow was coming down so thick and heavy, it was getting harder and harder to see. Nick knew he might have difficulty finding his way back to town if he continued his search for the Tower Motel. But he wasn't ready to go back. Daryl might make a big deal of his not showing up. He would probably say only wimps are afraid of snowstorms.

Still he hesitated. What would the girl do if they ran into her again? Nick was curious about her, but he also felt wary of her. He didn't know what to make of the closed look on her face, the way she had disappeared after helping him at the pet shop, his certainty that she had lied about the

Tower Motel being "somewhere over there," and the way she had made him promise not to tell anyone about her and the dogs. One thing was clear, though. She knew how to handle her dogs, and as long as they were around, he'd better be careful. Even though the girl had helped him save the goldfish and had told him to keep quiet if he cared about fish and other animals, he sure didn't want to find himself and Wags on the wrong side of the fence with those dogs.

If we run into her again, I'll ask her why she lied. If we don't run into her and we find Daryl.... The thought trailed off. He clapped his mittens together, suddenly determined. "Come on! Let's go!"

Wags wagged. She was as eager as he was to get moving.

"We're going to find the motel. We're going to show him!" Nick punched the air. "If we can't make it back to town, we'll hole up somewhere, just like Peter told me."

Wags wagged some more and grinned. Nick ruffled her fur quickly. She wasn't as smart looking as the black and white dogs, but she was worth the whole pack.

They climbed back to where the girl had said good-bye. She wasn't in sight. The paw prints and footprints were quickly being covered over with fresh snow.

When they reached the open hill, Nick could

barely see more than a couple of feet ahead. He shielded his eyes with his arm and peered into the whiteness as he moved. Nothing. Nobody. They inched their way along up the hill, in what Nick was sure was the direction of the stone wall. He figured if he could find the wall, the road on the other side would lead him to the motel.

The ground leveled off a bit, then rose again. The going was slow. Wags kept stopping to pull with her teeth at the balls of ice forming between her toes. Nick removed his mittens a couple of times to help her. He was beginning to worry that they were lost, when he saw a cluster of trees in the distance. He stumbled up to them and found they were about three feet from a tiny house with boarded-over windows.

Nick's heart sped up. He knew he'd found the Tower Motel and was looking at the back of one of the cabins. After years of avoiding the place, he was there. He had half expected to come upon the charred, splintered skeleton of a house, but this cabin—though it was somewhat dirty—was yellow with green trim. The gray boards nailed over the windows looked like rows of bandages.

The snow slackened briefly as Nick rounded the cabin. Then the wind hit him full blast, nearly blowing his hat off as he came out in front. He grabbed at his hat and at the porch railing. Wags huddled against his legs. An open space with snow-covered lumps on it—Nick couldn't tell if they were rocks or lawn chairs—was just barely visible. Beyond it was a gray-white void. He guessed they were now at the top of the bluff looking out over Route 77 and the hills beyond.

On Nick's left were more yellow cabins—he counted four. On his right was another cabin and, beyond that, the faint outline of a two-story building with an odd, boxy, windowed room perched on top. That must be the tower, he thought.

Nick turned left again and shivered. The cabins looked ghostly in the storm. He squinted to see if there was anything left of the one that had been destroyed by the fire.

Suddenly, hands grabbed his arms from behind. Nick instinctively pulled forward to get loose while twisting to see who was there.

"You ss..neak!" Nick yelled as he broke loose, stumbled, and landed facedown in the snow. Nick was so angry at being taken by surprise, he scrambled back onto his feet and turned, with his mittened hands clenched tight in fists.

There were four or five kids. Daryl, baseball cap on his head, had one arm raised high in the air. Nick saw the gleam of an ax in Daryl's hand. He saw that Wags had sunk her teeth into someone's jacket and wouldn't let go. Nick knew the ax was aimed at his dog.

"No! NO!" Nick screamed. "STOP!"

Wags let go and turned to look at him.

The ax paused in the air and then was slowly lowered.

Daryl looked at Nick, the grin on his rubbery lips.

"Wags!" Nick called.

The look on the dog's face said, "Are you sure?"

"Come here!" Nick slapped his leg as he called.

Wags did as she was told.

The kid—the girl from his English class—quickly backed away.

Daryl said something.

Nick couldn't see Daryl's lips well enough to get the words because of the swirling snow and because Daryl stood at a distance. He was clearly afraid of Wags.

Daryl spoke again.

Nick stared at him helplessly. His plan to out talk the older boy and his gang evaporated. How could he start talking when he didn't know what they were saying? Nick's mind was really buzzing: *What's he's saying? What's he want? What should I do?*

Daryl pointed at Wags.

Nick put a hand on his dog's collar.

Daryl nodded, and with quick motions of his head and hands, made it clear Nick was to follow, holding the dog. Nick felt he had no choice but to do as he was told. There were five of them, and Daryl might throw the ax or something if he got angry.

They waded single file through the snow, in the direction of one of the farther cabins. The wind was fierce.

Nick gritted his teeth to keep them from chattering. What was going on? He noticed that the guy in front of Daryl carried an armful of twigs and branches. *Have they been getting wood for a fire? Is that why Daryl has an ax?*

Nick stopped abruptly as six years of fears about the Tower Motel suddenly washed over him. *A fire? A fire! This isn't a nightmare, this is real! I've got to get away!*

The person behind Nick bumped into him before he could decide whether to make a dash to the left or the right. Wags barked. The fur on the nape of her neck stood up straight.

Daryl turned and advanced with the ax.

"Go!" Nick pushed at Wags.

The dog hesitated, bewilderment in her brown eyes.

"GO!" Nick kicked his foot out in her direction as Daryl stepped up, flourishing the ax.

Wags crept away. Nick watched her disappear into the falling snow, her tail between her legs, her ears flat back against her head.

Daryl straightened up. He was close enough now for Nick to see his mouth. "Freaking dogs...all over!"

"What do you want with me anyway?" The words burst out of Nick. "I haven't said anything to anybody."

Daryl grinned. "No ratting, no problem."

Then he came up close and bent over, his mouth inches from Nick's face. "You understand?"

Nick fought the urge to punch Daryl in the mouth. He couldn't belive Daryl had forced him to come all the way to the Tower Motel just to repeat his threat.

Nick didn't nod. "Is that all?" he growled.

To his surprise, Daryl widened his eyes and gave a comical shrug. Then he threw his head back and laughed. It was the same careless laugh he gave after he'd done a neat turn on his skateboard.

"So," Daryl said, "You wanna help us?"

Help them? Nick wasn't sure he'd gotten the words right. "What do you mean?"

"We've been watching you."

Nick frowned. What was Daryl getting at?

"You're smart," Daryl continued. *Real* smart. We could use you."

Nick stared at him.

Daryl winked, grabbed Nick's arm in a conspiratorial manner, as though it were just the two of them, and added, "Let's get inside before our butts freeze!"

Baffled, Nick followed.

* * *

They crowded into the cabin. Nick saw chairs, a table covered with bulging paper bags, a rusty Franklin stove, a pile of newspapers, and a couple of backpacks. The air reeked of a sharp odor Nick couldn't identify. Two doors at the back of the cabin opened into what Nick guessed were bedrooms. The light in the main room was dim because all but one of the windows were boarded up. Half of the unboarded window had layers of plastic taped over it.

That must be how they got in, Nick decided. *Broke the window and undid the latch.*

Despite the broken window, the cabin was quite warm. Embers glowed faintly in the open mouth of the stove. Daryl dug in one of the bags before pulling out a box of cocoa and tossing it onto the table in front of Nick.

Nick shook his head stiffly, still on guard.

Popcorn, chips, orange juice, milk, cereal, nuts, raw hamburger, candy, and cookies were added to the pile as Daryl emptied one bag. There was plenty to eat. *Where'd they get all this stuff? Is this a hideout or something?*

Daryl talked to the others as he moved around. Nick couldn't get the words, but he guessed Daryl was telling them what to do. They added more wood to the stove, took clean glasses from the sink, opened and closed cupboards, and stuck candles in wine bottles and placed them on the table.

Peg, the girl Wags had nipped, put a hand out for Nick's parka. She was the one who was in his English class. She always sat on the side of the classroom near the door, had shoulder-length, brown-blond hair, and wore dark-rimmed wire glasses. Nick couldn't believe she had been watching him like Daryl said. As far as Nick knew, Peg had never paid attention to him in the classroom or elsewhere.

Nick shook his head. He didn't want to take his backpack or his jacket off. Peg shrugged and rolled her eyes, as though she had offered him a $20 bill and he had been crazy enough to refuse.

Nick looked past her to the two guys. The one with the pale face, chipped front tooth, and long hair Nick couldn't remember having seen before. He stood close to Daryl, slouched a bit, his hands in his pockets. Nick recognized the other guy, who had been in the pet shop with Daryl the day before. He was short and stout, with hardly any neck. His dark eyebrows grew together, giving him an intense, almost worried, expression. Was he the guy who had been spray painting the wall of the bridge with Daryl? Nick wasn't sure.

The fifth person, the last one, was the girl from Nick's bus. She was usually on it when he boarded, so he didn't know where she lived. But he'd guessed her name was Missy because the words "Daryl & Missy" were scribbled all over her notebooks. She looked small enough to be in sixth grade, but her face was strangely old. Her thinness, the tightness of her mouth, and the black eyeliner around her unsmiling eyes made her look at least twenty.

"Sit down," said Missy, who was seated. She pointed at one of the two empty chairs. Nick looked at Daryl. The older boy grinned and nodded for him to sit down. It seemed more of an invitation than a command. By this time, Peg was seated cross-legged on the floor by the stove, One Eyebrow squatted beside Missy, and Chipped Tooth leaned against the wall.

Nick glanced around quickly before perching on the edge of the chair. Now what?

"Here's our little house," Daryl spoke, very slowly. "No dumb parents...no cattle-herding teachers...no counselors..."

The others added comments Nick couldn't follow.

Were they living there? he wondered. How could they live there? What about the motel owners?

Missy suddenly gestured at Nick to get his attention. "The door's behind you," she said.

They were all watching him.

Yes, he knew the door was right behind him. Were they telling him he could leave if he wanted to? He didn't say anything.

Daryl grinned and said something Nick couldn't get.

"Take off your pack," said Missy.

Nick wasn't going to take his backpack off. He pretended he hadn't understood her.

"Hey, Kid," Daryl said, one hand deep in another shopping bag. "Just relax."

Hey, Kid? Nick drew his breath in. *My name is Nick, not Hey Kid.*

Daryl pulled a Colt 45 from the shopping bag and held it out to Nick. Nick couldn't hide his surprise. *Beer? How'd they get beer?*

Daryl grinned. "Never had beer?"

Nick wasn't going to be pushed around because he hadn't drunk beer. He leaned forward. "How come you go around painting walls?"

Daryl leaned forward too, his grin gone. "I don't go around painting any ol' wall. I know what I'm doing. I could paint cars if I wanted to...." He yanked the tab of the beer can off and took a sip. "But I don't. I bring concrete to life!"

Nick knew he had to keep going. "What you said outside—about helping?"

"Now we're talking!" Daryl tipped the beer can at Nick. "We could use your eyes."

"My eyes?"

"We're a crew," Daryl explained with a nod at Missy and the others. "We're gonna be who we are. Forget the dumb world…"

He nodded at Missy, who drew a box of cough drops out of the pocket of her jeans and handed it to Nick.

Nick opened the box. Inside were four thin cigarettes, bunched close together.

Of course! Pot! Nick realized. *That's what I smelled when I came in.*

Nick had often seen high school kids smoking on the town green. He'd noticed the smells varied. There was a range of regular tobacco smells, and there was the other, stronger smell. It had all clicked in his head one day when he was watching a TV program about marijuana. When he'd mentioned it to his mother, she'd put her mug down so hard her tea had spilled. She had told him to stay far away from pot or he might become a feeble-minded dropout.

Nick had put both hands up. He had no interest in smoking. Smelling was almost, for him, another way of hearing. Cooking smells, animals smells, outdoor smells, human smells— they all told him things. When tobacco was around, it was hard to smell anything else.

At the same time, he was puzzled by his mother's reaction. He couldn't believe that the adults on the green, reading their newspapers or walking their baby carriages and their dogs on leashes, didn't smell it too. It was obvious, yet no one seemed to care. Nothing was done about it.

They're selling pot, Nick knew as he handed the box back to Missy. *Where do they get it?*

Daryl grinned at the others. "I bet 20 bucks Nicky's never had weed or beer. Anyone wanna bet?"

They all laughed.

The door's behind me. Nick stood up.

One Eyebrow and Chipped Tooth stood too.

"We're making bucks," Daryl continued. "We could use your eyes. Unless you'd rather have more of the same."

"More of the same?"

"At school. The pet store." Daryl paused before adding, "I know where your mom works."

Nick stared at him. *Is he saying he'll do something at the health food store?*

"I know things about you," Daryl added. He jerked his thumb at the others. "They do too."

Suddenly a gust of cold air blew in behind Nick.

Daryl, Peg, and Missy jumped up.

Nick turned.

The girl he'd met on the hillside was standing in the open doorway, a rifle in her hands!

chapter 6

Nick was pretty sure the rifle was a Marlin. His father had one that he used during the deer hunting season in Maine. During the rest of the year, it hung over the fireplace. Once, when he was younger, his father had taken it down, had shown him where the bullets went, and had put it in his hands. Though he knew it weighed only seven and a half pounds, it felt a lot heavier.

The girl spoke to Nick. "Come on." She gestured with the rifle. Daryl and his friends stood frozen, their eyes glued to the rifle.

"Who, me?" Nick asked to be sure.

She nodded even though her eyes were on the others.

Nick moved toward her.

"Out the door," she said without looking at him.

Nick went past her and out the door.

There, at the base of the porch steps, was Wags, her tail going in happy, helicopter circles. She threw herself on him as he stepped down onto the snow.

"Wa...gggs!" Nick mumbled. As he bent down, she covered his face with warm, wet kisses. How had she known where he was?

The girl's large black and white dog, the leader, was there too, standing stiffly to the side and looking a bit like a police officer while the snow swirled all around.

The girl came out, the rifle in one hand. She gave Nick a dark look. "I told you to go home."

Nick rolled his eyes. "You don't understand!"

"I don't?" she challenged him.

Nick rolled his eyes again, too tired and confused to argue.

"Come on," she snapped. "Follow me!"

They waded through the shifting snowdrifts. Wags stuck so close to Nick's legs that he almost tripped over her. This was no joke, he realized, as he struggled to keep up with the girl. *This* is *a blizzard!* He wondered what his mother was doing and if she had been in touch with Mrs. Firth and was worrying about him. What would she do if she learned he wasn't at the pet shop? Would she contact Peter, the police, both?

This is weird! Nick thought, as he followed the girl up the steps of the main building—the building on which the tower was built. *Here's Daryl with a bunch of kids in one house, and here's this girl with a bunch of dogs in another. She doesn't seem to like Daryl, certainly not if she's got a gun! What in the world is going on?*

Wags shrank back a bit when the girl pushed open the door, and the other dogs bore down on them in a wave of black and white fur, feathery tails, and bobbing black eyes and noses.

Then, as suddenly as the dogs had rushed forward, they drew back and sat down. The girl had put the rifle down. Her mouth was puckered, and one hand hovered in the air. Nick realized again, with amazement, that they were responding to her commands.

"How'd you do that?" he asked.

She turned briefly so he could see her lips. "Work."

All the dogs lay down at once.

"Amazing!" Nick whispered.

"We work every day, sometimes a couple of hours a day."

"For what?"

"They're sheepherding dogs," the girl explained as she kicked off her boots. "You know anything about sheepdogs?"

"Yeah!" Nick remembered the story Peter had done in the fall about a sheepherding contest in western Connecticut. His mother had gone along to watch. Nick had wanted to go, but Mrs. Firth had been counting on his help at the store. "A friend told me about them. How they know where to go by a single whistle."

"They're the best!" The girl's face softened as she looked at her dogs.

"How many are there?"

"Seven."

"Gosh! And you trained them all?"

"All but Fergus." She nodded at the one that had accompanied them back to the house. "He's their father."

Nick looked around. *Where are* her *parents?*

She sensed his curiosity. Without looking him in the eye, she gave a casual upward nod. "My grandmother lives here. She's busy now."

Nick said nothing. Again he had the feeling she was hiding something.

"So," she challenged him, "why didn't you go home like I told you?"

Nick flushed. "You...you make it sound like I'm dumb or something!"

"Anybody who gets involved with him is dumb," she shot back. She'd pulled off her hat. Nick thought he could almost hear her wiry brown hair crackling.

"You mean Daryl Smythe?"

"Who else? Thinks he's such a big shot. He's nothing but a bully trying to push people around. Messes with drugs. Hasn't got the sense of a dog—like yours."

Wags wagged as the girl looked in her direction.

Nick felt a pang of envy. *Wags likes her. She sure knows dogs! How does she do it?*

"You might as well take off your coat." The girl said. "You're not going to be able to get home now."

Nick knew she was right, but he had to challenge her. "I'm not?"

She shrugged. "You can try if you want to. I'm not going to rescue you again."

Avoiding her eyes, he lowered his backpack to the floor and looked around as he unzipped his parka. They were standing in a kitchen with three large windows covered by checkered green and white curtains, a round wooden table, a sofa against one wall, a high ceiling with a fan, and walls covered with maps and dozens of photographs. The photos were nearly all of dogs and people with dogs. *I've landed in dog-land, that's for sure!* Nick thought as he made his way around the sheepdogs to take a look at one of the maps.

It was a map of Great Britain, covered with dozens of little green marker circles. Nick turned to the girl for an explanation.

"Sheep farms."

"Sheep farms?" said Nick. "Wow! There's a lot of them. Have you been over there?"

She shrugged. "What's your name, anyway?"

Nick paused. She really made him feel dumb. Then he realized she was always changing the topic, steering it away from herself.

"Nick. Nicholas Wilder. What about you?"

"Ionie."

"What?" Nick wasn't sure he'd read her lips right.

"I-*oh*-nee." The last syllable looked to Nick like the word "knee."

"Never heard a name like that."

"I wouldn't think so. It's an unusual name. Actually my real name is Iona, for the island of Iona."

"Where's that?"

She ran a hand impatiently over her hair. "You don't know a thing!" Then she pointed at the map. "Right here, off the coast of Scotland."

Nick squinted. All he could see was a tiny speck of land with a green circle on it. "Um..." He didn't know what to say. He'd never met anyone before who had been named after an island.

Her mouth and eyes became solemn. She stood up a little straighter. "It's a *very* special place."

Then she walked over to the stove, her back to him, and began fussing with the switches. Nick was pretty sure, from the way his mother sometimes behaved when she was preoccupied, that she didn't want him to see her face.

"Have you got a last name?" he ventured. "Or is your last name Island?"

Her shoulders and thick hair shook.

Nick punched the palm of his left hand. *You fool! That was a dumb thing to say!*

When Ionie turned, he saw she was laughing. "Ionie Island? That's a good one! I like that!"

Nick's face got warm.

"My last name is Hunter," she continued. "Iona Margaret-Ann Hunter for full. You want some hot milk tea?"

Hunter, Nick thought. *The people who owned the motel and knew the man who died in the fire.*

Ionie put her hands on her hips. "Did you hear me?"

Nick nodded. "Sure." Hot milk tea sounded funny, but the mention of food made him realize he was famished. He waded back across the room, around the dogs, picked up his backpack, and unzipped it. Immediately the dogs' ears perked up, and seven pairs of eyes became riveted to the paper bag as he pulled it out.

"Mind if I give Wags her biscuits?"

Ionie shook her head.

Nick took two biscuits from the bag. The sheepdogs' noses twitched. Their eyes were bright and expectant, their tongues hanging out of their mouths. They looked close to drooling.

Nick had never known Wags—who was now wagging hopefully—not to be interested when there was the possibility that she might get something to eat. It was the same with the dogs at the

80

pet store. They would yap and wag and push eagerly against their cages. He knew every one of the sheepdogs wanted the biscuits, but they were holding back. Or were they being held back? He glanced at Ionie.

She was standing by the oven, waiting for the kettle to boil while watching her dogs. There was a stern look on her face. Nick wondered what she was telling them.

Ionie nodded for Nick to give Wags the biscuits. But he didn't. It didn't seem fair. He put them back in the bag. "You going to feed yours soon?"

"Fed them this morning," she replied. Her face was tight again. Closed.

"How *do* you feed them all, anyway? Do they all have their own bowls? And what are their names?"

"They share bowls. Three big bowls."

"Don't they fight over the food?"

"Not when I'm around. Fergus eats alone, though."

"Where do you work them?

Ionie frowned. "You sure ask a lot of questions."

Nick felt his face getting warm again. He couldn't see what was offensive about his question. Hadn't she said she worked them every day? "I thought you said something about working with them. Did I hear you right?"

She nodded. "I work them."

"In here?"

"Oh sure. On top of the table."

Her mouth stayed straight, but her eyes were laughing. Nick knew she was kidding. "Seven dogs on top of the table," he said. "Do they wash the dishes too?"

Ionie's mouth broke into a grin. "Right. They wash the dishes, sweep the floor...everything. That's how well they're trained."

Nick grinned back.

Wags nudged Nick with her nose, asking for the biscuits. "How'd you find my dog?" he asked.

"She found *me*," said Ionie. "I was upstairs, and the whole pack got hyper. I figured it was the storm. Sometimes they get hyper when the weather is bad, like they're responsible for all the lost sheep in the world. I told them to lie down, and they lay down and whined. If your dog barked, I didn't hear her because of their whining. And because of the wind. Can you hear the wind?"

Nick shook his head.

"It must be hard not being able to hear."

Nick shrugged. "You find other ways of hearing, like with your eyes."

She gave a thoughtful nod. "I think I know what you mean. Most of the time, I hear my dogs with my eyes. Fergus especially. He's the one who told me your dog was there."

"How'd he do that?"

"He kept looking at me, trying to catch my eye, then he went downstairs."

"Wow! So you went to the door and there she was?"

Ionie nodded. "I brought her in and offered her water, but she wasn't interested. She went back to the door. I heard that! I heard how she was worrying about you. I figured you'd gotten lost on your way back to Route 77."

"Gosh! I'm sorry. Did you go all the way down there looking for me?"

"No, she wouldn't let me. She went in the other direction, toward the cabins. I figured out where you were and got the rifle."

Nick was going to ask if she'd ever barged in on Daryl before with a gun in her hands, but what she'd said about him asking a lot of questions kept him quiet. He looked at his watch. It was after 3:00. It would be getting dark soon, and the snow was still coming down. What was going to happen with Daryl? More importantly, what was going to happen with him? Should he try to contact his mother?

Ionie carried a large teapot to the table. "Sit down," she said when she'd finished pouring two cups of dark tea.

Sure is bossy, Nick thought as he sat down. *What would Mum think of her?*

Ionie stirred a spoonful of white stuff into her tea and pushed a big jar over to Nick. It was powdered milk.

Nick hated the stuff. He'd used it when he was camping—the milk always came out looking weak and watery. He shook his head and took his sandwich out of the paper bag. As he bit into it, he realized Ionie was watching him.

"Want this?" He gestured at the other half of the sandwich.

Ionie shook her head and sipped her tea.

"It's cheese and tomato. The cheese comes from the health food store. My mother made the bread. She makes all our bread."

She shook her head yet again and looked away, out the window.

She's almost acting as if she's afraid to look at my sandwich, Nick thought.

"I've got nuts and raisins," he added. "And two tangerines."

"So..." Ionie turned her face back to him. "Why'd you come up here?" Her expression was cool, almost cold. It was hard to believe she'd been smiling a few minutes earlier.

Nick paused. She was definitely changing the topic. He took a deep breath and then shoved the paper bag across the table. "Have some. Have all you want!"

Ionie caught the bag. Her face was startled.

"Go ahead," said Nick. "Don't lie. You're hungry, aren't you?"

For one long second they stared at each other.

The color had drained out of Ionie's face. She looked scared.

"I'm *not* a liar," she finally said.

"I...I don't know," said Nick. "But you look hungry and your dogs look pretty hungry too. Have you got enough food for them?"

She stared at him some more, her face blank.

"There's lots of food in that cabin where Daryl Smythe is," Nick continued. "I saw bags and bags of food on the table. Can't you get some from them?"

To his surprise and dismay, Ionie put her head down on her arms and began to cry.

chapter 7

"I've shot seven squirrels, three rabbits, and a couple of crows for the dogs to eat," Ionie said. Her face was puffy and her eyes were red, but she was no longer crying. "Dad left two rifles—a 35-caliber and a 22-caliber. I almost shot a deer." She put the tips of her fingers on her forehead as though trying to hold back a bad memory. "But I couldn't. I just couldn't."

They were still at the kitchen table. Ionie had eaten both tangerines and the nuts and raisins Nick's mother had put in his lunch bag. She wouldn't touch the other half of his sandwich, not even when he offered her half of the half.

Nick stole a look at the gun leaning against the wall. Though he'd never liked like the idea of hunting, he was impressed. She must be a pretty good shot.

"What about your grandmother?" he asked.

Ionie looked away. She didn't speak until her eyes finally came back to his. "She's in Scotland with my dad."

"Oh," Nick said. He saw some uncertainty in her face. So she was alone with all the dogs. What was going on?

Ionie fingered her teacup. Nick changed his position again. He had been leaning over the table to see her lips better, but now he sat back against the chair. He had felt like leaving when Ionie started crying but hadn't, partly because of the dogs. All seven of them were watching him. And Fergus not only watched, he sat beside Ionie, leaning against her, his muzzle nearly resting on the tabletop.

Nick didn't think the dogs would attack him, but they still frightened him a little. It wasn't just that there were so many of them, it was their stillness. There was a power to their stillness. They behaved like they understood everything Nick was saying and were waiting to see what he would do. Fergus especially.

Ionie nodded her head to catch his attention. "I'm *not* a liar. I know you think I'm strange."

"I didn't say you're strange!" Nick protested.

"Your face says it!" She was sounding bossy again. "You said you hear with your eyes. Well, I do too."

87

Nick flushed in his confusion. "Well...." He threw up both hands and shrugged. "I don't know how many people in the world own this many sheepdogs and shoot squirrels to feed them. I don't know why you have to shoot squirrels anyway, or why you're hungry when there's so much food in that cabin Daryl's in. Or why your father and grandmother are in Scotland, or why I'm not supposed to tell anyone about you."

Ionie sipped her tea. He could see she was thinking hard.

"I'm glad you remember the promise," she said. "Because now you're really bound to it."

"Fine!" Nick put his hand down hard on the tabletop the way his mother did when she wanted to get his attention. He wanted her to talk straight and simple. To tell him why she was there and what was going on rather than changing the topic, looking friendly one minute and hostile the next. It was tiring to have to listen to her in so many different ways.

Ionie smoothed her hair a bit. "I've been living here with the dogs since Thanksgiving."

"All by yourself?"

She nodded.

How come? Nick wondered. He was afraid to ask. Another question came out instead. "What about school?"

"I'm not going right now."

"I thought all kids have to go to school till

they're sixteen."

"I am sixteen. I got my driver's license in July. Nobody knows I'm here except Daryl and his friends."

Nick scratched his head. "I don't get it. What's going on?"

"My father took my grandmother to Scotland," Ionie explained.

Nick waited.

"Gammy hasn't been well. She wanted to go back to see her sisters, my great aunts. My father came up from Virginia—that's where our farm is—to take Gammy to Scotland."

"I don't see why you're here if you have a place in Virginia."

"OK. OK." Ionie leaned toward him. "I'll tell you why. It's because of the dogs. They're among the best sheepdogs in the world. They've won awards all over. Even the Queen of England knows about them. We breed them, raise them, train them, sell them. We have buyers as far away as New Zealand. Five of these are already spoken for."

"Spoken for?" Nick asked, not sure he'd read her lips right.

"We've got deposits on five in this batch." Ionie looked at the dogs and ran five strange-looking names off on her fingers. The dogs' heads went up in response, but they didn't move.

"One of them will be going to Australia in

January when the training is over, three out west, one to Kentucky."

"Do you put them in crates and ship them?"

Ionie shook her head hard. "Oh no! The buyers come and get them. Or they send someone to get them." She gave Nick a fierce look. "People want them. They want them so bad they'll steal them if they can. That's why Dad left us, here where nobody knows about them."

Wow! Nick thought to himself. *What would Mum say? What would Mrs. Firth say? Peter would flip if he knew about this.*

Ionie sat back, her face flushed. Nick noticed how her hand now rested on Fergus's shoulder. It was the first time he had seen her pet one of the dogs. Up until then, he had only seen her giving commands.

"Two dogs have been stolen," Ionie added. "One was taken last July. Then Star—she's the mother of most of them—was stolen in September."

"How?"

"It happened one morning when Dad was out working them in the field. I was in school. When Dad came in at lunchtime, Star was gone."

"Someone just came and took her?"

"Someone just came and took her," Ionie said grimly.

"She didn't wander off?"

"Star never wandered off."

"Do you know who took her?"

"Dad's pretty sure it was a man who used to work for him. His name was Telio, and he got weird. He drank a lot. He got violent. That's why Dad fired him. Telio knew Star and the other dogs, and they knew him. He knew how Dad worked, when he'd be out of the house, how to forge the dog papers, things like that."

"Why would he want to steal her?" Nick asked.

Ionie gave a snort. "To breed her or sell her, for goodness sakes! What else? People don't get our dogs for pets! They get them to work."

"Oh." This time Nick felt silly.

"After Star disappeared, Dad said he wasn't going to leave me home with the dogs, even if friends came to stay with us. That's why we're here. Dad left food, wood, a full oil tank. I've got our car, but it's almost out of gas. Dad said they'd only be gone ten days."

"And?"

"Gammy had a stroke."

Nick was afraid she was going to cry again. "So when's your father coming back?" he asked quickly.

She shrugged. "He called the day before yesterday. He said Gammy wouldn't be coming back, because she can't talk or eat or anything. He said he'd try to be back before Christmas, but I knew when he was talking how much he wanted to stay with Gammy. So I told him we were doing fine."

Nick's eyebrows went up. "You didn't tell him you were out of food?"

Ionie shook her head. "He has enough to worry about. And look...I *know* Daryl has food, but I can't go there. A couple of them are always there, and even if I have a gun..." Her words trailed off before she added, "Daryl hasn't got any right to the cabin."

She's really on her own, Nick thought. "What about money?" he asked. "Haven't you got any?"

Ionie shook her head again. "That's the dumb part. I had $350 Dad gave me. But someone came in when I was working the dogs and took my fanny pack. I should have known better than to put it all in one place."

"You didn't tell your father about that either?"

"No!" Her eyes were angry. "I told you, he has enough to worry about. That was *my* stupid mistake."

"You think Daryl took your money?"

She nodded. "I went to the cabin with the dogs and a gun and asked them if they had my pack. They acted like they didn't know what I was talking about. I don't think Daryl knows what the dogs are all about, but he figured we were hiding. He said he'd tell on me if I told on him. So that's why we're both here, minding our own business. You know about the pot?"

"I found out today," said Nick. "Where does he get it?"

Ionie shrugged. "I don't want to know. I don't want anything to do with him. I can't wait for Dad to come back and chase him out." She regarded him for a minute, "You still haven't told me what *you're* doing here."

Nick's story seemed tame compared to hers, but he told her anyway. When he came to the part about the rabbit pellets in the fish tank, Ionie gave a grim nod. "I'm sure Daryl's gang did it. When I saw him there, I left." She sighed and added, "Now that you know about the pot and Daryl and about me, what are you going to do?"

Tired from all the lip-reading, Nick stood and stretched. It was getting dark, and the light in the kitchen wasn't very good. Wags popped up and began wagging expectantly. He thought of all the bags of dog meal in the pet shop and all the jars of nuts, dried fruits, rice, and granola in the health food store. He felt pretty sure his mother and Mrs. Firth would want to help Ionie. "I'll get food for you and the dogs," he said.

"I told you I have no money. When I was at the pet shop the other day, I was trying to figure out a way I could charge the food to my dad. Then Daryl came in, so I left."

He scratched his head. There was plenty of food in both stores. "I'll find a way," he told her.

"How?"

"If you can drive me to town, I'll get it."

She thought awhile, her eyes on the dogs,

before nodding. "The dogs really need the right food, and I know Dad will pay for it when he gets back and hears what happened. The van's in Gammy's barn on Route 77. I hid it there because the road up is pretty bumpy and because I didn't want Daryl messing with it. Let's go when the storm stops."

She went to the window and looked out, Fergus at her side. Nick felt for the pet store key in his pocket to make sure it was there. It was. He wasn't sure how he'd get into the health food store. His mouth suddenly felt awfully dry. *What am I getting myself into?* he wondered.

* * *

It was still snowing an hour later. Ionie was on her knees on the kitchen floor, brushing the dogs in long, slow strokes, from the tops of their heads to the tips of their tails. Not knowing what to do with himself, Nick kept looking out the window, then examining the photos and maps on the wall, then turning to Ionie to see if she wanted to talk.

"How come you keep looking at me?" she demanded the fourth or fifth time he glanced her way. "You're making me nervous."

Nick shrugged.

"What are you thinking?"

"My mother's probably worrying," Nick replied.

"What about your mother? Where's she? Can't she help you?"

Ionie paused, the brush in the air. "My mother died when I was seven."

"Oh," Nick croaked.

Ionie didn't blink. She put the brush down. "She had cancer—first breast cancer, then cancer of the spine. I remember being glad when it was over. She was sick a long, long time. It was like forever. I know this sounds awful but, afterward, I felt life could finally move on."

"Oh," Nick croaked again. "Don't you miss her?"

"Of course!" Ionie snapped, her eyes angry again. "After she died, I kept dreaming of her. Dreaming she was well and could walk around and talk with me. She couldn't talk during the last two months, but in the dreams, we talked like...like you and I are talking right now."

She sighed before adding, "When I was eleven, the dreams stopped. That's when I realized she was gone. That's when I began missing her. And now Gammy can't talk...and...and I don't know if I'll ever see her again."

Things were getting thick. Nick turned to the window.

Ionie tapped at his arm after a few minutes. Her eyes were dry. Her face was closed. "You were talking about your mother. Why don't you call her, or can't you talk on the phone?"

Nick explained about the TTY and how his mother thought he was at the pet shop.

"Hmm..." Ionie was thinking. "I can call her for you, but wouldn't she want to know who I am and where you are?"

Nick scratched his head. Then he remembered something. "I know! She'll think we're at the pet shop, so you won't have to say where we are. If she asks who you are, tell her Mrs. Firth hired you to help during the Christmas rush. I told Mrs. Firth yesterday how you helped with the fish. She was thinking about hiring you if you came by again."

"Really?" Ionie smiled.

Nick nodded.

Ionie looked pleased. "I'd love to work in a pet store."

"It's great! If your father doesn't come back soon, maybe you could work for her, and she'd give you the dog food."

Ionie shook her head. "If I worked there, she'd want to know where I live and all that. Then she'd find out about the dogs. I wouldn't be doing my real job if that happened."

"I bet she knows your grandmother. She knows everyone in town."

Ionie gave a quick shake of her head. "No. I promised Dad I'd take care of the dogs and wouldn't let anyone know about them. You're the only person who knows. The dogs are Dad's life. I have to be with them. Besides, he could come back *any* time...like tomorrow. And we'd have to go home."

Minutes later, after she'd dialed Nick's number, Ionie put her hand over the phone and told him, "There's no answer at your house. Shall I leave a message on the answering machine?"

Nick stared at her. "Are you sure there's no answer?"

Ionie nodded. "I can try again in a couple of minutes, if you want."

"Yeah. Let's do that."

There was no answer the second time either.

"Leave a message on the answering machine," Nick decided. "Say I'm OK. Say I'll be home as soon as the storm stops."

He went back to the window and peered out again, anxious. *Where's Mum? She wouldn't have gone to get a Christmas tree without me, not in this snow. Where could she be? Is she looking for me?* And then, *Is she OK?*

chapter 8

"I think about Peter all the time," Nick's mother said. She was wearing her purple Icelandic sweater, the one she'd knitted herself the year she and Nick had driven to Prince Edward Island. Her blond hair was drawn back into a ponytail. The familiar turquoise studs shone like little round blue pools in her ears. Her gray-blue eyes were sad. Nick wanted to reach out to hug her, but somebody was pulling at his arm.

His eyes fluttered open. A yellow light was shining in his eyes. Somebody really *was* pulling at his arm.

A strange face was near his—he couldn't see it clearly at first because of the brightness in the background. Then he saw the eyes were dark, much darker than his mother's. There was an urgency in them.

The mouth below the eyes moved. "We've got to go!"

Nick blinked. Wags's wet, warm tongue passed over Nick's chin, telling him he wasn't dreaming.

The girl, Nick remembered. *Ionie Island.*

Wags stepped onto his chest and sat down, wagging all the while. Nick pushed her aside as he struggled to sit up. His head weighed a ton, his stomach felt hollow, and there was a bitter, acid taste in his mouth.

He was on the floor of the kitchen in the main house of the Tower Motel, surrounded by the lumpy forms of sleeping dogs. He and Ionie had dragged a mattress down from one of the bedrooms after Ionie had tried reaching his mother on the phone. The upstairs rooms were freezing cold because Ionie had turned the heat down and closed the doors. To conserve the fuel oil, she had been living only in the kitchen with the sheepdogs.

Ionie spoke, but Nick couldn't get what she said. "What?" he asked, as he fumbled to turn on his hearing aid.

"It stopped snowing."

"What time is it?"

"Quarter to five."

Nick groaned. Despite all the tea they had drunk while playing cards the night before, he had gone out like a light the minute his head hit the mattress.

Mum would say I'm on overload, Nick thought. His mother used the term when he looked as though more things were coming at him than he could understand. Only it wasn't, just now, a matter of being able to understand through his hearing aid or through lip-reading, it was a matter of being able to understand what in the heck was going on and what he should do.

How could he explain the missing dog food to Mrs. Firth if Ionie didn't want anyone to know about her dogs? What about food for Ionie? What about Daryl? Nick was pretty sure Daryl was going to be nasty again, especially now that he knew about the beer and the pot. And Nick's biggest question of all: What about his mother? Where was she?

Nick wanted to ask Ionie to try calling his home again, but he didn't. If they did reach his mother, there would be a thousand questions. If they didn't reach her, well, he wasn't ready to think about that.

"Tea?" Ionie asked.

Nick shook his head. "How about orange juice?"

"Oh sure!" she snapped. "I'll get you some eggs and bacon, too." She clearly wasn't in a joking mood.

I have about a gallon of tea to get rid of, Nick

thought as he stumbled out to the bathroom.

Back in the kitchen, he found the dogs up, facing the door, all ready to go.

"They're coming with us?"

Ionie nodded.

"All of them?"

She looked angry, as if he had asked yet another dumb question. "I'm not leaving them here."

Nick gritted his teeth as he pulled his boots on. Ionie had beaten him flat at cards the night before. She had played as though she were playing only to keep him amused. *Who does she think she is? Do I really want to go through this trouble for her?*

It was fiercely cold outside. A thin sliver of moon hung low and bright in the sky. Nick could just barely see the smooth swells of new fallen snow. It was dry snow, at least two and a half feet deep.

Nick glanced anxiously at the cabins, but there was no sign of life in any of them. Ionie brought two pairs of snowshoes out. She'd told him in the house that he would have to use her grandmother's pair, even though they looked old enough to be in a museum. She helped Nick strap them to his boots. Although he couldn't see the dogs clearly, he was aware they were diving and leaping in and out of the snow all around like a pod of seals. When Ionie had finished with the snowshoe straps, she held her small flashlight close to her mouth so he could read her lips. "Follow me."

Nick nodded.

"Go slow," she advised. "Feel your way, so you don't fall off the bluff or walk into a tree."

I wouldn't be that stupid, Nick thought.

He took two steps and nearly toppled over. The snowshoes were like enormous, oversized flippers. *What's snowboarding going to be like?* he wondered.

He tried again, taking smaller steps, shuffling a bit. This time he was concentrating so hard on moving the right way, he walked into a hedge.

Nick backed out. He didn't like being slow and clumsy. He peered around. Had Ionie had gone on without him? Darkness made him really deaf. *How can I follow her if I can't hear or see her?*

No sooner had he wondered about that than she stepped up beside him. She switched the small beam on. "You'd better take this," she said, handing him the flashlight.

Soon they were on their way again. Ionie, who was clearly at home on snowshoes, started down what Nick decided was the road. He could just barely see the shadowy movements of the sheepdogs following Ionie. The dogs crunched through the snow, making a trail for Nick and Wags. To their right was an open area that stretched out over the valley. Nick couldn't see any more than black shadows and white fields. On the left he faintly saw a row of tall old oaks and a few snow-clad evergreens.

As the night silence settled on Nick, he grew warmer. It was great to be outside! The snow, the stars, and the moon all reminded him of Christmas. For a minute, he wanted to whistle. He could almost smell the Christmas tree and his mother's roast Cornish hens, wild rice, orange-cranberry sauce, and apple-pecan pie. His mouth began to water at the thought of all the food.

Down and down they went. Nick hopped and ran to keep up with Ionie, but she was always eight or more feet ahead of him. Then, by chance, he discovered if he sat back on the snowshoes, he could slide downhill. It wasn't a fast slide, but it was easier and more comfortable than walking. When he realized Wags was struggling to keep up with him, he stopped, gathered her in his arms, and pushed off again.

It took them over thirty minutes to reach Route 77. Nick saw a huge pile of snow in front of him that had been created by the snowplow, then realized where they were. He could just barely see the hemlock where he had left his bike. Should he get it? Ionie shook her head when he asked her and gestured for him to unfasten the snowshoes, climb over the drift, and follow her north. The snow on the road was lightly packed and crunchy. The dogs moved behind Ionie like a dark, fluid pool of ink.

Another ten or fifteen minutes brought them to a wooden building quite close to the road. Nick watched Ionie fiddle with something on the door—he realized she was opening a lock—then she used one of her snowshoes to push the snow away.

There was a minivan inside. All of the dogs, including Wags, disappeared readily into it while Ionie found a pair of shovels.

Nick helped her clear a wide path to the road. Fergus was in the front passenger seat of the automobile when Nick opened the door to climb in. Nick couldn't see Ionie's face well enough as she addressed the dog to know what she said, but Fergus reluctantly surrendered his space to Nick. Minutes later the headlights went on, cold air blew up from the dashboard, and they shot forward out of the barn, skidding this way and that.

Whew! thought Nick as they eased onto the road. *It would take a tow truck to get this elephant out of a drift!*

Ionie drove carefully, hunched over the big steering wheel, one hand on the stick shift. *She knows what she's doing,* Nick thought, impressed. *When I'm sixteen I'm going to drive a standard transmission.*

He wanted to ask Ionie if this was the first time she had driven in snow, but he kept quiet. He could hardly see her face, and he didn't want to distract her.

Though the road had been plowed, it was still slippery. They drove slowly along the lake, past the public beach and other familiar—but now not entirely familiar—spots. They were rounding a curve when Ionie stepped on the brakes so suddenly that two dogs tumbled right over the seat top onto Nick. The car spun around 180 degrees before it came to a halt.

A snowplow was stopped on the side of the road up ahead. Once Ionie turned the car back around, its bright headlights shone straight at them while an orange warning light on top of its cab flashed in circles. A man standing in the road turned to look at them before waving for them to pass.

"Looks like someone got ditched," Nick said as Ionie inched her way forward.

The rear end of a car could just barely be seen on the right side of the road. As they went past it and the man who was waving them by, Nick saw first a bald head, then two dark, frowning, peering eyes. Then Nick felt their car roaring and skidding as Ionie suddenly pressed down on the accelerator.

"Whoa!" Nick yelled as the car lurched this way and that, dog fur flat against his face, obscuring his view. Ionie paid no attention. She was in a fearful hurry. All Nick could do was hug both dogs to his chest with one hand, while clutching at the seat with the other.

On they went without a stop, skidding left and right but without further mishap, all the way into town, into the half-plowed parking lot, right in front of the darkened windows of the pet store.

The dogs returned to the back seat as Ionie switched on the interior light. Her eyes looked frozen. "It's him!" she cried.

"Who?"

"Telio! The man I was telling you about—the man who stole our dogs. That was his car by the side of the road. I saw the Virginia license plate. I saw him."

"The bald man looking at us?"

Ionie gave a grim nod.

Nick stared back. "How?"

"I don't know!" Ionie cut him short. "I can't go back to Gammy's. He knows where the motel is. He came up once with Dad."

Nick tasted acid in his mouth again.

Ionie grabbed his mittened hand to get his attention. "Do you know a place where the dogs and I can stay?"

She was awfully strong! Nick pulled his hand out of her grasp. "Can't you ask the police for help?"

Ionie rolled her eyes. "Of course not! Not without Dad. They might take the dogs away. They might take the van away. What if they put me in a foster home or something? My license was taken when the money was taken, so I can't prove I'm sixteen. I can't prove anything. You've got to help me!"

Nick turned from her. *What have I gotten myself into?* he wondered again. *If I'd stayed home I would never have gotten into this mess.*

Ionie grabbed his hand again. "You're the only person I know here! Do you have a garage at your house where we can hide till Dad comes back?"

"No, not without my mother finding out."

She squeezed his hand. She was really desperate. *"Please*, Nick, think of something...someplace!"

Nick looked at her helplessly. "What if your father comes back and you're not at the motel?"

"My father would look for me. He wouldn't stop until he'd found me." She regarded him for a moment before putting both hands high on the steering wheel. "I see you don't want to get mixed up with me and the dogs. You'd better get out so I can get going."

Nick drew back against the front passenger door. She had not called him any names the way Daryl did, yet her words right then had almost the same effect. "Where will you go?" he asked.

Ionie shrugged. "I'll find a way. I've managed this far."

She turned abruptly away from him and glanced out the rearview mirror, as if expecting the car with the Virginia license plates to pull up beside them.

Nick saw her wiry hair, her razor nose, and the set line of her lips. He knew he could get out right there and leave her. That way he wouldn't have to have to worry about taking food from Mrs. Firth or the health food store. But that didn't feel right. Not just because he had said he would get the food or because she was in a fix, but because, even if Ionie was awfully bossy, he had to admit he liked her. She was unlike anybody he'd ever met.

"I think maybe I do know a place where you and the dogs can hide," he said, remembering Esmeralda's dog grooming salon in the basement of the pet shop. Esmeralda wouldn't be back till mid April, and Mrs. Firth hardly ever went down there.

Ionie looked at him. Her lips didn't move, but her face asked, "Are you sure?"

Nick peeled a mitten off and felt in his pocket for the store key. He took it out. "Drive around to the back."

They circled the customer parking lot, and Nick got out to look. The plow had created a mountain of snow by the Dumpsters. Nick was just able to see through the small space between the Dumpsters, the pile of snow, and the edge of the building that the back lot had not yet been plowed.

"If you can get back there," Nick said, as he got back in the van, "there's a place where you can hide."

"Easy," said Ionie.

Before Nick could say anything more, she put the car in gear and pressed the accelerator. They shot past the Dumpsters and the edge of the building, skidding a bit as they went, and seconds later, pulled up before the back entrance to the pet store.

chapter 9

Ionie was afraid her dogs would get sick if they ate too much dog meal all at once, so she measured out the food from the twenty-five-pound bag Nick gave her very, very carefully.

Despite their good manners, the dogs pushed the plastic buckets from wall to wall, knocked them over several times, and pulled up bits of Esmeralda's pale blue rug, trying to get pellets that spilled between the fibers. They were certainly hungry!

Nick shut his eyes tight. What was this place going to look like when Esmeralda came back in the spring?

Ionie grabbed his arm and squeezed it. Her cheeks were red. "Nick, you sure came just in the nick of time!"

He didn't smile.

Noticing his glum expression, Ionie squeezed his arm again. "My father will pay for *everything* when he comes back," she promised.

When's that going to be? Easter? Nick turned to go upstairs to check the pets and find out when Mrs. Firth had last been there.

Again Ionie grabbed his arm. "He will! We Scots keep our word!"

Nick was too tired to say anything.

"I'm sorry I got you into this, really, I am," Ionie continued. Her brown eyes were dead serious. "Wouldn't you rather be mixed up with me and the dogs than with Daryl and his gang?"

Nick shrugged. Just because he was mixed up with her and the dogs didn't, as far as he could see, mean he was all through with Daryl.

"Daryl won't bother you again."

"How do you know?" Nick demanded. "You don't live here. You don't go to my school."

Ionie took hold of the front of his jacket. "You've got two things working for you, Nick. First, you know stuff about Daryl that he doesn't want people to know. Second, he can't drive you all over."

She let go of him and turned back to her dogs.

Can't drive me all over? What does she mean? Nick wondered as he went upstairs.

A message written in red marker on a large sheet of paper was taped to the front door:

NICK WILDER:
IF YOU COME IN, BE SURE
TO READ THIS!

Where have you been? We're all worried. I called your mother to tell you not to come because of the storm. She said you'd already left. I waited two hours and called her back to tell her you never got here. If you come in, please call home *immediately*, even if you don't have your special machine. Say you're here so we'll know.

Mrs. Firth
2 p.m., Dec. 22

It was almost 7:00 in the morning. Nick couldn't think right then what to do about the note. He went from cage to cage, pen to pen, and tank to tank checking on the animals and cleaning things up. The puppies wiggled, squirmed, and tumbled all over each other in an effort to reach and lick his fingers. The ferrets and rabbits paid no attention to him. The fish darted, circled, and floated about as always in their watery worlds. All, including the special goldfish in the big tank, seemed content and well fed. It looked as though Mrs. Firth had doubled, and in some instances tripled, the food rations in case she couldn't get in to feed them. Then, since the cockatiels appeared to be irritated by the lights going on so early, Nick flicked them off again and headed for Mrs. Firth's tiny office. He knew his boss loved black tea—she drank half a dozen mugs of it a day—and had a plug-in kettle.

Please, he prayed, as he switched the light on, *let there be more than tea!*

There was a big box of saltine crackers, a jar of peanut butter, and a large baggie filled with packets of instant soup mix. Nick unscrewed the jar of peanut butter, dug a finger in, then popped it in his mouth. It was supermarket peanut butter and was a lot sweeter than the stuff his mother got, but he couldn't have cared less. He would have cleaned the entire jar out on the spot with his finger, except he knew how hungry Ionie was.

Fifteen minutes later, they were seated side by side on the wooden bench in Esmeralda's reception area, munching peanut butter cracker sandwiches and sipping hot chicken soup. The dogs watched intently.

"Mrs. Firth doesn't come down here?" Ionie wanted to be sure she was safe.

Nick shook his head, "Hardly ever. She doesn't like Esmeralda. She calls her a pip sweet— whatever that is. She only does it this way because Esmeralda is her cousin and they own the place together."

"What about the back entrance?" Ionie asked.

"I'll have to take the dogs out sometime to go to the bathroom. Won't Mrs. Firth see the tracks?"

"She comes in the front door." That reminded Nick of the message Mrs. Firth had left for him. He showed it to Ionie.

"I left that message on your answering machine saying you're OK and you'd be home as soon as the storm stopped," she reminded him.

"But you left it. If Mum got it, she'll want to know whose voice it is. She'll want to know who you are."

Ionie didn't reply.

"My mother won't let me alone till I've told her *everything*," Nick continued. "She's like that. She knows when I'm not telling the truth."

Ionie folded her arms over her chest. "You tell her the truth."

Nick frowned. "But you don't want anyone to know you're here, do you?"

"No." Ionie shook her head. "Of course not."

She had this superior, I'm-older-than-you look on her face. Nick almost punched her. "What do you mean?"

"It's simple. You say you can't tell her because you've made a promise not to tell."

Nick groaned. "You don't know my mother. She wouldn't take that."

"How do you know?"

"She wouldn't! I know she wouldn't."

"You'll have to try it!" Ionie snapped. "If she

114

loves you, she trusts you, the way Dad trusts me. It's that simple. Dad trusts me with all the dogs. Almost $40,000 worth of dogs!"

Nick groaned again. It was impossible arguing with her. "But this is different. You're older than I am, you're sixteen, your father knows what's going on. Or he should know."

Ionie ignored the last comment. "I don't see how it's different because I'm older than you. Dad trusted me when I was ten just as much as he trusts me now."

She stood up and brushed the crumbs off her clothes. "I'd better take the dogs out before Mrs. Firth comes. You're sure nobody will be coming in the back way to see the van and the dog tracks?"

Nick shrugged. He knew Mrs. Firth always parked in front and came in the front door, but he wasn't sure about the other storeowners. "It depends how soon they plow back there."

"Um," Ionie suddenly looked distant again. "I'm going to have to do some thinking. Are you going home now?"

Home? Nick hadn't thought about that, but he nodded. Yes, he wanted to go home.

"When will you be back?"

"Later today or tomorrow. I'll bring some bread and stuff."

"Um," Ionie said again. She put out her right hand to shake hands while looking Nick square in the eye. "OK. Thanks again, Nick. You're a good kid."

A good kid? Hadn't Daryl Smythe called him a kid too? Nick could feel his neck and face getting warm.

Ionie was still holding out her hand.

Nick couldn't stop himself. His fist shot out, landing hard on the shoulder of Ionie's extended arm.

She stumbled backward, her eyes shocked, her mouth half open. Fergus leaped into the space before her, teeth barred, daring Nick to come closer.

Nick went hot, then cold. He sucked his breath in quickly. He'd forgotten about the dogs. He was unable to take his eyes off Fergus, but he was aware the other dogs were every bit as ready to defend their mistress. And Wags, where was she? He was too scared to look around. He knew Wags would be mincemeat if she tried to help him.

Nick sank down onto his knees, hoping the lead dog would take this as a gesture of submission.

Fergus slowly lowered his lips. Nick knew Ionie was talking to the dog, but he didn't dare look at her until Fergus sat down.

"Why'd you do that?" Ionie asked, her left hand on the spot where Nick had socked her. "I was saying thank you and then whammo, you came down on me like a snowplow!" She didn't look angry. She looked genuinely surprised.

Nick shrugged.

"Come on! Why'd you hit me?"

Nick shrugged again. His throat was beginning to sting.

"Was it something I said?"

"I'm *not* a kid," the words burst out of him. "I'm sick of being talked down to, bossed around, bullied. Why can't people leave me alone?"

Ionie was smiling faintly now. How dare she?

"I want to get things straight, by myself..." Nick could feel the pressure from the tears welling up in his eyes. *I can't cry! I can't!*

"And?" asked Ionie.

"Everything...gets...more...and...more... mixed UP." The last word surged up and out on a hiccup as the tears rolled down his cheeks. *I'm a wimp and a fool!* Nick buried his face in the crook of his arm, on his knees.

Ionie put an arm around him and held him close. Her hair smelled piney and was softer than it looked.

Nick tried to draw back. But Ionie wouldn't let go.

"I'm...I'm...O—K!" Nick hiccuped again as he looked up.

Ionie let go and drew back. "You're not a baby, Nick. I didn't mean it that way when I said you're a good kid. You got me wrong. You're a good person, that's what I mean. I trust you. With me, that means a whole lot."

Nick didn't know what to say. Trust was obviously a big word in her vocabulary. He'd never thought about it much before.

"You could be a h.......," Ionie continued.

"A what?" Nick asked, wiping his eyes on his jacket sleeve.

"A h a n d l e r." She moved her mouth slowly to be sure he got the word. "The handler is the person who gives commands to the dogs."

Nick's heart gave a little jump as he stared at her. Was she saying he could work with sheep-dogs? *Wow! That would be neat.*

Ionie tapped at Nick's arm. "I think you could do it, not only because you hear with your eyes and you love dogs—I think you could do it because you're not afraid."

Not afraid? Nick stole a glance at Fergus. The lead dog had lain down. His head was on his paw, but his eyes were on Ionie.

"A sheepdog needs a handler who can keep cool under pressure. The handler has to keep looking for openings when the going gets rough and the sheep are all over the place. You weren't afraid to meet Daryl on his turf, and that says a lot—although I'm sure glad I came along when I did!"

"Me too!" said Nick.

Ionie suddenly glanced toward the door. Nick knew she heard something.

"What is it?" he whispered.

She put a hand on her lips. "Somebody's upstairs. You'd better go—quick!"

Nick grabbed his jacket and motioned to Wags. He looked back before shutting the door behind them. The dogs were gathered around Ionie. Her face was apprehensive—it looked like a white island in the middle of a dark sea of dog fur.

I'm going to help her! Nick thought as he bounded up the stairs.

chapter 10

"Mum! *Mum?*" Nick let out a whoop as he and Wags entered the pet store from the rear.

Peter and Mrs. Firth were with her, but Nick hardly saw them as he made for her in her half-zipped parka and the familiar purple Icelandic sweater he'd seen in his dream.

"Where were you?" Nick croaked, as she opened her arms.

"Where were *you?*" she asked, after they'd hugged. She had him at an arm's length. Nick saw the circles under her eyes and the anxiety in them and knew she probably hadn't slept all night. The realization made him feel both guilty and glad.

"I...I was downstairs." Nick hoped his voice sounded OK. After all, it was true. He *had* been downstairs.

She pushed his hair back from his forehead. He knew from the line of her mouth that she wasn't sure she believed him.

"I don't know how you stand it down there!" Mrs. Firth wrinkled up her nose. "But it's surely better than freezing in a snowdrift!"

"We've been terribly worried. The police are still looking for you," Nick's mother said with a glance at Peter. Peter nodded so vigorously the brown woolen ski cap flew off his head and landed in one of the aquariums before he could catch it.

Nick and his mother both laughed.

Mrs. Firth, however, wasn't amused. "My angels! My guppies! My neons!" she exclaimed.

Nick dropped his parka and quickly, gingerly, pulled the hat out of the bowl, making sure no fish were tangled in it. He handed the soaking mass to Peter, who went to the back sink to squeeze it out.

"You found my note?" Mrs. Firth asked Nick.

"When did you get here?" added his mother. "We came here half a dozen times, but we never thought of looking downstairs."

Mrs. Firth poked at his arm. "I was going to stay yesterday, but the police told me to get out before my car was buried by the snowplow."

Nick's mother brushed his hair off his forehead again. "Thank God you're OK. Did you get much sleep? Are you starving?"

They sure had a lot of questions!

"I came in the back way, so I didn't find your note till this morning," Nick told Mrs. Firth. "And I'm sorry.... I ate all your peanut butter and crackers."

Mrs. Firth put her hands on her hips and cocked her head. "I thought you ate dog food!"

Nick gave a small grin. He knew she was joking, but the mention of dog food worried him. How soon would she realize that a twenty-five-pound bag of meal was missing from the storeroom? The thought made him shiver.

Nick's mother saw the shiver, reached out, and pulled him close again. "We have a lot of talking to do, sweetheart. Let's go home. I bet you want a big breakfast. How about buckwheat pancakes?"

Nick only gave a small nod. Pancakes would be nice, but talking? He wasn't looking forward to that.

"I'll drop you two off at your house," said Peter when he returned from calling the police. He looked awkward standing there with the limp wet cap in his hands, a shy, uncertain expression in his eyes.

Have they been together all this time? Nick wondered, turning from Peter to his mother.

She clapped her hands. "Come on Wags!"

Wags took the cue, leaped into the air, and trotted eagerly toward the front door.

Nick, however, hung back. He was anxious about leaving Mrs. Firth in the store. What if she went downstairs? What if Ionie's dogs barked? How was Ionie going to know when she could take her dogs out back?

"I checked the cages and cleaned them," Nick told his boss. "Everything looks good. There's plenty of food and water. I fed the fish too. You aren't going to open up today, are you?"

"What! Not open on December twenty-third? I'd be CRAZY not to! The roads are plowed. The folks who made down payments on the puppies and birds will be coming by." She paused, her bun wobbling a little. "I was going to close at five this afternoon, but now I think it will probably be later."

Nick's mother turned and nodded at Mrs. Firth in agreement. "Ralph is counting on plenty of last minute shoppers. I'm sure you need Nick. I can bring back him at noon, when Ralph expects me."

Nick wanted to protest—he hated his mother arranging his day—but he kept quiet. He knew it was important for him to be at the store to protect Ionie, and this would give him a chance to get food to her.

"That would be good," Mrs. Firth agreed. She poked Nick in the arm. "Can you shovel the sidewalk in front of the store now, before you go home?"

"Sure."

He noticed, after getting the shovel from the storeroom, how Mrs. Firth and his mother stopped talking when he came back up front. *What are they talking about? What's going on?* he wondered as he followed Peter out the front door.

Peter used a broom to help Nick clear the walkway.

"Nick," Peter said when they'd finished, "I hope you didn't run away or anything last night because of me."

Nick shook his head.

Peter's mouth broke into a relieved grin. "Do you want to talk?"

Nick shook his head again.

Peter's mouth drooped. He looked very much like Wags when she'd been scolded.

"Not now," Nick said quickly.

"Oh, OK." Peter nodded to show he under-stood. "Where's your bike? Want to put it in the trunk of my car?"

Nick cleared his throat awkwardly as his mother came out the front door of the pet shop. "It's...buried. I'll get it later."

Nick's mother insisted he sit in the front passenger seat on the way home. When they got to the main road, Nick twisted around to look at her in the back seat. Wags was on her lap because there was no other space in the pile of notebooks and cameras. She wasn't paying attention to the dog, though. She was staring out the window, a strange expression on her face.

Nick looked away quickly. *Is she mad at me? Did she get the phone message Ionie left? What's she going to say when we get home?* He looked at Peter, who shot a friendly glance at him and grinned. "Beautiful snow."

Nick nodded.

"We'll have to go snowboard—*Whoops!*" Peter clamped a hand over his mouth quickly and took a peek through the rearview mirror at Nick's mother before winking at Nick.

Nick had to laugh.

"A class one storm," Peter said. "All the airports from New Jersey to Boston are closed. Hundreds of Christmas travelers are stranded in them. Wait till you see the turnpike."

When they came to the bridge over the turnpike, Peter stopped and jumped out to get photos of the abandoned cars and trucks down below. Most were on the side of the road, but some had gone right over the edge and would have to be towed. Nick's mother waited in Peter's car with Wags.

"Look like a lot of lost sheep, don't they?" Peter said between shots.

Lost sheep? Nick peered at him. Funny Peter should mention sheep now. That made Nick want to tell him all about the sheepdogs and how Ionie, as a handler, managed them.

H A N D L E R, he mouthed the word silently to himself as they went back to the car. *Do you know what that means, Peter? You should see the way Ionie handles her dogs. It's amazing. And she thinks I could do it!*

He was the first one out when they got home. When his mother didn't appear, he opened her door to let Wags out.

"Coming, Mum?"

She nodded but went on talking to Peter in the car.

Nick climbed the stairs to the front door, only to discover he didn't have his own house key. He looked back. His mother was still in the car, still talking. He shrugged and stamped his feet a bit. What was the fuss? Why didn't they come inside to talk if they wanted to talk so much? Forget the pancakes. All he wanted was a big bowl of granola!

When she finally joined him, she was alone.

"Where's Peter?"

She ignored the question and led the way into the house.

"Where were you last night?" Nick asked when they were in the kitchen.

"Where were YOU?" She pointed a finger at him. "That's the question. If you left home at nine in the morning and didn't get to the pet shop until late last night or this morning...well... where were you?"

Nick looked down at his boots. He wished Peter had come in with them. There was something funny about him, even when he wasn't trying to make people laugh.

Nick's mother lifted his face by the chin so their eyes met. "Have you any idea how worried we were? We were driving all over, *skidding* all over, looking for you. I can't remember a worse night in my life! I'd better call Ralph to let him know. He was looking too."

She went to the phone without waiting for his response and dialed. She was really upset.

Nick swallowed. His throat was starting to sting again. "Mum," he told her, when she had finished calling and had peeled her jacket off. "I left a message on the answering machine."

"I know. I got it at 10:30 last night. I was glad to get it, but still..." She threw up her hands.

Nick waited for her to ask who had called for him. When she didn't, he realized she probably thought Ionie was a relay operator. Relief washed over him.

"So, where were you?" she asked.

"I can't tell."

She slumped down in one of the kitchen chairs. "You disappear in a blizzard, six policemen, the town rescue squad, Mrs. Firth, Ralph, Peter, and I go looking for you and then—thank goodness—you reappear, and you can't tell us where you've been. Really! I've just about had it.

What *is* the matter with you? You've been moody and rude and secretive for weeks now."

Nick swallowed again.

There were tears in her eyes. "Please, Nick!"

"I can't tell you, Mum," Nick tried again. "I promised."

"Promised what?"

"Not to tell."

She wiped a tear away from one eye. Nick could see she was curious. "Who did you make this promise to?"

Nick shrugged awkwardly.

"Why did you make such a promise?"

"Because..." Nick bit his lip. Once again he wanted badly, so badly, to tell her everything.

"Why?"

"Because I'm trying to help someone, and I can't tell about her until—" He stopped abruptly. Had he said too much? Had he actually named Ionie? He was so tense he couldn't remember.

His mother was waiting, listening.

No, I didn't say her name, he assured himself. "I can't tell you now, Mum."

She didn't nod, shake her head, smile, or answer. She didn't even blink. For one awful minute, he wondered, *Does she still love me?*

Then he remembered what Ionie had said about trust and added, "Please, Mum, you've got to trust me."

She got up, came to him, and put both hands

on his shoulders. She looked him square in the eye. "Nicholas Wilder, I believe you and trust you. I've always trusted you. Even if you have a crazy way of getting yourself in tight spots."

"Mum—"

"Let me finish what I'm saying." She was squeezing his shoulders hard now. "If you can't tell me where you've been and who you're helping, if I have to wait to find out, then I'll wait. But please, PLEASE, don't do anything too crazy. And I want to help if I can. OK?"

Nick nodded and walked into her arms for another hug.

chapter 11

Hot water had never felt more wonderful. Nick stood in the shower with his eyes shut, the water streaming over his upturned face and down his chest, arms, stomach, and legs.

I wish I could take a hot shower to Ionie. He grinned at the thought. How could you take a hot shower to someone? Put it in an empty milk carton, wrap it in a towel, tie it with a ribbon?

Nick's grin faded. *What am I going to take her? How can I take food without Mum knowing?* He had always been free to have what he wanted from the refrigerator and cupboards, but thinking about taking food to Ionie made him feel like a thief.

When he was eating his pancakes, his mother had her turn in the shower. He figured if he took a little bit of this and that she wouldn't notice. He filled a bunch of Baggies, one by one, putting each in his backpack the minute he had what he wanted. Bread was in the first, cheese in the second, granola in the third, pecans in the fourth, and rice in the fifth. He would tell Ionie where Mrs. Firth's hot plate was so she could cook the rice that night when she was alone in the store.

He was poking about in the refrigerator, wondering about butter or vegetables to go with the rice, when his mother appeared with her wet hair bound up in a towel.

"Aren't the pancakes enough?"

"Yes..." Nick stammered. "I...I was thinking about something to take to work."

Her eyebrows went up.

He knew that she knew he was lying.

She regarded him for a minute before pointing at his plate on the table. "Finish your breakfast. I'll make your lunch."

Nick shoved the pack behind his chair before sitting down. His face was hot. He was grateful his mother had not pointed out that she always made his lunch and often had to remind him not to forget it at home.

"Are you and Peter...um...?" he stammered again after he'd finished the pancakes.

She turned from the counter so he could see her face. "I'd rather not talk about Peter and me."

"Why not?"

"Because of what's going on with you. That comes first right now."

Nick pushed his plate away. Did this mean she was going to be following him around everywhere, never letting him out of sight, telling people to keep an eye on him? How was he going to be able to help Ionie if she was going to be like that?

"Mum—" he started to say.

She put a hand up to silence him. "Trust me," she said.

* * *

The pet shop was jammed at noon, just as Mrs. Firth had predicted. Nick motioned to his boss that he would help her as soon as he put Wags in the apartment downstairs.

"Ionie?" he whispered, with a soft knock on the downstairs door. "It's me, Nick. Open up."

Ionie peeked out to make sure it was Nick before letting him in. Her eyes were anxious. Her loose hair rose up around her face like a dark, wild, brambly bush.

Nick stepped into the salon office as Ionie switched on the overhead light. The shades had been drawn and the furniture had been moved back against the wall. All of the dogs jumped up as Wags came in hesitantly, her tail between her legs.

"How are you doing?" Nick asked.

"OK," she said. "When will the store be closing? The dogs are going to need to go out before long."

Nick looked at the sheepdogs. They were milling around, obviously eager to get out for a romp, if not to go to the bathroom. *Cripes!* he thought. *That would be the end of Esmeralda's rug.*

"Mrs. Firth was going to close at 5:00, but it might be later."

Ionie frowned as she gathered her hair together and applied the rubber band. "Can you get me some old newspapers or paper bags?"

"I'll look upstairs."

"The dogs are paper trained," she explained. "It can be smelly, but they can do it if they have to."

Nick emptied out the contents of his backpack on Esmeralda's desk. His lunch bag looked unusually large. He peeked inside. There were two of everything: two apples, two sandwiches, two molasses cookies, and two bags of nuts and raisins.

"Looks like my mom put lunch in here for you too," he told Ionie.

Her mouth tightened. "Does she know about me?"

Nick shook his head, put one hand over his heart and raised the other as a pledge that he hadn't broken his promise. He didn't tell Ionie, though, that the two lunches made him uneasy.

He could feel his mother trying to figure out what was going on. And she could be pretty sharp. How long would it be before she found out about Ionie?

"I'll be back at closing time," he promised.

Ionie put one hand over her heart and promised in return, "Don't worry, Nick, I'll have figured out by then what I'm going to do. I won't stay here long. And I do think Dad will be back soon."

*   *   *

Back upstairs, Nick found a pile of newspapers, added some shopping bags, and slipped them quickly through the door to Ionie before getting to work.

Mrs. Firth had Nick fetching all kinds of things for the customers as well as transferring birds from large to small cages and fish from tanks to carry-home cartons. He had just finished placing a box with a hamster in a lady's car and was trotting down the shoveled sidewalk to the store when he caught sight of something near the front door: the gray baseball cap with black lettering.

Nick turned away. He wasn't quick enough, though. Peg, the one from his English class, saw him and said something.

Daryl swung around. The boy with the one long eyebrow was with him too.

"There he is," said Daryl.

The others didn't respond. Their faces were blank. Were they stoned?

As they stared at each other, a strange thought came to Nick: *He's not all that big!* Daryl Smythe actually looked small standing by the door while adults passed behind him on their way in and out of the store. He no longer looked like the cool skateboarder, the daring graffiti artist.

Nick almost rubbed his eyes. What had happened to make him look so different?

"Where is she?" Daryl asked.

"Who?" asked Nick.

"You know."

Nick did know, but he pretended he hadn't understood what was being said.

"Come on now," Daryl wasn't grinning. His lips looked thicker than usual and sagged a bit at the edges, as though they had been pulled out of shape. "Where's the girl? You know—the girl with all the dogs."

Nick continued to play deaf.

Daryl muttered something to the others, rolled his eyes, and glanced briefly, quickly, to the left.

Nick followed his glance and saw the car parked near the curb. He saw the out-of-state license plate. He saw the man in the driver's seat watching them from behind sunglasses, his arm on the opened window. He saw, too, the frightened face of a girl in the front passenger seat. The one who rode on the bus with him, Missy.

In a flash, Nick understood. The man Ionie had fled was trying to find Ionie and her dogs through Daryl.

"Where is she?" Daryl asked again. His eyes were pleading.

He's scared, Nick realized. *Daryl Smythe is scared. That's why he looks different.*

He remembered the way Ionie had told him about the dogs being stolen, and the way she had sped up that morning when she saw the man standing by the roadside. She sure had driven fast! One thing was clear to Nick: *This man isn't anybody to fool around with.*

Without taking another look at the car, Nick stepped up to Daryl, reached past him for the door handle, and said, "Let's go inside."

They all went into the store.

"Who's that man in the car?" Nick asked.

Daryl rolled his eyes impatiently. "I don't know! Where's the girl? Where are the dogs? Just tell me and we'll leave you alone."

"What about Missy?" said Nick. "Isn't she out there in the car with that man?"

"Yeah!" Daryl was so edgy he couldn't stand still. He looked nervously around the store, as if expecting to see Ionie.

Peg grabbed at the sleeve of Nick's T-shirt. "He won't let Missy go till we get the dogs. He'll—"

Daryl poked Peg hard with his elbow to tell her

to shut up. Peg slapped Daryl's arm. The two would have started fighting if One Eyebrow hadn't put both of his arms down between them. People were turning to see what was going on.

"You blabbermouth!" Daryl hissed at Peg.

"You got us in this mess, idiot!" Peg shot back.

"My boss will call the police," Nick warned.

"You know where the dogs are, don't you?" Daryl demanded.

Out of the corner of his eye, Nick saw Mrs. Firth by the cash register, waving frantically at him.

"I've got to help my boss," Nick told Daryl. "You wait right here. OK?"

"No!" said Daryl. "Tell me where the dogs are...please!"

"Wait right here," Nick told Peg and One Eyebrow.

To his surprise, Peg nodded.

One Eyebrow neither nodded nor shook his head. Nick felt certain, though, from the look in his eyes that the guy would do as he'd been asked. Daryl's hold on his friends appeared to be unraveling.

What am I going to do? Nick thought as he hurried over to the cash register.

"This is *not* the time to hang out with your buddies!" Mrs. Firth really mouthed the words to make sure he understood. The bun on top of her head trembled as she spoke. "Get this gentleman a ten-pound bag of puppy chow *immediately*. Do you understand?"

Nick nodded and made for the storeroom at a trot, trying to figure things out as he went. If he told Daryl he didn't know where Ionie was, the man might come after him because it was clear he, Nick, was the last person who had been with Ionie. Should he warn Ionie? Would Daryl figure out that Ionie and the dogs were downstairs in the room he had hidden in two days ago? Should he try to get Mrs. Firth's help? How could he possibly explain everything to her when she was already mad at him?

Nick paused for a minute in the storeroom. He leaned against the door with his eyes shut tight. He felt sick with anxiety and confusion. He could not see any clear way out.

chapter 12

Go slow. The words sounded faintly within Nick as he leaned against the door. He opened his eyes and peered out of the storeroom, down the length of the store. He could see beyond the customers to where Daryl, Peg, and One Eyebrow stood waiting by the front window of the pet shop. Daryl's baseball cap was now on backward. He stood with his arms folded high and tight over his chest, awaiting Nick's return.

Go slow. Nick heard the words again. That was what Ionie had said when they had started off on snowshoes.

Go slow. He realized that, even though he still didn't know what he was going to do, the words made him feel better. As if he'd been able to catch his breath. He reached for the bag of puppy chow. But how *could* he go slow? Mrs. Firth certainly did not want him to go slow. Nor did Daryl Smythe.

As he came out of the storeroom with the bag in his arms and made for the cash register, he felt a glimmer of understanding. It was like snowshoeing in the dark. If he couldn't see where he was going, he slowed down. It was that simple. He slowed down so he wouldn't fall off the bluff or run into a tree. And now when he couldn't see what he should do, even though it was daytime and the sun was shining, he had to try to slow things down somehow. If he did that, the way would become clear.

Mrs. Firth gave a curt nod of thanks as Nick lifted the dog food onto the counter. Then she asked him to show the customer their selection of dog collars and leashes while she tended to someone else.

Across the room, Daryl watched Nick with a desperate look on his face and his arms still folded over his chest. Peg and One Eyebrow appeared to be looking out the window, checking on Missy.

"Get some filter bags for this gentleman," Mrs. Firth told Nick when he came by the register.

Nick got the filter bags.

Daryl stayed by the window, shifting his weight from one foot to the other, keeping an eye Nick all the while.

Nick was helping a little girl pick a turtle for her brother when he realized Daryl was standing beside him.

"The dogs..." Daryl began.

Go slow, Nick told himself.

"I told you I'll leave you alone. Honest!"

"Why do you do it?" Nick asked.

Daryl gave him a bewildered look. "What?"

"Drugs."

"Do we have to talk about that now? Can't you see?" Daryl rolled his eyes as he put a hand up. "He's blackmailing me. Where...where are the dogs?"

"Sorry." Nick spoke low, even though his heart was booming loud and hard in his chest. "I'm not telling. My boss will call the police if you touch me."

Daryl's hand jerked down again as he restrained himself. The eyes of the little girl Nick was helping had widened. Nick knew she had heard everything.

Daryl snorted and glanced in the direction of the front door. "He took all the pot, the cash—everything. And he's...he's gonna take Missy if we don't get the dogs."

Nick said nothing.

"Please!" said Daryl.

Nick paused. He certainly wasn't going to let Ionie or her dogs be hurt in order to help Missy. But shouldn't he do something?

"Can't Missy get away?" Nick asked.

Daryl shook his head and moved closer to speak in Nick's ear. His jacket smelled greasy.

"I have to read your lips," Nick reminded him, stepping back.

"He's got a gun!" Daryl mouthed the words silently, desperately. Then he grabbed hold of Nick's arm and nodded in the direction of the front door.

Missy had come into the store. The bald man with the dark glasses was behind her, one hand on her shoulder, the other out of sight at her back. A casual observer might have thought they were father and daughter out for some Christmas shopping together, but Nick saw the fear in Missy's small pale, tight face. The sick, confused feeling washed over him briefly again. *Oh my God! Does he have a gun? Is there going to be a shooting?*

He glanced around quickly. Daryl edged his way back against the wall like a cornered creature. The little girl Nick had been helping had disappeared. Where was she? Then he saw what he couldn't hear: The little girl was crying and pointing at Daryl. Everyone in the store was looking in the direction of the eighth grader.

Suddenly Nick knew what he had to do: He had to switch from slow to fast. He dropped down, slid around the turtle tank, edged past the birdcages, and came out a bit behind the bald man with the sunglasses.

"You want the dogs?" Nick asked gruffly.

Startled, the man swung to the left.

But Nick was too quick. He stepped to the right of the man, near Peg and One Eyebrow. Both looked dazed.

"Get Missy!" Nick hissed.

His words brought them to life. Peg grabbed Missy by the arm while Nick and One Eyebrow lunged at the man. There was a scuffle, arms flew up in the air, something fell to the floor, then the man turned and ran out the door—nearly colliding with two customers who were on their way in.

Nick and One Eyebrow both looked down. There was a gun, a chunky handgun, on the floor. Nick had never seen this kind of a gun.

"Don't touch it!" Nick warned One Eyebrow.

One Eyebrow stepped back, both hands up, as though Nick had pointed the gun at him.

"There are fingerprints on it," Nick explained.

Missy, Peg, and others were all staring at the gun. Mrs. Firth elbowed her way through the crowd to where Nick stood. A part of her bun, which was still pinned to the back of her head, had unraveled into a wispy, white, birdlike plume.

"WHAT in the world is going on?" she demanded.

Nick nodded at Missy.

"That man was holding a gun to my back," said Missy.

Mrs. Firth saw the gun on the floor. "GOOD GRIEF! What's going on in my store? Someone call the police!"

Nick remembered then that, though Missy had been saved, Ionie was still in danger. He ran out of the store onto the sidewalk, his breath coming out in big white puffs. He stood on tiptoes, his eyes sweeping over the parking lot in every direction. The car with the out-of-state license plate was gone.

Minutes later two policemen arrived at a run. One slipped the gun into a plastic bag. The other took a notepad out of his pocket and was talking with Mrs. Firth and Missy when Nick's mother burst into the store. She hadn't even bothered to put on her parka.

She made right for Nick. "What is it? Are you OK?"

Nick nodded, though his legs felt rather like Jell-O.

"Someone said a girl was being held hostage."

Nick nodded at Missy. Peg and One Eyebrow stood close by her. Peg was holding Missy's hand. One Eyebrow's head was bent. He appeared to be staring at his Nikes.

Nick realized then that Daryl wasn't with them.

"I've got to find someone," he told his mother.

"Wait a minute!" she grabbed hold of his arm,

144

her blue eyes never leaving his face. "You know all about this, don't you?"

He nodded.

"Well, I'm not letting you out of sight now, Nicholas Wilder. Not if there's a madman around here."

Nick shrugged.

They made their way out of the crowd that had gathered by the front door. Daryl was not at the back of the store where Nick had last seen him. He was nowhere in sight.

Oh no! Nick put both hands to his head. Daryl must have gone out the back way. That meant he would find the dog's footprints and Ionie's van.

"What is it?" Nick's mother asked. "Tell me who we're looking for."

"Daryl Smythe," Nick replied.

"Daryl Smythe?" she repeated, puzzlement all over her face. "Who's that?"

Nick didn't stop to answer. He turned and ran down the back stairs to the rear entrance. The door was wide open. Nick ran out into the middle of the parking lot. He knew Daryl had fled this way, but saw, with relief, that the minivan was still there.

Nick's mother had followed. She grabbed at his arm again. *"Please* tell me what's going on!"

Nick paused. Should he tell her about Ionie? *Could* he tell her? Was he bound to his promise forever?

She called something into the air to someone else.

"Peter's coming," she explained as he appeared on the back steps.

Nick saw the relief on Peter's face as he hurried up to them, his feet sliding around a bit as he went.

"You're all right?" he asked Nick.

Nick nodded.

"I drove like a lunatic when the police said Firth's Pet Shop," Peter continued, breathlessly.

"We're looking for someone," Nick's mother said. "But I don't even know what he looks like or what's going on." She faced Nick. "Can we go inside now and talk? I'm frozen."

I promised I wouldn't tell, Nick thought, as they headed back into the pet shop. *But what if that man goes after Ionie? What if he comes after me? What if Ionie's father never comes back?*

His thoughts were broken abruptly as he came in the door. Ionie was standing at the base of the back stairs. She turned as they entered. From her expression, Nick guessed that she'd been eavesdropping.

"The dogs?" The words rushed out of Nick's mouth before he could stop them.

Ionie's eyes traveled from Nick, to his mother, to Peter, and back to Nick. *Is she going to pretend she doesn't even know me?* Nick wondered. He wanted to tell her she could trust his mother and

Peter, but her face was distant again, like when he had first seen her.

Nick shut his eyes. He couldn't face-read people or figure them out for one more minute. He was so tired.

He felt an arm around his shoulder and knew by the light touch that it was his mother. He opened his eyes.

"Is this the person you've been helping?" she asked.

Nick shrugged.

"I'm Nick's mother," she said to Ionie.

Ionie was still closed off, far away.

"Nick never said a word to us about you," Nick's mother continued. "Not a word. He's great at *not* talking. Believe me, I wish he'd talk more! Especially now when we want to help."

Peter nodded hard in agreement.

Ionie was silent.

"We truly want to help," Nick's mother said again. "But first we need to know what's going on."

Ionie bit her lip.

Then she motioned for them all to follow her into Emeralda's office.

chapter 13

Nick had to grin when his mother and Peter walked into Esmeralda's office and got their first glimpse of Ionie's dogs. Peter nearly fell over backward. Nick's mother's mouth dropped open.

"Is something wrong with my eyes?" she asked Nick. "I've never seen so many dogs all at once before."

"There are seven, Mum."

The dogs covered the entire floor, from wall to wall. They were the picture of good behavior. All were lying down, facing the door, some with their heads up, others with their heads on their paws. Only Wags was up and about. She'd rushed forward to greet Nick when they came in, and now her tail was going around and around like an eggbeater whipping the air at top speed.

"They're sheepdogs, aren't they?" Peter asked.

Ionie nodded.

"They look smart," Peter continued. "And handsome. *Very* handsome. Especially that one." He pointed at Fergus.

Nick knew Ionie was pleased.

"Intelligence first, looks second," said Peter.

Ionie's face turned cautious as she looked at Nick.

"Peter's a newspaper reporter. He wrote a story about a sheepherding contest," Nick explained.

"Where?" asked Ionie, turning back to Peter.

Nick's mother mouthed questions silently to him while Ionie talked with Peter. "Where'd you meet her?"

Nick pointed to the ceiling. "Upstairs."

"She's fierce!" Nick's mother concluded, still using no voice.

Nick grinned, nodded, and mouthed the word, "Independent."

"Where's her family? Do they sell the dogs?"

Nick nodded again.

Distracted by the silent conversation, Ionie interrupted Nick's mother. "What are you talking about?" she demanded.

"I don't even know your name," Nick's mother replied.

"Iona—"

"For an island," Nick interjected.

"Iona Margaret-Ann Hunter. Ionie for short."

"Hunter's Herders?" Nick's mother asked.

Ionie's mouth fell open. "That's what we call them!"

"Hunter?" Peter exclaimed. "William Hunter?"

Ionie's eyes seemed to grow a shade darker. "William Hunter is my father."

Peter almost fell over again. "My gosh! The police got a phone call early this morning from a William Hunter in Scotland. He said something about having his mother's property checked out."

"The Tower Motel?" Ionie asked.

"Yes! He'd been trying unsuccessfully to reach someone there. Was it you?"

Ionie turned to Nick and smiled triumphantly. "My father called. I told you he wouldn't forget me." Then to Peter, "What did he say?"

"I don't know. You'll have to ask the police."

Ionie drew back suddenly, an anxious look on her face, as she, Peter, and his mother turned their faces to the door. All the dogs rose, as if to protect their mistress. Nick knew someone was talking through the door. He looked to his mother. "They're asking for you, Nick," she explained.

Peter spoke to Ionie before motioning to Nick. "Come on, Nick. The police probably want to talk with you about what happened upstairs. Your mother will stay with Ionie until you're through."

*　　*　　*

150

"WHERE have you been?" Mrs. Firth demanded as Nick reentered the pet store. "This place has been turned upside down! And what's all this talk about dogs?"

Nick didn't know what to say. If word got out about Ionie, would that endanger her further? Peter must have understood what was on his mind, because he spoke briefly to Mrs. Firth, who dropped back as three police officers converged on Nick. Missy and One Eyebrow were with them and looked pretty scared.

"Where's this girl with the dogs?" a police officer asked Nick.

Nick turned to Peter, who signed for Nick to tell them about Ionie.

"But..." Nick hesitated.

"We'll ask for police protection for her," said Peter.

"Will they take the dogs away from her?"

Peter shook his head hard. "Not while I'm around."

*   *   *

Mrs. Firth was speechless when she went downstairs with Nick and the police and got her first glimpse of Ionie's dogs.

"This is my boss," Nick said to Ionie.

Ionie was also unable to speak. She looked as though she had been betrayed.

151

"Don't worry," Nick assured her. "They want to help you."

Ionie stood close to Fergus, both hands on his back.

"I can't believe this," Mrs. Firth exclaimed when she had found her voice. "All these magnificent dogs were right downstairs, and I never knew it. How long have you been here? Have they got enough food and water?"

"I opened a bag of meal for them," Nick confessed. "I'll pay for it."

"Nonsense! I'm honored to have them here as guests! I can't wait to tell my cousin what she's missed!"

Ionie smiled. Nick could tell she liked his prickly boss.

The police had just finished questioning Ionie when Peter ran in. He evidently had important news to share, because the police officers talked together and then rushed out the door.

Ionie made for the door, but Peter stopped her. All of the dogs were up, ready to go. Nick could smell their doggy eagerness to get out.

"What's going on, Mum?"

Nick's mother turned to him. "There's a fire at the Tower Motel!"

"What? How?"

"The police discovered it when they went to check on the property."

Peter closed the door and stood with his back

against it, talking with Ionie. Nick could see she was upset.

"Is it bad, Mum?"

Nick's mother shrugged to say she didn't know.

"You two stay here with Ionie," Peter told Nick and his mother. "An officer is right outside the door, so you don't need to worry about anyone breaking in. I'm going to the motel and will be back as soon as possible. I don't think Ionie should go near there until we know what's going on."

"Do you think someone started the fire?" Nick asked Ionie after Peter had left.

Ionie didn't respond. She didn't even look at Nick. She seemed to be in shock.

Nick's mother went quickly to Ionie and put both arms around the girl. To Nick's surprise, Ionie turned and buried her head in his mother's shoulder.

The two talked together, Nick's mother stroking Ionie's hair all the while.

A fire? Nick punched the palm of one hand with his other fist. *Oh my God!* "There was a fire there years ago during a snowstorm," he blurted out. "A man was killed in that fire."

Ionie looked at him.

"That's what we're talking about," Nick's mother said. "It happened right around the time you lost your hearing. You remember it?"

Nick shivered. *Do I remember it?* "Of course I do!"

"So do I," said Ionie. "Some people said my grandparents started the fire. And it was a friend of theirs who died in it. He was reading and smoking on the bed and he fell asleep. It was pretty awful!"

She paused and added, "I never wanted to come here again. And when Dad left me here—"

Her words were interrupted by the phone. Nick's mother and Ionie both reached for it.

"It's her father!" Nick's mother mouthed the words to him and put a thumb up as Ionie took the receiver. "Let's go get some food and come back. I'm sure she wants to talk with him alone."

Nick was glad to see the police officer standing guard outside the door. He followed his mother up the stairs, Wags close behind.

Things were back to normal in the pet shop. To Nick's surprise and annoyance, Peg and One Eyebrow were helping Mrs. Firth. Peg was bagging. One Eyebrow was fetching things for customers.

"Where's Missy?" Nick asked.

"Gone home," Mrs. Firth answered. She cocked her head at Nick's annoyed expression and added, "Look here, Nick, no one can take your job from you. You're my hero! I can't wait to see those dogs again!"

Nick grinned. "I hope the rug downstairs hasn't been ruined."

Mrs. Firth waved her hand. "Don't worry about

it. Go do what you have to do now."

Peg gave a shy smile and waved good-bye to Nick as he left with his mother to go to the health food store.

She's acting like we're friends, Nick thought. He wasn't sure how he felt about it. *Can I trust her? Does she know about the fire? Did Daryl start it?*

"That eighth grader that was being mean," Nick's mother said, as they walked down the sidewalk. "What did he do to you?"

Nick shrugged. Right then the graffiti and Daryl's grimaces, notes, and threats seemed like years ago.

"I feel terrible about this. Why didn't you tell me?"

Nick stopped. "I almost did, Mum. But you were busy with Peter...and I couldn't."

"Why not?"

"I would've been a wimp if I'd told you."

She gave a thoughtful nod. "I understand what you're saying, but if anything like this ever happens again, I hope you won't clam up. I hope we can talk about it."

She linked her arm in his. "There are too many adult bullies in the world, Nicholas Wilder. Take the man you thwarted today. If people like that can get help early, when they're kids and they're hurting, they might not grow up to be so bad."

Peter's old Honda pulled up alongside the sidewalk before they reached the health food store.

Peter rolled his window down to speak. He looked excited.

"Did they put the fire out?" Nick wanted to know.

"Yes."

"Was it bad? Was anybody hurt?"

"No, and no again," said Peter.

"Whew!"

Peter's eyes became serious. "Thank goodness you and Ionie came to the pet shop this morning, Nick! I don't know what it would have been like if you hadn't."

"Why?" asked Nick.

"Because that guy from Virginia started the fire. If Ionie hadn't talked with the police, they wouldn't have known who to look for. When they caught up with him, they found a couple of tins of gasoline and a bag of rags in the back seat of his car. It looked as though he planned to burn down the place. The two officers Ionie talked with arrested him on Route 77 a little while ago."

Nick stared at Peter for a few seconds. Then he turned to his mother, let out a whoop, and threw his arms around her. Ionie and the dogs were safe—they wouldn't have to hide any longer!

chapter 14

Nick couldn't wait to tell Ionie the good news. But when he burst into Esmeralda's office, he found her curled up tight on the floor, with both arms around Fergus and a miserable look on her face.

Ionie said something, but Nick couldn't get it because her lips were hidden behind the dog's back.

What happened? Nick looked to his mother for an explanation, but she had gone straight to Ionie.

"Ionie's grandmother died yesterday," Peter told him.

Nick sighed and sank onto the swivel chair. He felt really bad about Ionie's grandmother. "I'm sorry," he said to Ionie.

Ionie's head was bowed. She didn't look up.

Nick sighed again. All he wanted, now that they didn't have to worry about the bald man anymore, was for things to slow down and get back to normal.

Nick's mother talked to Ionie, while Nick squirmed about, not sure what to do. What about Christmas? Would his mother invite Ionie for dinner? He hoped so. And what about their tree? Were any trees left at the Floyds' farm? Would Mrs. Floyd have time to make popcorn for them?

Ionie, Nick's mother, and Peter talked together. Then Peter caught Nick's eye and signed, "Let's go."

Nick's mother nodded for him to follow Peter.

"If Mrs. Firth doesn't mind your coming with me, we have a whole bunch of things to do," Peter told Nick out in the hallway.

"Like what?"

Peter put up his hands to count. "One, I've got to drop film off to be developed. Two, I've got to check my voice mail. Three, I want you to help me write a story for the paper—"

"What story?" Nick interrupted.

"About what happened this morning."

Nick started, amazed he had forgotten about Daryl. "Do you know what happened to Daryl Smythe?"

"The police found him and another kid in one of the cabins," said Peter. "They took him home."

"What will happen?"

"He'll probably be on probation because of the marijuana, the vandalism, and other things. He and his parents will be required to get counseling. Because he's a minor, his name won't be in the paper."

"What about Ionie's money?"

"She might get some of it back, but not all of it." Peter put a hand on Nick's shoulder. "How are you feeling about Daryl Smythe?"

Nick shrugged. He wasn't angry with Daryl anymore. The frightened look he had seen that morning on the older boy's face had been enough for him.

"You were pretty cool," said Peter. "A lot cooler than I was at your age. Once, when I was being harassed, I tried to run away. My bathing suit caught on the top of the wire fence I was climbing over and was ripped right off."

Nick laughed. "You had nothing on?"

"*Nothing*. And I landed in a cow pie when I came down."

Peter in a cow pie? Nick bent over laughing.

"It's funny now but it wasn't then," said Peter. Then he changed the topic. "By the way, after we write the story we're going to get a Christmas tree."

Nick stopped laughing. "But, what about the Floyds? What about Mum?"

"We're going to the Floyds'. Your mother asked

if we could get the tree. She has too many things to do."

That shut up Nick. He had never ever gone to get a Christmas tree without his mother. Nick and Wags followed Peter up the stairs.

Mrs. Firth was very busy. She nodded, smiled, and kept on working as Peter spoke with her. With a quick glance at Nick, she said, "Be here tomorrow morning at 9:00 sharp, OK?"

Nick nodded.

Wags hopped into the front seat of Peter's car and sat sandwiched between Nick and Peter.

Peter started the engine, but he didn't shift into first gear. Instead, he looked over Wags's head at Nick. "Your mother asked Ionie to come for Christmas."

Nick grinned.

"In fact, Ionie is coming tonight," Peter added. "The smoke smell is pretty bad in the big house at the motel. She'll stay with you till her father comes back in the next couple of days."

"The dogs too?"

Peter nodded.

Nick's grin got bigger. *All* the sheepdogs were coming to his place! He'd never, not even in his wildest dreams, imagined anything like this happening. Seven dogs! Wow! How was Wags going to like it? Nick put an arm around his mutt and pulled her close.

"Your mother is afraid it's going to be

crowded," Peter continued. "So, instead of going to your apartment, she's thinking about going somewhere else."

Somewhere else? Was he hearing right? Nick sat bolt upright.

"What do you mean?" he asked.

Peter ran his hand through his dark hair twice, as though trying to clear his mind. He looked worried.

"You'll like this other place, Nick. Your mother's been thinking about it for a while, even before she knew about Ionie, and it's available right away. There's a meadow out behind the house, and a river...."

Nick stared at him, puzzled. *A house with a meadow and a river behind it? Where would that be?* He knew Peter lived in an apartment over a grocery store in the next town, so Peter couldn't be talking about his place.

"There are lots of pines like the one you like to climb," Peter added. "I counted nine the other day."

Lots of pines? Nick was annoyed. So his mother had been thinking about another home for them without even telling him! How could she do that? They'd been in the apartment for ten years. Hadn't she painted their living room last spring and their kitchen the year before? And how could Peter assume any pine tree was like his pine tree?

161

The air was getting unbreathable. Nick put his hand on the door handle to go back into the pet shop to his mother, but Peter grabbed him by the arm. "Stay here, Nick. Ionie needs to talk alone with your mother right now."

"She's *my* mother! Why didn't she say anything about this to me?"

Peter's hand tightened on Nick's arm. "She wanted to, Nick. She had to figure out some details first. We...she was talking with the owners two days ago."

So that's where Mum was when Daryl was dumping rabbit pellets in the fish tank, Nick knew.

"She was going to take you to see it after you got the Christmas tree," Peter continued, "but that never happened."

"And we're moving there?" Nick said crossly.

"Nick..." Peter tried to explain.

Nick didn't want to listen. He looked away, one arm tight around his dog.

After a while, Peter started up the car, and they drove to his office without exchanging any more words.

"Want to come in?" Peter asked.

Nick shook his head. He didn't know what he wanted, except to go to sleep in his own bed, in his own room, in his own home. Even the thought of Ionie and the dogs coming to stay with them didn't excite him.

He must have dozed off, because the next thing

162

he knew, it was getting dark and he was lying on his side in the front seat with a blanket and Peter's parka on top of him. Wags was curled up in the back amid the photography equipment.

Nick sat up blinking. He felt better. He and Wags went into the building and found Peter where he usually was when they came by: hunched over the computer in his office.

Peter was glad to see him. "Have a good sleep?"

Nick nodded.

"You were so tired you fell right over. Shall we get the Christmas tree now?"

Nick shrugged.

They looked at each other, and Nick saw the anxiety in the older man's friendly eyes.

Peter's scared of me! Nick suddenly knew. *He's afraid I don't like him.* The realization didn't make him feel good or powerful. It made him feel like he'd been mean.

"If we get a tree, where would we take it?" Nick asked.

Peter smiled, leaned over and rumpled Nick's hair. "You'll see," he said.

*   *   *

They drove a couple of miles out of town, up Long Hill Road to the Floyds' farm. Nick loved Long Hill Road. It rose slowly along a ridge that looked out over the southern end of the lake.

There were apple orchards, pumpkin fields, maple woods, and the Christmas tree farm.

Mr. Floyd, dressed in his familiar blue overalls, boots, red Santa hat, and thick work gloves, came out to greet them. He slapped Nick on the back and talked with Peter as though he knew him well.

They climbed into the cart behind Mr. Floyd's tractor and rode through the snow into one of the farthest pine patches. Mr. Floyd shone a light on the trees to help them find the one they wanted.

Nick picked a bushy white pine a couple of inches taller than Peter. Together—without talking, because Nick couldn't see anybody's lips very well—they felled the tree and lifted it into the cart. The delicious pine scent reminded Nick of something. He couldn't remember what at first, but then Ionie's wiry hair came to mind.

What will it be like having her and the dogs with us for Christmas? Will she work them? Will she show me how to handle them?

Nick was so deep in his thoughts that he didn't notice at first that Mr. Floyd wasn't taking them back the way they'd come. Instead they went over a bridge and headed up a hill to a brightly lit house.

Suddenly Wags began barking, and Nick saw dark shapes circling around their cart. It took him a second to realize they were Ionie's dogs.

He squinted and saw Ionie at the top of the

hill. Although he couldn't see her face in the dark, Nick figured she was calling out commands to the dogs, because they left the cart and circled back up to her. Mr. Floyd drove the cart right to the front door of the house.

"Come on," Peter signed to Nick.

Nick smelled the popcorn as they opened the front door. His mother was standing in a big bare kitchen talking with Mrs. Floyd. Both turned as he walked in.

"I was beginning to worry you'd disappeared again," Nick's mother said. "How do you like it?" she asked with a sweep of her hand around the kitchen.

"Mum...?" Nick didn't know where to start.

"It belongs to the Floyds," Nick's mother said. "Their son moved to California."

Mrs. Floyd nodded hello to Nick and went to the oven. She, too, was wearing a red Santa hat.

"There's *lots* of space," Nick's mother said. "There's a big vegetable garden, and a flower garden, and a river down the hill...." Her cheeks got pinker and pinker as she talked.

"We were going to show it to you two days ago," she rushed on.

We? Nick turned from her to Peter. Hadn't Peter used the same word? Peter was standing behind Nick, his long arms hanging limp at his sides, the anxious look still in his eyes.

Nick turned again to his mother. He saw the

same anxiety, the same what-are-you-going-to-say? look in her eyes.

They love each other. They do want to get married, Nick knew. Hadn't he known that all along? Hadn't Mrs. Firth said they belonged together?

Strangely, amazingly, Nick didn't feel left out as he stood there between them. He knew he was a part of their belonging together.

"Well?" said Nick's mother.

"It's *big,*" said Nick. "Do you think maybe I could have another dog if we lived here? A dog like Fergus?"

She smiled. "You could."

Peter tapped Nick's arm to get his attention. "Wait a minute, young man," he warned, "I think you'd better check with someone else before you get a sheepdog."

"You mean Ionie?"

Peter shook his head.

Nick turned to his mother. She gave a little nod in the direction of the front hall. There stood Wags, her tail down, a bewildered look on her face.

"Wags!" Nick said, as he hurried over to let her know she would always be his best friend.

Nick's Mission
0-8225-0740-4

Nick's Secret
0-8225-0743-9

PUBLISHING GROUP

Lerner Publications   Runestone Press
Carolrhoda Books   First Avenue Editions
LernerSports   LernerClassroom

www.lernerbooks.com
Order toll–free 800-328-4929 • FAX 800-332-1132

Just turn the page for a sample of NICK'S MISSION!

Look for

Nick's Mission

by Claire H. Blatchford

Nick rowed and rowed. It was slow going, not only because the boat was getting heavier, but because of the waves. They got bigger and bigger. He rowed upwind, right into them. His bathing suit was soaked but the life preserver remained fairly dry and warm. He pulled as hard as he could at the oars while Wags sat facing forward, her ears flapping in the wind.

They were about twenty-five feet from the shore when the raft suddenly seesawed wildly. Nick swung around in time to see a dozen or more mallards flapping up and out from under long yellow-green willow hair. The ducks skimmed past Nick close to the surface of the water, their necks stretched out, their webbed feet held straight back against their bodies.

They'd been frightened by Wags, who had belly flopped into the lake and was paddling toward the shore.

Nick stared after them. There went his photos!

A second later, a mother swan swam out from under the willow, followed by three fluffy gray babies. Nick reached for the camera. Then he saw that Wags was going for the swans.

Nick lowered the camera. What did Wags think she was doing? She was headed for big trouble if she thought she could catch a swan. The mother swan's long white neck flattened out at Wags like the taut neck of a snake. She looked as though she was hissing.

Nick gave two quick hard claps and whistled.

Wags circled around and swam back toward the raft, her ears flat against her head.

Nick got a couple of photos of the swans as they moved on, downshore, in the direction of the boathouse. He didn't follow them because of Wags. He noticed, as he lowered the camera, that the boathouse was quite large and that all of the windows were shuttered. There were two large NO TRESPASSING signs on the lake side of the house.

Nick also saw that the brown growth that obscured the lower part of the house was a thicket of cattails. There were water-lily pads too, which meant there might be turtles. He squinted. Some of the reeds looked trampled. Was that a pathway through the cattails up to the house?

Nick's new orange raft was turning into a bathtub. He tucked the camera inside the life preserver against his chest, piled the snorkeling equipment in the bow, and slipped over the edge of the boat into the lake. The water came up over his knees.

The rocks were sharp underfoot after the sandy public beach. Nick towed the raft in. Then he dragged it out of the lake and up the stony shore to a grassy spot beneath one of the willows. Wags shook herself off and started zigzagging all around with lowered nose and an alert, upright tail.

Nick tipped the raft to empty it out. To his dismay, the hole was about the size of a dime. Had one of the dog's nails punctured the rubber? What could he do about it? He looked around. Rocks, brambles, old wood, grass, tangled bits of reeds, water lilies and duckweed. There wasn't anything he could use to patch up the raft. His watch read 1:10. How in the heck was he going to get the pictures and return by 3:30? Not only had Wags frightened all the birds away, she and Nick were stranded.

Nick decided to explore the shore area around the boathouse. He'd tell Wags to stay with the raft so she wouldn't scare off any more birds and he could take pictures. Then he'd swim back across the lake with the camera. He'd be going with the waves and would have his flippers. He was sure he could get back to the public beach by 3:30. He would figure out how to get his boat and the other stuff later. Wags would swim with him. It would be cold, but he knew he could do it. He'd be the first kid under fifteen to swim across the lake alone! His face got warm as he thought about it.

Nick clapped for Wags and gestured for her to stay by the boat. She looked disappointed, but did as she was told and lay down on the grass beside Nick's snorkeling equipment.

Camera in hand, life preserver still on, Nick made his way down the shore, hopping from rock to rock and climbing over fallen trees. He got a picture of some mallards but that was all.

When he reached the cattails, Nick saw that there was a path. The growth had been hacked back neatly. It had been done in such a way, though, that the path wasn't straight—it curved around into the heart of the thicket.

Curious, Nick followed the path. The earth was soft and muddy underfoot. He stopped as he recognized footprints in the mud. Faint human footprints. He squatted down and looked at them. His father had told him a little bit about reading animal tracks the last time he was in Maine. What could he read in a human footprint?

There were three different imprints. Two of the imprints were quite large. They looked as though they'd been made by heavy people wearing shoes or boots. The third set of prints was small and had a clover pattern in the middle. Nick knew the imprint must have been made with Vibram soles. He knew because his father had boots with the same clover pattern on the bottom.

The imprints led up the path toward the house and then back. The imprints that went in were older and fainter than the ones that came out. They puzzled Nick. Who would be going in and out? The nuns? In boots? Carlos? Maybe Carlos went fishing in the early morning or late evening.

Nick went on. The path began to curve again, this time toward the edge of the boathouse. He walked on the balls of his feet, softly, looking to the left and right. He stopped, rubbed his arms, and listened through his eyes. He felt strangely tense. There was nothing, nobody, only the wind bending the reeds and the clouds building up overhead.

Just before Nick reached the edge of the boathouse, he thought he saw something red out of the corner of one eye. He turned. Yes, there was something red under the reeds.

He stepped off the path, pushed past the cattails, leaned over, and looked. A red-pink feather about two and a half inches long lay on the mud. Nick picked it up. His heart sped up as he wiped it off. What kind of a bird would have such a bright feather? Not a cardinal—it was too pink. A scarlet tanager?

Something clicked in Nick's head a split second after he'd thought of the scarlet tanager. He remembered the newspaper photo in the pocket of his shorts at home. He could see the bird perfectly, lying limp in the hands of the police officer. His mouth fell open. Could it be? Could it possibly be the feather of a scarlet macaw?

CLAIRE H. BLATCHFORD lost her hearing overnight when she had the mumps at the age of six. She attended regular schools and colleges and became a teacher as well as a writer. She and her husband have two daughters, a dog named Ginger, and two finches named Nut and Meg. They live in Massachusetts.

Jacket illustration by Laurie Harden

$10

DAMAGED